William Hammond

The Marrow of the Church

the doctrines of original sin, justification by faith, and the Holy Spirit, fairly stated,

and clearly demonstrated, from the homilies, articles, and liturgies of the Church of

England. Fourth Edition

William Hammond

The Marrow of the Church
the doctrines of original sin, justification by faith, and the Holy Spirit, fairly stated, and clearly demonstrated, from the homilies, articles, and liturgies of the Church of England. Fourth Edition

ISBN/EAN: 9783337284664

Printed in Europe, USA, Canada, Australia, Japan

Cover: Foto ©Lupo / pixelio.de

More available books at **www.hansebooks.com**

THE
DOCTRINES
OR
ORIGINAL SIN,
JUSTIFICATION BY FAITH,
AND
THE HOLY SPIRIT,

Fairly Stated, and Clearly Demonstrated,

FROM THE

HOMILIES, ARTICLES, and LITURGIES
OF THE CHURCH OF ENGLAND.

Confirmed by Apposite Texts of Scripture. With proper Reflections, Inferences and Instructions, annexed to each Head.

Being the Substance of several DISCOURSES preached in
CAMBRIDGE.

By WILLIAM HAMMOND, A.B.

Late of St. John's College, in Cambridge.

The FOURTH EDITION, Corrected.

Speak thou the Things which become found Doctrine. Tit. ii. 1.

BIRMINGHAM:

PRINTED FOR THE EDITOR: AND SOLD BY
E. PIERCY, IN BULL-STREET.

To the READER.

THE Editor of the *Marrow of the Church*, knowing how precious to the Chriftian Reader are all Mr. *Bunyan's* Works, and how fcarce many of them are, purpofes to publifh the following in Weekly Numbers, that Perfons of all Situations and Circumftances may not lofe the Comfort to be had from reading them, viz.

1. Law and Grace
2. Water of Life
3. Bunyan's laft Sermon
4. Advocatefhip of Chrift
5. Chrift a Complete Saviour
6. Gofpel Truths opened
7. Vindication of Gofpel Truths
8. On the Law and a Chriftian.

Thefe are the moft fimple, inftructive, and beft approved Works of that great and good Man of God, Mr. *John Bunyan.*

THREE DISCOURSES

ON

INTERESTING SUBJECTS,

INTENDED BY WAY OF

SUPPLEMENT

TO

The MARROW of the CHURCH.

By WILLIAM HAMMOND, A. B.

Late of St. John's College, in Cambridge.

The great Scarcity, as well as extreme Importance,
from the very interesting Nature of their Subjects, of
the following Discourses, induced the Editor of the
Marrow of the Church, to solicit the Favour of two
pious and worthy Divines, in whose Hands they were,
to oblige him with them, in order to their Publication.

EXTRACTS, &c.

It is hoped that the following Extracts from the Author's Pre-
face to his Hymn Book, will be found to the comfort and
edification of the Church and Children of God.

AS the Apostle saith, *All Men have not Faith*, 2 Theff. iii. 2. so neither have all that have Faith, *a full Affurance of Faith.* What then? Shall we say, because they have not a full Affurance of Faith, they have no Faith at all? God forbid. This would indeed be condemning the Generation of God's Weak Children: And I wifh those who embrace such an Opinion would consult the Scriptures; for if Men neglect or forsake those infallible Writings, 'tis no wonder they run into Error and Extravagance. The Apostle *Paul*, in his Epistle to the *Ephefians*, tells us, that *to every one of us is given Grace, according to the Meafure of the gift of CHRIST;** and in his Epistle to the

---

* *Eph.* iv. 7.

Romans

Romans he faith, *GOD hath dealt to every Man the Meafure of Faith* ;* which fhews, that there are different Meafures or Degrees of Faith. Accordingly we find our Saviour making mention of thofe who have *little Faith*, Matt. vi. 30. viii. 26. xvi. 8. and of *great Faith*, Matt. viii. 10. xv. 28. Luke vii. 9. And the Apoftle before-mentioned, fpeaks of a Soul *weak in Faith*, Rom. xiv. 1. and ch. iv. ver. 19. fpeaking of *Abraham*, the Father of the Faithful, he faith, he was *not weak in Faith*; and then again, ver. 20. he *was ftrong in Faith*; and ver. 21. he was *fully perfuaded*; which full Perfuafion is equivalent to the *full Affurance*, mentioned Heb. x. 22. All this informs us that fome Believers have a little Faith, others have a great Faith; fome have a weak Faith, others a ftrong Faith. And I fee not how any can poffibly deny this, without at the fame Time denying the Holy Scriptures. And we may commonly take Notice, that thofe who deny this Doctrine, make either their own prefent Inward Senfations, or elfe the Principles which they have imbib'd from others, the Rule and Standard of their Judgment, inftead of the Scriptures of God. What I find deliver'd in the Word of God I muft believe; and I am obliged to fpeak and write accordingly, whether it pleafe or difpleafe Men. I do not write to pleafe a Party; If I did, I fhould not fpeak my Mind fo freely. I know fome abufe the Doctrine I have been fpeaking of, and from hence take Occafion to nurture themfelves in Sloth, Indolence, Lukewarmnefs, Worldly-Mindednefs,

nefs, Weak Faith, yea, perhaps, ('tis to be fear'd) too often in no Faith at all; for if Perfons have true Faith, they will continually cry for the Increafe of Faith, *Luke* xvii. 5. but if they habitually indulge themfelves in Doubts, Unbelief, and Defpondencies, and feek for no Increafe of Faith, this is one probable Evidence they have no Faith at all. But what is the Confequence? Shall Chriftians reject a Scriptural Truth, becaufe Infidels abufe it? Or becaufe Carnal Profeffors run into one extreme, fhall we, to avoid that, run into another? Yea rather, let our Moderation be known unto all Men. Scriptural *Wifdom is profitable to direct*, Eccl. x. 10.

As fome deny that there is any Faith without a Full Affurance, fo others deny that there is any fuch Thing as a Full Affurance of Faith; fo contrary do Men go to God's Word, and fo do they run a Tilt at each other. To talk of being affur'd of the Forgivenefs of our Sins, and to fay we are fure of going to Heaven, is, in fome Men's Efteem, the higheft Arrogance and Prefumption. The *Papifts* generally reject this Doctrine, and affert, that none can be fure of their Sins being pardoned, and of obtaining Eternal Glory, unlefs by fome fpecial and extraordinary Revelation, fuch as is not the common Privilege of all Chriftians, but vouch-

---

* *Rom.* xii. 3.

a 3   fafed

fafed only to fome peculiar Favourites of Heaven : and many, who are not of the *Roman*
Communion, yet fall into their Opinion, in
this particular Point.   Let us then hear what
our eftablifh'd Church fays upon this Head, for
fhe is excellently Sound in all the Doctrines of
Grace ; altho' 'tis too true alas ! that many of
thofe, who at prefent are called her Preachers
and Minifters, attempt to fully her Beauty, and
eclipfe her Glory.   In the 6th of the *Lambeth*
Articles, fhe declares her Judgment in thefe exprefs Words : " A Man who is a True Believer,
" that is, endu'd with Juftifying Faith, is Sure,
" with a Full Assurance of Faith, of the
" Forgivenefs of his Sins, and of Eternal Sal-
" vation by Chrift."   Here you fee the Full
Assurance of Faith is afferted in the ftrongeft
Terms poffible.   Are you then of the eftablifh'd
Church ?   Why then do you not receive the
Doctrine which fhe profeffedly maintains ?   Or
why fhould you ftop fhort of this Affurance,
which is the common Priviledge of juftified
Perfons ?

But you perhaps will fay, " I don't mind
" any Church, nor any Man."   Well then, do
you regard the Holy Scriptures ? If you will
not believe Man, will you believe God ? Are
you willing to ftand or fall by the Determina-
tion of the Sacred Writings ? Then hear what
the Word of God fays, Col. ii. 2. *That their*
Hearts might be comforted, being knit together in
Love, and unto all Riches of the Full Affurance of
Underftanding.——And Heb. vi. 11.   *And we*
defire

defire that every one of you do fhew the fame Dili-gence to the Full Affurance of Hope unto the End. And again, ch. x. ver. 22. *Let us draw near with a true Heart, in Full Affurance of Faith.* And as this Privilege of Affurance is fo plainly fet forth in Holy Scripture, fo the Saints both of the Old Teftament,* and alfo of the New, were poffefs'd of it.   So *David*, Pfal. xxxi. 14. *I faid, thou art my GOD.*   He does not fay, I faid, thou art God, in a general indefinite Way, but thou art *my* God, which denotes the Full Perfuafion he had of his Intereft in the Divine Favour: this the Pfalmift declares to the Lord himfelf, Pfal. xvi. 2. *O my Soul, thou haft faid unto the LORD, thou art my LORD.*   Of this Faith was *Job* a bleffed inftance, as we learn from Job xix. 25. *I know that my Redeemer liveth.* And in fhort, *Abel, Enoch, Noah, Abraham, Mofes,* and all the Believers mentioned in the Eleventh Chapter to the *Hebrews,* had this Af-furance; the Apoftle *Thomas* had this Affurance, *John* xx. 38. and fo had all the Apoftles, as they themfelves declare, John vi. 69. *We believe and are fure that thou art that CHRIST.*   And the Apoftle *Peter* exhorts all Chriftians in gene-ral, to *make their Calling and Election fure,* 2 Pet. i. 10. but how could this be, if there was no fuch thing as Affurance ?

The Martyrs both of antienter and later

----

* Compare *Heb.* iv. 2. with *Cant.* ii. 16. and 2 *Cor.* v. 1.

Date enjoy'd this Full Assurance of Faith, else how do you think they could have look'd Death in the Face with so chearful a Countenance? How could they have endur'd Racks and Stakes, Fire and Sword, and have clapp'd their Hands in the midst of the Flames? Do you think they could have so undauntedly encounter'd Death, if they had not been sure of entering into Eternal Life? I only ask you yourself, Reader, are you not afraid of Death? And yet you must own you should not be afraid to die, if you was sure of going to Heaven. You see then that this Assurance of Faith gives us Victory over Death; and 'tis for want of this Assurance that you are so fearful of Death; and you always will be afraid of Death, till you have this Full Assurance of God's Love to you. I only ask you, should you be willing to burn at a Stake for Christ, unless you was fully persuaded and absolutely assur'd that he loved you? Therefore, let the Indigence and Infelicity of your present Condition, convince you of the Necessity and Happiness of this strong Confidence in God, this Fulness of Faith in Christ. Never rest short of it; look to Christ, and he will give it you: Doubting is no part of Religion; (altho' some People seem to make it of the Essence of their Religion to doubt) 'tis the want of Religion that makes People doubt. *He that doubteth is damned*, saith the Apostle: and *he that believeth not GOD, hath made him a Liar*, saith the Evangelist: and *he that believeth not is condemned already*, saith our Saviour. If therefore you have not this Belief in Christ, you

are

are in a State of Condemnation. And be not
satisfied with a small Degree of Faith, but press
forward after a Full Assurance. How many
People deceive themselves, and under the pretence of Little Faith, have no Faith at all ?
For a *Little Faith* is in Comparison *no Faith*,
Mark iv. 40. And how many, under the Co-
lour of Weak Believers, are found Infidels in
the Sight of God ? Therefore wait upon God
for an undoubted Evidence of his Love to you,
call upon the Lord Jesus to give you his wit-
nessing Spirit *to bear Witness with your Spirit,
that you are a Child of GOD,* * then you will
be rooted, settled, and established in Christ,
then you will be quiet, easy and comfortable
in your Soul, and never till then. For this
Reason it is, I have so frequently insisted upon
this Doctrine, and so earnestly inculcated it in
these Hymns ; because I know when Souls experience the Truth, Life, Power and Efficacy
of it, they are indeed truly happy ; they then
fear not Death, they fear not the World, they
fear not Men, they fear not Devils ; they fear
nothing. The love of Jesus shed abroad in
their Hearts comforts them under all Tribulations, carries them thro' all Temptations, and
gives them Victory over all Enemies.

As the Lord Jesus is made unto us of God,
Wisdom and Righteousness, so he is also made

Rom. viii. 16.

our

our *Sanctification*, Cor. i. 30. Chrift in himfelf is infinitely Holy, and admits of no Degrees, more or lefs. So that our Sanctification, confider'd as fubfifting in Chrift, or as
Chrift is made to us of God Sanctification, is
Perfect and Inftantaneous; fo that the Moment we believe in Chrift, and poffefs him by
Faith for our Juftification, that Moment we
poffefs a Perfect and Compleat Sanctification in
him. Yet our Lord faith, John xvii. 19. *For
their Sakes I fanctify myself, that they alfo might
be fanctified.* Not only is our Saviour fanctified, but we alfo muft be fanctified; and we are
fanctified in him and by him: For *if the Firft
Fruit be holy, fo alfo* is the whole *Heap, and if
the Root be holy,* fo alfo *are the Branches,* Rom.
xi. 16. And if the Head is holy, fo are all the
Members.

The Author of our Sanctification is God,
yea, even the whole facred Trinity. Therefore fometimes we find this afcribed to God the
Father, thus Exod. xxxi. 13. *I am the* LORD
that doth fanctify you; and Jude, ver. 1. Chriftians are faid to be *fanctified by* GOD *the Father.*
In other Places of Scripture our Sanctification
is attributed to God the Son; fo Eph. v. 25,
26. CHRIST *loved the Church and gave himfelf
for it, that he might fanctify and cleanfe it with
the wafhing of Water by the Word.* And again,
Heb. ii. 11. *For both he that fanctifieth, and they
who are fanctified are all one.*—Now who are
they that are fanctified, but Perfons fanctified?
So that here we hear of perfonal Holinefs or

Sancti-

Sanctification, as also in *John* xvii. 19 1 *Theff.*
v. 23. *Heb.* xiii. 12. *Acts* xxvi. 18.   This is
wrought in us by the Holy Ghoft ; fo faith the
Apoftle, Rom. xv. 16. *That the offering up of*
the Gentiles *might be acceptable, being fanctified*
by the Holy Ghost ; and 1 Cor. vi. 11. *Ye*
are wafhed, ye are fanctified, ye are juflified in the
Name of the Lord Jesus, *and by the* Spirit *of*
our God.   So that you fee God the Father, the
Lord Jefus, and the Holy Ghoft, are all concerned in our Sanctification.

We may obferve further, the Blood of Chrift
is fometimes mentioned as the Caufe of our
Sanctification ; thus Heb. xiii. 12. *Wherefore*
Jesus *alfo, that he might fanctify the People with*
his own Blood, fuffer'd without the Gate; and ch.
x. ver. 29. *and hath counted the Blood of the Co-*
venant wherewith he was fanctified. We are all
by Nature Unholy and Unfanctified, but we
are fanctified by the Blood of Chrift.   That
very Blood which Chrift fhed without the Gates
of *Jerufalem* is the Ground and Foundation of
our Sanctification.   The Greek Prepofition fignifies Caufality, and fhews plainly that the
Blood of Chrift is the meritorious Caufe of our
Sanctification.   It is therefore called *Precious*
Blood, 1 Pet. i. 19. for *unto you which believe he*
is Precious, 1 Pet. ii. 7.   If Chrift had not fhed
his Blood for us, we muft have continu'd Unholy and Unfanctified for ever.   But now when
we fee ourfelves Unfanctified, we look to the
Blood of Chrift, and by Faith apply it to our
own Hearts. *The Blood of* Christ *cleanfeth us*
from

from all Sin: herein and hereby we are fanctified. We fee in Chrift all the Sanctification
we want, and by Faith we poffefs it, and appropriate it to ourfelves ; and fo we ftand perfectly Holy and perfectly Sanctified, before the
Face of our Heavenly Father.

Every Believer in Chrift is fanctified; therefore the Apoftle ftiles the Chriftians at *Corinth,*
them that are fanctified in CHRIST JESUS, 1 Cor.
i. 2. In Chrift dwells all Fulnefs. And all
our Sanctification is in him and from him.
Hence our Lord calls himfelf *the Fountain of*
living Waters, Jer. ii. 13. xvii. 13. Chrift is
a Fountain of Grace and Holinefs; and as
Water from a Fountain fupplies or fills all the
Streams, fo Holinefs or Sanctification flows
from Chrift, and fills the Hearts of all his
People.

The Means whereby we are fanctified is
Faith, therefore are the Difciples of Jefus faid
to be *fanctified by Faith that is in him,* Acts xxvi.
18. Faith is the Eye of the Soul, whereby fhe
looks to Chrift : and as the Eye receives Light
into it by looking at the Sun, fo does the Soul
receive Holinefs or Sanctification by looking to
Jefus Chrift by Faith. And as the Sun of the
World is always equally bright in himfelf, fo is
Chrift the Sun of Righteoufnefs, always equally
glorious in himfelf; but Souls have greater or
lefs Degrees of Light, according as they look
nearer to or farther from him. Hence, therefore, as Perfons increafe in Faith, they alfo in-

creafe

creafe in Holinefs : fo faith the Pfalmift, Pfal. lxxxiv. 7. *They go from Strength to Strength——* And *Solomon* affirms the fame Thing, Prov. iv. 18. *The Path of the Juft is as the fhining Light, that fhineth more and more unto the perfect Day :* and the Apoftle *Paul* fays, *the Inward Man is renewed Day by Day,* 2 Cor. iv. 16. The Expreffion Day by Day feems to denote a gradual Renewal or Renovation of the Heart, and fo acquaints us that our Sanctification, as confider'd wrought in us, or manifefted to us by the Holy Spirit, is Progreffive, and proceeds by certain Steps and Degrees. And this is agreeable to Experience, for faithful Souls find daily more and more Power over Sin ; they feel their Hearts more dead to Sin, and more alive unto God. Hence the Apoftle *Jude* defcribes the Saints as *building up themfelves in their moft holy Faith,* ver. 20. After the Foundation is laid, the Superftructure is to be erected. So after we have laid Chrift the Foundation, Souls are to be built up in Faith and Holinefs in him, which makes the Apoftle call it the moft holy Faith. The Apoftle *Peter* exhorts Chriftians *to grow in Grace, and in the Knowledge of our* LORD *and Saviour* JESUS CHRIST, 2 Pet. iii. 18. whereby he informs us, that Believers not only grow in Faith, which is exprefs'd by the Knowledge of our Lord and Saviour Jefus Chrift, but alfo in Grace, that is in Love, Joy and Peace, and all the Fruits of the Spirit mentioned *Gal.* v. 22, 23. Believers are called *Trees of Righteoufnefs ;* * for as Trees increafe in

---

* *Ifa.* lxi. 3.

Strength,

Strength, Stature, and Fruitfulnefs, fo do the People of God increafe in Light, Power, Faith, and Purity of Heart. The Church of Chrift is called his Body, 1 *Cor.* xii. 13. *Eph.* i. 23. and is faid to *increafe with the Increafe of* God, Col. ii. 19. Now if the whole Body increafes, each particular Member muft increafe in his proper Meafure and Proportion : to affert therefore that the Members of Chrift's Body myftical do not increafe in the Divine Life, in Faith, in Strength, in inward and outward Sanctity, is falfe, and contrary to Scripture. As Plants or Shrubs grow up till they become Trees, or as Children grow up to Manhood, fo do the Children of God grow up till they become Perfect Men, till they arrive *to the Meafure of the Stature of the Fulnefs of* Christ, Eph. iv. 13.

We are not to live upon the Sanctification that is wrought in us, but upon the Sanctification that is in Chrift : Otherwife we fhall live upon the Streams inftead of the Fountain. All true Religion is not a Burden, but a Privilege. There is no fuch Thing as a Curfe to them that are in Chrift Jefus, for Chrift was *made a Curfe for them,* Gal. iii. 13. *There is therefore now no Condemnation to them which are in* Christ Jesus, Rom. viii. 1. *And there fhall be no more Curfe,* Rev. xxii. 3. Therefore happy are the People that are in fuch a Cafe; yea, bleffed are they who have the Lord Jefus for their God. They are truly happy who live by the Faith of the Son of God. Bleffed are they who fee Chrift their all in all, and who fee nothing at all, yea,

and

and defire to fee nothing at all but Chrift alone.
While the Eye of the Soul is fteadily fixed on
Chrift, that Soul is perfectly happy, fo happy
that it cannot be happier, unlefs in the full
Fruition of Chrift in Glory.   But the Moment
we take our Eye off from Chrift, and look after
fomething elfe befide the Lord Chrift; that Moment, I fay, our Souls are unfettled, confus'd,
darken'd and diftrefs'd.   We then become quite
uneafy, and utterly miferable; nor can we find
any Comfort or Satisfaction, till we return to
our Reft, that is, to Chrift.   This is agreeable
to the Experience of the Pfalmift, who, after
he had wander'd from God, and was thoroughly reftlefs and unhappy, fays to his Soul, *Return unto thy Reft, O my Soul*, Pfal. cxvi. 7.
And the Lord Jefus, the good Shepherd of the
Sheep, calls and invites, prefies and exhorts,
yea, and in the moft loving and affectionate
Manner befeeches his ftray Sheep to return to
him again: obferve he repeats the Invitation,
Return, return, O Shulamite, return, return, Cant.
vi. 13.   And Jer. iii. 14, 22. *Return ye back-
fliding Children, for I am married unto you, and
I will heal your Backflidings*—Oh that all who
have left their firft Love, and have forfaken
Chrift and turned afide unto fome Idol, would
reply with the faithful Souls in the Text, *Behold, we come unto Thee, for thou art the* Lord
our God. God loves his Children freely, he
heals their Backflidings.   When therefore your
Soul is healed, and your Spiritual Strength reftor'ft, fin no more, left a worfe Evil come
upon Thee; never turn thy Eye from Chrift
any

any more, but keep looking to him continually; behold him as the Author and Finisher of thy Faith; look upon him as *the Alpha and Omega, the First and the Last, the Beginning and the End of thy Salvation,* Heb. xii. 1. Rev. i. 8, 11. And look at nothing else, either within thee or without thee, but Christ; for in him thou art *complete,* Col. ii. 10. in him thou art *perfect,* Col. i. 28. in him thou art *washed,* in him thou art *sanctified,* in him thou art *justified,* 1 Cor. vi. 11. He is *made unto us of* GOD, *Wisdom, Righteousness, Sanctification and Redemption,* 1 Cor. i. 30. In him we are *Perfect and Entire, wanting nothing,* Jam. i. 4. And this is properly Christian Perfection; because indeed this Perfection is not inherent in us, but it subsists in Christ, and is ours only by Virtue of our Union with Christ. Every Christian, truly so call'd, is one with Christ,* and therefore *purifieth himself even as he is pure,* 1 John iii. 3. He *is righteous even as he is righteous,* ver. 7. He is *merciful as* GOD *is merciful,* Luke vi. 36. He is *holy as* GOD *is holy,* 1 Pet. i. 15, 16. He is *perfect as his Father which is in Heaven is perfect,* Matt. v. 48.

---

* 1 *Cor.* vi. 17.

THE

PREFACE.

WHEN I was firſt convinced of the Truths maintained in theſe Papers, and ſaw them ſo generally oppoſed by thoſe of the eſtabliſhed Communion, I was induced to ſearch more narrowly into the Conſtitution of our Church; whereupon I carefully peruſed her Articles and Homilies, and ſoon perceived the Judgment of our Reformers as to theſe Important Heads of Chriſtian Divinity; and the frequent Mention and ſtrenuous Vindication of theſe Evangelical Truths, gave me an equal Degree of Pleaſure and Surprize. The Preaching of this or that particular Perſon is not the Rule whereby we are to

A 2

judge

judge of our Church, but her profefs'd Articles
and Homilies are the Standard; and fince thefe
Doctrines are therein contained, they may truly
and properly be called the Doctrines of the
Church of *England.*

'Tis a Rule in Philofophy, that a Fountain
can rife no higher than its Source. 'Tis a Rule
in Divinity, that a Preacher can preach no
more of Chrift than he hath experienced in
his Heart. Hence we find fo many Preachers
mentioning nothing of the Corruption of the
Heart, becaufe they feel it not: They feldom
fpeak of the Doctrine of Juftification, unlefs it
be to expofe or deprave it: And as for the Effufion of the HOLY SPIRIT, this with them
is Madnefs and Enthufiafm. *Father, forgive
them, for they know not what they do.* When
a Preacher is influenced by the HOLY GHOST,
he fpeaks as the SPIRIT gives him Utterance,
and he feels every Word he fpeaks: his every
Word is Light, Life, Power and Demonftration. He is never at a Lofs for Quicknefs of
Apprehenfion, Accuracy of Expreffion, or Af-
fluence of Elocution. He can fpeak with
equal Facility upon any Evangelical Subject
whatfoever.

I know this Performance will gain me no
Credit or Repute with fome fort of People: I
fhall pafs with them (as I already do) for a
Philofophic Divine, a Perfon of clear Notions,
a fpe-

a fpeculative Preacher, that hath a confiftent Scheme of Doctrines in the Head, but little or no Fund of Grace in the Heart. This is a fevere Cenfure; yet I freely forgive thofe who pafs it upon me. With me it is a very fmall Matter to be judged of *Man's Day.* And whatfoever Thoughts fuch Perfons may entertain of me, ftill I love them, and hope the beft of them; and this I defire, even the Salvation of their Souls.

Others perhaps may carry the Matter further, and be ready to efteem me a Madman, a Fool, an Enthufiaft, or an *Antinomian.* As to the two firft of thefe I have no reafon to be offended, becaufe greater Perfonages* than I have been branded with them: Yea, Jefus Chrift, my Lord and Mafter, was called by a Name as bad, or worfe than any or all thefe put together, *Mark* iii. 22. As for Enthufiafm, if it be counted Enthufiafm to have a Poffeffion of the Spirit of God, and a fenfible Enjoyment of his Comforts, then let me live and die an Enthufiaft; and I wifh my Enemies no worfe Evil than that they may do fo too. Our Church faith of true Chriftians, " They dwell in Chrift, and Chrift in them; " they are one with Chrift, and Chrift with " them."† But if by Enthufiafm you mean
a falfe

---

* See 2 *Kings* ix. 11. *Jer.* xxix. 26, 27. *John* x. 20. *Acts* xxvi. 24.
† Communion Service.

a falſe Pretence to the Spirit, (as I ſuppoſe
you do) then how will you know a Man to
be an Enthuſiaſt, if he be orthodox in Faith,
and blamelefs in Converſation? Hence therefore learn not too haſtily to brand any Man
with this odious Appellation. As to the Charge
of *Antinomianiſm*, I have carefully avoided this
Error, by inſiſting upon the Neceſſity of Good
Works, as the proper Produce and genuine Effects of Juſtifying Faith.

I know there is in Man a natural Enmity to
theſe Spiritual Truths, which will always exert
itſelf in a Manner ſuitable to its Nature and
Quality. Hence the Oppoſition of ſome Men
to theſe Chriſtian Principles, and their way of
manifeſting that Oppoſition, does but confirm
me in the Truth of them. I remember once
when I was in great Doubt and Concern about
the Trinity, I met with theſe Words of
Lucian; " The moſt high God, Great, Im-
" mortal, Heavenly, the Son of the Father,
" the Spirit proceeding from the Father, One
" of Three, and Three of One." This ſcur-
rilous Paſſage of the *Pagan* Scoffer was a
Means of removing my Doubt, and confirmed me in the Doctrine of the holy Trinity.
Juſt ſo, in the preſent Caſe, the Rage and
Raillery, the Ridicule and Drollery, the Mad-
neſs and Blaſphemy, wherewith ſome oppoſe
the Doctrines now under Conſideration, juſt
ſerves to convince me of the Truth of them,

and

and withal shews me the Badness of the Adversaries Cause, which requires so much Sin, Folly and Extravagance to support it.

I am sensible that many Objections are leveled against these Doctrines: But I purposely decline burdening the Reader with them, for two Reasons; First, because I design to make this Work as little controversial as possible. Secondly, these Objections are chiefly borrowed from the Papists, and have been solidly confuted by judicious Protestant Divines, both domestic and foreign.

I have taken Care, in the ensuing Pages, to cite some of the most learned Divines of the last Age, and the beginning of this; such as Archbishop *Usher*, Bishop *Hall*, Bp. *Reynolds*, Bp. *Sanderson*, Bp. *Wilkins*, Bp. *Burnet*, Bp. *Beveridge*, and Dr. *Edwards*, in order to shew the Reader what learned Men have embraced these Principles, and with what good Authority they are back'd, And if our modern Preachers and Ministers will not hear them, whom will they hear? Especially if we add, that these learned Bishops speak none other Things than what Christ and his Apostles spoke and taught before them.

My Design in insisting on some particular Truths is not to exclude others, such as Christ's Incarnation, Satisfaction, Resurrection, &c. &c.
which

which are generally neceffary to be known in
order to our obtaining eternal Life :   But the
profound . Ignorance of fome, and the virulent
Oppofition of others againft thefe Gofpel-
Truths, makes it needful to vindicate and eftablifh them at this Time.   Indeed I wifh this
Work had been done by fome abler Hand.
But I fay, as *Peter* in another Cafe, *Such as I
have give I thee.*   And how ungrateful foever
this Undertaking may be to fome Pharifaical
Chriftians and heterodox Preachers, yet I am
willing to hope it will find a favourable Reception with all thofe who have a hearty concern
for the honour of Chrift, and an inward Experience of the Gofpel-Salvation.

T H E

THE
DOCTRINE
OF
ORIGINAL SIN.

CHAP. I.

ORIGINAL SIN is fo called, becaufe it is the Sin of *Adam*, who was our Head and Origin; and from him it is derived to us. This Sin, confidered in relation to *Adam*, confifts of two things; 1. His actual Tranfgreffion in eating the forbidden Fruit: 2. The corruption of his Nature confequent thereupon. Accordingly Original Sin, fo far as it affects us, confifts, *1ſt.* In the Imputation of Adam's actual Sin to us: *2dly*, In the inherent Pollution of our Natures; upon both which Accounts we fall under the Curfe of God, and become the objects of his eternal Difpleafure. This, therefore, I fhall demonftrate at large: And that may render what I have to fay upon this Subject more eafy and intelligible, I fhall divide my matter into the three following Propofitions; and fhew,

B   I. That

I. That *Adam's* Sin is imputed to all his Posterity.

II. That all Men derive an inward Pollution or Depravation of Nature from him: And therefore,

III. Are juftly liable to the Torments of Hell for ever.

I. I am in the firft place to prove, that *Adam's* Sin is imputed to all his Pofterity.

The Homily on the Mifery of Man hath thefe exprefs Words, " In ourfelves (as of " ourfelves) we find nothing whereby we may " be delivered from this miferable Captivity, " into the which we are caft through the En- " vy of the Evil, *by breaking of God's Com-* " *mandment in our firft Parent* Adam." This Paffage is plain and clear to our Purpofe; and if I was to alledge no more, this is fufficient to fhew the Judgment of our Reformers in this Point. Here is exprefs Mention made of our *breaking God's Commandment in* Adam, which can no better be underftood than of our ftanding in *Adam* as our common Head, and Reprefentative; and fo, confequently, when he *broke God's Commandment*, we are faid to have broken it *in him*; becaufe his Breach or Violation of the divine Command is imputed unto us. This, I think, is a clear explication of the Words; and no unprejudiced mind can deny it.

The

The Homily on the Nativity of CHRIST, speaks the same Language, and affords us another evident Proof of our present Proposition. Thus it is said, " As in *Adam* all Men *sinned* universally, so in *Adam* all Men universally received the Reward of Sin." Here we are informed, that all Men, without Exception, sinned *in Adam*, which could be no otherwise than as he was their Head in Covenant, and so his Sin was charged upon them all. And lest, by *sinned* in this Place, some should understand our suffering Death, which was a Consequence of *Adam's* Sin (as is the common Way of our *Pelagian* and *Socinian* Adversaries) it is very seasonably added " In *Adam* all Men universally *received the Reward of Sin*." Where we see there is a plain Difference made between *sinning* and *receiving* the Penalty of Sin: the former denotes the Imputation of *Adam's* Crime to all his natural Descendants, the latter the Punishment due to us thereupon. And a little afterwards the Church laments the Misery of our fallen State in these Words: " Oh! what " a miserable and woeful State was this, that " *the Sin of one Man* should destroy and condemn all Men "---But how could the Sin of one *Man* destroy and condemn all Men, unless it was imputed to them all? Besides, observe, the Word *condemn* implies and presupposes a Crime for which we are *condemned*: Guilt and Condemnation go together; this latter passes upon all Men, all therefore are guilty; and in what Instance? We are here informed in the

Sin

Sin of *one Man.* This therefore is a clear Demonstration, that the Guilt of that one Man's Sin, viz. *Adam's* is transferred to all Men.

We see then the Judgment of the Church of *England* upon this Head. Let us now enquire into the Scripture-account of this Matter. The Apostle *Paul* largely and designedly treats of this Doctrine in *Rom.* v. He begins at the 12th Verse, saying, *Wherefore as by one Man Sin entered into the World, and Death by Sin; and so Death passed upon all Men, for that all have sinned.* Sin entered into the World first, and Death followed after; both these came in by *one Man,* viz. *Adam:* but then death did not terminate upon him only, but infected and flew the whole Race of Mankind, who were included in him, *in whom* (as it should be translated, and as we find it rendered in the Margin) all have sinned. All Men were included in *Adam,* as the Plant is contained in the Seed, or the Branches in the Root: their wills were included in his Will, their Act in his Act; hence his Sin becomes their Sin; they stand convicted of it, they are condemned for it, and suffer Death as a Punishment thereof. This seems to me the genuine Meaning and Purport of the sacred Text, though I know some endeavour to understand it otherwise. The Followers of *Samosatenus* say That the Greek Expression, which the Apostle uses, does not signify *in whom,* but *for that,* or, *forasmuch as;* which is so far from weakening, that it

even

even confirms our Opinion. For thus the Reason is assigned why Death passed upon all Men, yea, upon infants themselves, *ver.* 14. to wit, because all sinned, namely, in that Sin which entered into the World by one Man, Now they did not sin that Sin in their own Person, because they did not exist; therefore they sinned it in Adam.

The Apostle prosecutes this argument thro' ver. 14. *Nevertheless Death reigned from* Adam *to* Moses, *even over them that had not sinned after the Similitude of* Adam's *Transgression.* --- Death reigned over Infants who had never committed any actual Sin, they therefore died upon account of Original Sin. --- The Apostle adjoin , *who is the Figure,* or Type, *of him that was to come.* Adam was a common Head and representative of all Mankind; he personated all his Seed natural; and in this respect he was a Type of Christ, who took human Nature upon him, and represented all his Seed spiritual. Agreeably to this Adam the Protoplast is called the *first* Adam, and Christ the *last* Adam; the one is called the first Man, the other the second Man, 1 *Cor.* xv. 45, 47 for which no other Reason can be assigned but this, Adam and Christ were both public Persons and Representatives; the one represented all Mankind universally, the other was the Representative of all true Believers. *Adam* is the Head, we are the Members: Now what the Head does, the Members are supposed to do; the Sin therefore which

B 3

Adam

Adam committed, all Men are looked upon as having committed: So in the Cafe of a Reprefentative, his Actions are accounted theirs in whofe Stead he is conftituted. Adam was our Reprefentative when he finned againft God; we therefore finned in him, and fell with him in his firft Tranfgreffion. His Sin becomes ours by Imputation, becaufe God imputes Adam's actual Difobedience to all his natural Pofterity: I fay, imputes, becaufe the Act itfelf was a tranfient Thing, nor did it cleave to us as it did to Adam; but it is moft juftly imputed to us, becaufe we all finned in him as our Head and Root. This the infpired Writer declares again and again, in Terms as clear as the Light: fo that one would wonder how any can avoid feeing it, unlefs they are wilfully blind. *If through the Offence of one many be dead;---the Judgment was by one to Condemnation.---By one Man's Offence, Death reigned by one---By the Offence of one, Judgment came upon all Men to Condemnation.* And *by one Man's Difobedience many were made Sinners,* ver. 15, 16, 17, 18, 19. They were *conftituted Sinners, viz.* in the divine Order and Appointment; for God was pleafed to conftitute Adam a Head of the whole human Race, and fo upon his Default charged all his Pofterity with the Guilt of his Sin. This Chapter therefore is a fufficient Proof that Adam's firft Sin is reputed the common Sin of all Mankind.

This Truth we have again delivered in 1 *Cor.* xv. 22. *As in* Adam *all die.*---But how could
all

all die in Adam, unless all had sinned in him?
To evade this, some Persons of a *Pelagian*
Dye are pleased to say, that *Death* was a Punishment to Adam for his Sin, but that it
befals his Posterity only as an accidental Evil
or Calamity. But what saith the Apostle?
The Wages of Sin is Death, Rom. vi. 23. Death
is the true Desert, the exact Stipend, or just
Wages of Sin. By this he informs us, that
Death is the proper Punishment of Sin. It
passeth upon none but Sinners, and for nothing
but Sin. Now punishment implies and presupposes Sin: *All die* (saith the Apostle)
i. e. suffer the Punishment of Death, and that
in Adam; this therefore implies that all sinned
in Adam, or else they could not consistently
with the divine Justice *die in him*. And when
the divine Writer says *all*, he includes Infants
and Adults; Men, Women and Children;
all universally and unexceptionably: they all
have the Guilt of their Forefather's Sin upon
their Heads. And since they had no personal
Existence at the Time he committed the Offence, how could they sin in him any otherwise
than as they have his Sin imputed unto them?
Thus Archbishop *Usher* explains this Matter?
" Q. *What is Sin imputed? A.* Our Sin in
" Adam, in whom as we lived, so also we
" sinned; for, in our first Parents, every one
" of us did commit that first Sin which was
" the Cause of all other; and so we all are
" become subject to the Imputation of Adam's
" Fall, both for the Transgression and Guilti-

" ness

" nefs.*" This therefore may fully fatisfy us, that all the Sons and Daughters of Adam are Partners with their great Predeceffor in his Apoftacy, as well as in the penal Effects and Confequences of his Rebellion againft God.

I know the Mouths of natural Man are wide open againft this Doctrine: they think it an hard Saying, and cannot fee how it is confiftent with the divine Juftice or Goodnefs to charge the Sin of one Man upon all Men. This puzzles their natural Reaſon, and therefore Original Sin is a difficult Pill (as one calls it) for them to fwallow; and fome of them abfolutely reject it. But now to remove this Scruple, and to fhew in fome meafure the Reafonablenefs and Equity of God's imputing Adam's Sin to all his natural Offspring, it may be confidered,

Firft. All Men were in the Loins of Adam at the time of his Fall, and fo all fell in him, and are juftly accountable for his Sin. Levi is ſaid to have paid Tythes in Abraham, becaufe he was in Abraham's Loins when Abraham paid Tythes to Melchifedec, *Heb*. vii. 9, 10. In like manner all Men may be faid to have finned in Adam, becaufe they were in the Loins of Adam when he finned againft God. This is clear. And this is the arguing of the Holy Spirit in the former Cafe, and feems to me equally applicable in the latter. Accordingly this Argument hath been frequently made ufe of for this Purpofe, by many Orthodox Divines,

------

* Subftance of the Chriftian Religion.

vines, and Theological Writers. But I am aware this Objection may be ftarted: "If the "Sin of Adam is imputed to us, becaufe we "were in his Loins at the Time of his Difobe-"dience; then why are not the Sins of our "immediate Parents reckoned ours, feeing we "were in their Loins before our Birth, and "while they committed many Sins? But the "Sins of our immediate Progenitors are not "plac'd to our Account*; therefore why fhould "Adam's?" In anfwer to this Objection we rejoin,

Secondly, That Adam was our Covenant head, and therefore his fin is imputed to us; but our immediate Parents are not.Covenant heads, and therefore their fins are not charged upon us. *The* LORD GOD *commanded the Man, faying, of every Tree of the Garden thou mayeft freely eat, but of the Tree of the Knowledge of Good and Evil, thou fhalt not eat of it; for in the Day that thou eateft thereof, thou fhalt furely die.* Gen. ii. 16. 17. Thefe Words have the nature of a Covenant; for here God gives Man a Command, and annexes a Threatning to the Violation of it, which implies that a Promife was added to the Obfervation thereof. Adam actually confented to this Covenant; he accepted the Terms and Conditions of it, and entered into it, not only for himfelf, but alfo for all his natural Progeny. Confequently if Adam had fulfilled the Conditions of this Covenant, all his Children would have enjoyed the Benefits of it; but fince he broke the Law

---

* Ezek. xviii. 20.

Law GOD gave him, he involved not only himself but all his Offspring in eternal Mifery and deftruction, *i. e.* rendered them juftly obnoxious thereunto.   We were all one in Adam and with him; in him legally in regard of the Stipulation and Covenant between GOD and him we were in him parties in that Covenant, had Intereft in the Mercy, and were liable to the Curfe which belonged to the Breach of that Covenant*.   And herein appears the Juftice of GOD; for as on the one hand. if Adam had ftood, all Men would have fhared in the Bleffings of the Covenant; fo on the other, fince he fell, it cannot be thought hard or unjuft, that they all fhould be Partakers of the Curfe and Penalty thereof.   If Adam had kept the Covenant, Men would have liked well enough to have been his Companions in Happinefs; why then, fince he broke it, fhould they murmur or repine at their being followers of him in his Mifery? Does it not argue too much Partiality to make a Diftinction here? If Men admit one of thefe, why fhould they not admit the other? Are not thefe Terms very fair and equitable? But then proud Nature is ready to afk, how could GOD make Adam our Head in Covenant without our Confent? Or how can we juftly fhare in the Penalties of a Covenant to which we never confented? To folve this Difficulty, let it be obferved, that actual confent cannot be had in perfons who do not exift.   It may be afked then, could they be obliged without

their

---

* Sinfulnefs of Sin by Bifhop *Reynolds.*

their Confent? The Anfwer is, Adam was the Reprefentative of all Men, he confented, and fo they are looked upon as confenting in him. Their confent therefore was included in his, and his Act is imputed to them. Hence they fuffer. the penal Effects of his firft Tranfgreffion.

Thirdly, GOD is Sovereign of all: He created Man at firft, and he was at liberty to fix his Happinefs upon what Terms and Conditions he pleaf'd. Since therefore our Almighty Creator chofe to appoint Adam to be a fœderal Head of all the Human Race, fo that if he ftood, they fhould ftand in him; if he fell, they fhould fall with him; we ought to fubmit our Wifdom to the Wifdom of GOD. and bow our Wills to the Sovereignty of his Will. GOD was under no obligation to create Man at all; and when he did create him, he placed him in what circumftances he thought beft: And it does not become fuch Mortals, and withal fuch finners as we to cavil or find fault with the Difpenfations of our Maker. Yea, I believe, had it been poffible for the whole bulk of Mankind to have been confulted upon this important Affair, they would infinitely fooner have chofe to have been created upon thefe Conditions than not to have exifted at all.

Indeed GOD could (if he had pleafed) have prevented the fall of Adam; but his infinite Wifdom did not think fit. The LORD knew upon the whole, that by the Fall of Adam, the Divine Glory and human Happinefs would be moft promoted. The LORD brings Light
out

out of Darkneſs, Good out of Evil. According-
ingly by means of the Lapſe of our Great
Anceſtor, an effectual Door is opened for the
diſplay of God's vindictive Juſtice, and of his
infinite Mercy: The one upon thoſe to whom
the Goſpel is the Saviour of Death unto Death,
the other upon thoſe whom it is the Saviour
of Life unto Life. 'Tis true, if we had ſtood
in Adam, our Happineſs would have been
great. But as we ſtand in CHRIST, our Happineſs is infinitely greater. We have no Reaſon
therefore to quarrel with GOD, for imputing
Adam's ſin unto us, but we ought to bleſs
him for providing a Redeemer for us. The
Redemption of CHRIST muſt needs ſilence all
our Complaints, and ſwallow up all our Cavils
and objections at once.

Many Preachers ſpeak much of the Corruption of human Nature, and inſiſt frequently
and earneſtly upon that Topick; they ſet forth
the natural Depravation of the Soul, and our
Obnoxiouſneſs to GOD's Wrath upon that Account. But then they ſeldom mention the Imputation of Adam's Sin to his Poſterity. Perhaps then it may be aſked of what Uſe is this
Doctrine? it hath ſeveral uſes: *Firſt*, it ſhews
the extreme Miſery and deplorable Condition
of Man by Nature, and ſo is a proper Motive
to Humiliation and ſelf-abaſement. This will
eſpecially appear if we conſider, how exactly
we tread in the Steps and imitate the Rebellion of our firſt Parents. How often do we
believe the Devil before GOD? How often do
we doubt of the Truth of GOD's Promiſes, and
the

the Execution of his Threatnings? How bafely
are we enflaved by our fenfual Appetites? Efpecially how frequently are we drawn away
by the Luft of the *Eye** to covet forbidden
Fruit? And how common is it for Men to deftroy themfelves by an inordinate fondnefs for
Wifdom? And how ready are we all to defire a
Thing if for no other Reafon, yet for this,
becaufe it is forbidden us? *Laftly,* how greedily
do Men commit fuch fins as ruin not only
themfelves, but alfo hurt and deftroy their
Pofterity? All thefe are Footfteps and Traces of
our forefather's Apoftacy. And Minifters fhould
perpetually fhew how Adam and his Children
refemble each other in Wickednefs. *Secondly,*
Preachers are to declare this Doctrine becaufe
it greatly enhances the Value of the Gofpel Salvation, for the greater our Mifery, and the
deeper our Diftrefs, the greater is the Mercy of
the Son of God manifefted in delivering us.
Thirdly, The imputation of Adam's fin and
Christ's Righteoufnefs run parallel each to
the other (as we fhall fhew more at large afterward) and in proportion as we are convinced of
the Reality of the former, we fhall fee the Excellency and Neceffity of the latter. Contraries
mutually illuftrate and fet off each other. Win-
ter makes the Summer appear more pleafant;
and the Night makes the Day more agreeable
and delightful. Therefore the Apoftle fpeaks
of the Imputation of the Sin of the firft Adam,
and the Imputation of the Righteoufnefs of the
fecond

---

* *Gen.* iii. 6.

second Adam both together: He oppofes the one to the other, and draws a long but agreeable Parallel between them. *Rom.* v. 15---21. He choofes to fpeak much of Adam's fin imputed to *all Men for Condemnation*, that he may thence take occafion to magnify and extol the abundant Grace of God, in imputing the Righteoufnefs of his Son Christ to *all Men for Juftification of Life.* ver. 18.

II. I come now, *Secondly*, to fhew that all Men derive an inward Pollution and Depravation of Nature from Adam. We have before cleared up the Doctrine of Original Sin, as confifting in our having Adam's fin imputed to us. Now therefore we are to fpeak of another Part of Original Sin *viz.* that innate Defilement of the Soul which is derived from Adam to all his Sons and Daughters, in fucceeding Generations. Of this the Homily of the Mifery of Mankind fpeaks thus, " We " cannot think a good Thought of ourfelves, " much lefs can we fay well, or do well of " ourfelves." And can we neither think, fpeak, nor do well of ourfelves? Is this the prefent Condition of Man? And did God create him in fuch a weak and imperfect State? The Scriptures forbid us thus to think; they acquaint us that God created Man in his own Image, *Gen.* i. 27. *i. e.* Upright as the wifeft Man tells us, *Eccl.* vii. 29. If Man was thus created at firft, how comes it to pafs, that he is now fo Impotent and Helplefs, as to be unable to think a good Thought? This therefore

fhews

ſhews that Man's Nature is ſpoiled, that his Original Righteouſneſs is loſt, and all the Powers and Faculties of the Soul weaken'd and debaſed.

In the next Page of the ſame Homily, it is ſaid, " Wherefore he (i. e. *David*) ſaith, " mark and behold I was conceived in ſins; " he ſaith not ſin, but in the plural Num- " ber, ſins; foraſmuch as out of one as " a Fountain ſpring all the reſt." The one here ſpoken of as the Fountain, is before called the original Root and ſpring Head, and ſo juſtly points out to us that inbred Corruption of the Heart from whence all outward Ini- quities have their Riſe. Of this our LORD himſelf ſpeaks, ſaying, *From within out of the Heart of Men proceed evil Thoughts, Adulteries, Fornications, Murders, Thefts, Covetouſneſs, Wickedneſs, Deceit, Laſciviouſneſs, an evil Eye, Blaſphemy, Pride, Fooliſhneſs: All theſe evil Things come from within, and defile the Man.* Mark vii. 21, 22, 23. This ſhews the Wick- edneſs of Man's Heart, and informs us, that there is no ſort of ſin which Men commit, but what was firſt conceived in that Womb of Iniquity. A learned Divine* ſpeaking of this Depravity of the Heart, calls it " The " Root and Fountain of all other ſin, from " whence every actual Abomination does pro- " ceed. Atheiſm, and Pride, and Baſeneſs, " and Cruelty, and Profaneneſs, and every " other Vice which the moſt wicked Wretch
" in

---

* Biſhop Wilkin's Gift of Prayer, Chap. vii.

" in the World is guilty of, doth proceed from
" hence.   Hell itfelf, which is the proper
" Place 'of Sin, is not more full of Sin, for the
" kind of it than our Natures are."

In the fecond Part of the fame Homily we
have thefe Words; " Of ourfelves, and by
" ourfelves, we have no Goodnefs, Help or
" Salvation, but, contrariways, Sin, Damna-
" tion, and Death everlafting."   And again;
" Hitherto we have heard what we are of our-
" felves, very finful, wretched and damnable,
" ---fo that we can find in ourfelves no Hope
" of Salvation, but rather whatfoever maketh
" unto our Deftruction." We have here the
Sinfulnefs and Weaknefs of human Nature
plainly fet before us, and Damnation mentioned as the juft confequence thereof.   One
would think fuch paffages as thefe fhould ftrike
with fome degree of Evidence and Conviction
upon the Minds of all who read thefe Homilies;
and one might juftly wonder, that any who
fet their Hands to them, fhould either deny
Man's natural Depravity, or palliate it in the
leaft; feeing it is fo plainly profeffed and exhibited by that Church, of which they would
be thought Sons and Minifters; yea, and for
which they pretend to have fo great a zeal
and Affection.

I fhall add one Paffage more from the Homily on CHRIST's Nativity, which is fo clear
and full to the Purpofe, that it may juftly put
the matter beyond all Doubt.   " As before,
" he (viz. *Adam*) was moft beautiful and pre-
" cious; fo now he was moft vile and wretched

" in the Sight of his Lord and Maker. In-
" ftead of the Image of God, he was now be-
" come the *Image of the Devil*, inftead of the
" Citizen of Heaven, he was now become the
" *Bondflave of Hell*, having in himfelf *no one*
" *Part* of his former Purity and Cleannefs,
" but being *altogether* fpotted and defil'd, in-
" fomuch that he now feem'd to be nothing
" elfe but a *Lump of Sin*, and therefore, by the
" juft Judgment of God, was condemned to
" everlafting Death." This is a true, but at
the fame Time a very awful Defcription of
Man fince the Fall. Obferve by what Names
he is here called, *a Bondflave of Hell, the Image
of the Devil, a Lump of Sin*; and yet fome People are apt to think we delineate human Nature in too black Characters, and make Man a
much worfe Creature than he is. But do thefe
Names juftly fuit Man, or do they not ? If thefe
Characters are juftly affixed on Man in his fallen
State, what Names can be too bad for him ? Or
how is it poffible to reprefent Man worfe than
he is ? Let the Preachers therefore of the Eftablifhed Church take care to fpeak the fame Language, and give the fame Defcription of Man
in their Sermons, as is here give in this Homily.
And left any fhould think this was the Cafe of
Adam, but not of his Pofterity, the following
Words are worth our Notice. " This fo great
" and miferable a *Plague*, if it had only refted
" on *Adam* who firft offended, it had been
" much eafier, and might the better have been
" borne. But it fell not only on him, but alfo
" on his Pofterity and Children for ever ; fo

C

that

" that the *whole Brood of* Adam's *Race* should
" suftain the *felf-fame Fall and Punifhment,*
" which their Fore-father by his Offence moft
" juftly had deferved." Here we fee the *Plague*
i. e. the Infection of Sin defcends to the *whole*
Brood of Adam, and they all fuftained the *felf-*
fame Fall and Punifhment with himfelf.

It is now Time to alledge the Teftimony of
the Ninth Article, entitled,

Of ORIGINAL SIN.

" Original Sin ftandeth not in the following
" of *Adam* (as the *Pelagians* do vainly talk)
" but it is the Fault and Corruption of the Na-
" ture of every Man, that naturally is engen-
" dered of the Offspring of *Adam,* whereby
" Man is very far gone from Original Righ-
" teoufnefs, and is of his own Nature inclined
" to Evil, fo that the Flefh lufteth always
" contrary to the Spirit."---This is an accu-
rate Account of the innate Corruption of the
Soul, which *Adam* contracted in his Fall;
which was in him originally, and is in all his
Natural Offspring derivatively.   The Terms
here ufed to exprefs this are clear and explicit;
they need no Glofs or Commentary to render
them plainer; let them but ftand before an
impartial Judge in their native Simplicity, and
he will prefently fee they carry in them the
true Notion of Original Sin, and are the genuine Language of thofe who hold that Doctrine.   As for thofe who fweat and toil, to
give this Article a different Turn, and endeavour to make it fpeak two or three Languages,

they

they seem nearly related to the *Pelagians* *
who are condemned in the front of it. In the
Conclusion of this article, the Doctrine of inherent finless Perfection is exprefsly contradicted ; " *This Infection of Nature doth remain,*
" yea *in them that are regenerated,* whereby the
" Luft of the Flefh, which fome do expound
" the Wifdom, fome Senfuality, fome the Af-
" fection, fome the Defire of the Flefh, is not
" fubject to the Law of God."

C 2   This

---

* It was the Doctrine of the *Pelagians* in primitive Times,
that Man's Nature was not corrupted by the Fall of *Adam*; that
his Sin was not any ground to his pofterity, either of Death, or of
the Merit of Death ; that Sin comes from *Adam* by Imitation, not
by propagation ; that Baptifm doth not ferve in Infants for Remiffion of Sin, but only for Adoption and Admiffion into Heaven ;
that as *Chrift's* Righteoufnefs doth not profit thofe who believe
not, fo *Adam's* Sin doth not prejudice nor injure thofe that actually fin not ; that as a righteous Man doth not beget a righteous
Child ; fo neither doth a Sinner beget a Child guilty of Sin ;
that all Sin is voluntary, and therefore not natural ; that Marriage is God's Ordinance, and therefore no Inftrument of tranf-
mitting Guilt ; that Concupifcence being the Punifhment of Sin,
cannot be Sin likewife. Thefe and the like Antithefes unto orthodox Doctrine, did the *Pelagians* of old maintain : And (as it
is the Policy of Satan, to keep alive thofe Herefies, which may
feem to have moft Relief from proud and corrupted Reafon, and
do principally tend to keep Men from that due Humiliation, and
thorough Conviction of Sin, which fhould drive them to CHRIST,
and magnify the Riches of CHRIST's Grace to them) there are
not wanting at this Day a Brood of finful Men, who notwithftanding the evidence of Scripture, and Confent of Antiquity, do
in this Point concur with thofe wicked Hereticks, and deny the
Original Corruption of our Nature to be any Sin at all ; but to
be the Work of God's own Hand in Paradife, nay, deny farther
the very Imputation of *Adam's* Sin to any of his Pofterity for Sin.
Thus far Bifhop Reynolds. And this brief Schedule of the *Pelagian* Tenets I fet before the Reader, in order to caution him
againft them.

This Doctrine spreads itself through the whole Liturgy, as the following Petitions and Confessions may satisfy us; *there is no Health in us*--We be tied and bound with the Chain of our Sins†---Through our Sins and Wickedness we are sore let and hindered in running the Race that is set before us§---May it please Thee that by the wholesome Medicines of the Doctrine delivered by him, all the Diseases of our souls may be healed‡---Through the Weakness of our mortal Nature we can do no good thing without Thee**----Without Thee we are not able to please Thee‡‡.* All these Passages, and many more that might be extracted from the Book of Common Prayer, plainly declare the Original Corruption of Man's Nature, and the Insufficiency of his Natural Will.

There are two Places in the Liturgy which deserve a particular consideration : The first is, *Dearly beloved, for as much as all Men are conceived and born in sin.*---Here the Doctrine of Original Sin is clearly asserted, and it is said to be convey'd to us in our Conception and Birth. And this is advisedly placed at the beginning of the Baptismal Office ; because the inherent Pollution of our Nature is one valid argument for the Use of Baptism. Baptism (saith our xxvii. Article) is a Sign of our Regeneration or New Birth.

---

* Order for Morning Prayer.
† Prayers upon several Occasions.
§ Fourth *Sunday* in *Advent.*
‡ Collect for St. *Luke's* Day.
** First *Sunday* after *Trinity.*
‡‡ Nineteenth *Sunday* after *Trinity.*

Birth. Now unless we were born in Sin, we should have no need of a Regeneration, or second Birth; much less should we stand in need of Water-Baptism (which is only a Type or Figure of the Baptism of the Spirit) unless we were originally depraved and corrupted. Therefore the Doctrine of Baptism and of Original Sin, stand or fall together, and those who deny the latter, evacuate the Necessity of the former, and so condemn the Usage of the present as well as the Primitive Christian Church.

The other Place is in the Catechism, where the Question is proposed, "What is the Inward and Spiritual Grace?" The Answer is returned, "A Death unto Sin, a New Birth "unto Righteousness; for being *by Nature* "*born in fin,* and the Children of Wrath we "are hereby made the Children of Grace." Here we have a brief Account of the Regeneration of the Spirit, which is typically represented by the external washing of Water in Baptism. When we are said to be *by Nature born in fin,* what Words can be plainer to express our Birth-Sin, or the innate Corruption of the Heart? I know some by the Term in *Eph.* ii. 3. are willing to understand strong and inveterate Habits of Vice contracted by long Custom of sinning; for, say they, Habit and Custom are second Nature, and therefore may fitly be express'd by that Term. But the Word cannot be so taken here, because it is joined with being *born,* unless our *Pelagian* Opponents will say that Men are *born* with inveterate Habits of Vice, acquired by long Custom

and

and Practice, which seems too preposterous for any reasonable Man to affirm. Therefore our *being by Nature born in sin*, must mean our being *born* of sinful Parents, and deriving a vitiated Nature from them.

The Scriptures attest this truth in innumerable Places. Thus, *Gen.* v. 3. *Adam begat a Son in his own Likeness, after his Image.* Like begets Like: Adam, in his corrupted State, begat a Son, and therefore his Son was as corrupt as himself. So *Job* xiv. 4. *Who can bring a clean Thing out of an unclean?* And xv. 14: *What is Man that he should be clean? and he-which is born of a Woman that he should be righteous?* The argument is plainly this, as is the Cause, such will be the Effect; as Parents are, such will their Offspring be; but Parents *are unclean*, Men and Women are unrighteous, and so their Children derive an innate Unrighteousness, a spiritual Uncleanness from them. Our blessed Lord declares the same Truth. *John* iii. 6. *That which is born of the Flesh is Flesh.*--Lions do not beget Lambs, nor Wolves Sheep; no more do fleshly Parents beget spiritual Children; but as Serpents produce Serpents, and Vipers beget Vipers, and all manner of wild and venomous Creatures bring forth Creatures as wild and venomous as themselves, so carnal and impure Parents beget Children as carnal and impure as themselves. This follows upon the established Laws of Generation. As to the *Modus**,

how

---

* Many Divines have lost themselves here. Since the Soul is not *ex traduce*, some have supposed it is created pure and
holy

how this fpiritual Contagion is conveyed to us,
I do not pretend to determine it: That we are
polluted Creatures from the Womb is plain;
the Fact is too vifible to be denied. We are
not therefore fo much concerned to know how
we came by the Difeafe, as how or where we
may procure a Remedy.

The Pfalmift *David* had a deep Experience
of this finful Infection, this native Stain of the
Soul: wherefore he cries out, *Behold, I was
fhapen in Iniquity; and in fin did my Mother
conceive me*, Pfal. li. 5. The Spirit of God
generally convinceth Sinners firft of their actual
Sins, and then of their original Depravation.
As we trace back the Streams to the Fountain,
fo we trace back our actual Tranfgreffions to
the innate Corruption of the Heart, which is
the Root and Source of all outward Sins. Accordingly *David* having confeffed his actual
Offence in the Matter of *Uriah*, ver. 4, he proceeds to lament that Vitiofity of Nature which
he brought into the World with him; *Behold,*
faith he, *I was fhapen in Iniquity, and in fin
did my Mother conceive me.* He introduceth
his Lamentation with a Note of Attention, *Behold*, in order to make us take more Notice of
it. In acknowledging himfelf to be *conceived
in fin*, and *fhapen in Iniquity*, he plainly owns,

C 4

that

holy by God, but becomes depraved by virtue of its Union
with the Body, as pure Liquor is tainted by being put into an
impure Veffel. Others have ventured to affirm, that God ju-
dicially creates Men's Souls without Original Righteoufnefs
and Holinefs. Many pious Divines have unwarily fell into
this latter Opinion, altho' it is fo contrary to the divine Attributes and hath neither Scripture nor Reafon to fupport it.

that he was tainted with the hereditary Pollu‑
tion of Nature we are fpeaking of, and fo bears
ample Teftimony to the Doctrine of Original
Sin.   I know indeed fome endeavour to dilute
thefe Words by a Hyperbola, and fay, that *Da‑
vid* thereby only intends an Aggravation of his
actual Offence: But this is all an Evafion. There
can be no Hyperbola here, becaufe the infpired
Writer fpeaks neither more nor lefs than the
exact Truth.   " Thefe Words (faid a learned
Divine) are not an hyperbolical Aggravation of
David's actual fins, as the *Pelagians* of old, the
Socinians and fome others of this Day vainly
pretend, only to make them confiftent with
their Scheme of Religion; for they fet forth a
Sin of quite another kind; a Sin in our very
Frame and Conftitution, and are a plain and
pofitive Affertion of the Catholic Doctrine of
Original Sin.   Now, if there be no fuch fin,
thefe words are fo far from being an Hyperbo‑
la, that they contain a mere Fiction; they do
not aggravate what is, but acknowledge what
has no Reality at all*.   When Men feel that
Preffure and Burden of fin which the Pfalmift
felt when he penned thefe words, they will not
refolve them into an Hyperbola, or any Figure
of Speech, but to a Senfation of the Heart;
and they themfelves will make the fame Con‑
feffion, and become Advocates for the fame
Truth.   So long as Men continue ignorant of
that Mafs of Corruption, that World of Iniquity
that is within them, it is no Wouder they op‑
pofe

---

* *Dr. Delaune*'s Sermon on *Pfal.* li. 5.

pofe this Doctrine, though at the fame time their Blindnefs and Obftinacy, in rejecting fo felf-evident a Truth, are but too vifible Effects of that Apoftacy which they contradict, and labour to difprove.   If Men did but truly know and deeply feel the State of their own Hearts, they would find this Doctrine *written* there *with a Pen of Iron, and with the Point of a Diamond*; or, as holy *Job* expreffes it, *graven with an Iron Pen and Lead in the Rock for ever.*   Their inward Experience would then convince them, that *every Thought*, every *Imagination* of Man's *Heart* is *Evil, only* Evil, *continually*, Evil, *Gen.* vi. 5. viii. 21.

The infpired Pfalmift delivers the fame Truth, *Pfal.* lviii. 3. *The wicked are eftranged from the Womb.---*This Alienation or *Eftrangement* of the Creature, Man, from his Creator, is *from the Womb*, or *from his Youth*, Gen. viii. 21. which implies that it is born with him, and in him; he derives it from his Parents in a Way of natural Generation.   The Pfalmift adds, *They go aftray as foon as they are born, fpeaking Lies.*   Children are inclined to all Vice in general, but to *Lying* in particular: You may catch them in this Sin as foon as they are able to fpeak: and this Sin makes them the Children of the Devil, if you will believe our Saviour, *John* viii. 44. *Ye are of your Father the Devil, and the Lufts of your Father ye will do.---When he fpeaketh a Lye, he fpeaketh of his own; for he is a Liar, and the Father of it.*   You fee then how nearly Children in their natural State are related to the Devil.   Hence
Solomon

Solomon, faith, *Foolifhnefs is bound in the Heart of a Child*, Prov. xxii. 15. By *Foolifhnefs*, the wife man means fin, and efpecially the fin of our Nature; and when he faith *bound*, he lets us know how intimately it adheres to the Child; it is wrapt up in his Heart, it is interwoven with his very Nature and Conftitution. Accordingly we find GOD himfelf thus addreffing his People; *I knew that thou wouldft deal very treacheroufly, and waft called a Tranfgreffor from the Womb*, Ifa. xlviii. 8. God does not give Things empty and infignificant Names; if therefore he calls his People *Tranfgreffors*, it is becaufe they really are fuch; and *from the Womb*, denotes as much as from their Birth and Conception; and fo informs us, that in their very Rife and Original, they were defiled with this in-bred Depravity. What then becomes of the *Pelagian* Hypothefis, which fuppofes that Children are born innocent and free from fin, and are only corrupted by the ill Example of others? Thefe Texts teach us another Leffon; they tell us, that the *Wicked* (and fuch we are all by Nature) *are eftranged from the Womb*; that the People of GOD, as well as others, are *Tranfgreffors from the Womb*; and that *Foolifhnefs*, or fin, which fo early appears in Children, is not barely owing to the Influence of the bad Example of others, but is *bound* up in their little degenerate Hearts. And all this is confirmed by daily Experience, for we fee Children running into Wickednefs as greedily as to their natural Food; they drink Iniquity like Water, and are never better pleafed

than

than when they are committing Sin. Their Wills are bent upon Evil; and they delight in doing Mifchief. And although wholfome Inftructions are adminiftred unto them, and Examples of Piety and Virtue fet before them, yet you will find they take infinitely more Pleafure in Vice than in Virtue: their Natures are wild and ungovernable : they are fullen, felf-will'd, unruly Creatures; and they will do what they pleafe in fpite of all Arguments and Perfuafions to the contrary. *Man is born* (the Note of Similitude is not inferted in the original *Hebrew*) *a wild Afs's Colt, i. e.* a wanton, skittifh, favage, untractable Creature ; and the Gradation of the Words is obfervable (faith Dr. *Edwards*) Man is a *Colt*, an *Afs's Colt, a wild Afs's Colt*, Job xi. 12.

The Apoftle Paul frequently mentions this. Thus *Rom.* iii. 10. *There is none righteous, no not one :* that is, none are fo by Nature; but, as he tells us, *ver.* 9. both *Jews* and *Gentiles* are all *under Sin*, viz. under the Guilt of *Adam*'s actual Tranfgreffion, and under the Diforder of a vitiated Nature, upon both which Accounts *all the world is become guilty before* GOD, ver. 19. Again, the Apoftle faith, *All have finned and come fhort of the Glory of* GOD. The *Greek* Word which is here tranflated *come fhort*, is properly expreffive of our Fall in *Adam*, and of the Default of our Nature confequent thereupon : It denotes our Lofs of the divine Image, our Lofs of the divine Favour,
our

our Lofs of all that Happinefs and Holinefs which we poffefs'd in Adam : it expreffeth our Lofs of Communion with GOD, and our Lofs of the Enjoyment of GOD both prefent and future. Some think the Apoftle, in this Chapter, is defcribing the general Decay of Religion among the Jews, and the univerfal Declenfion of Manners that had overfpread the Gentile World. This is true ; but then he fpeaks of the Corruption of the Heart alfo. This appears, *firft*, becaufe the 10th, 11th, and 12th Verfes are taken from the xiv and liii *Pfalms*, the Contents of both which inform us, that therein *David defcribeth the Corruption of a natural Man.* Accordingly he begins, *the Fool hath faid in his Heart*, and he fpeaks chiefly of the depraved State of the *Heart* in the three firft Verfes, and then proceeds to defcribe the Wickednefs of their Lives, *ver.* 4. where he calls them *Workers of Iniquity.* The Apoftle takes the fame courfe : he firft defcribes the Sinfulnefs of Men's Hearts, *ver.* 10, 11, 12, and then he fhews the Sins of their Lives and outward Actions, *ver.* 13, 14, 15, &c. The Apoftle therefore and the Pfalmift both give their Suffrages to the Truth of our Doctrine. They both pourtray the Ignorance, Impiety, Infidelity and Atheifm of the Heart, as well as the Sins and Follies of the external converfation of Men. *2dly*, I would remind the Objectors of the exclufive Terms, *no not one.* Now, do they think none abftained from outward Sin in *David*'s or St. *Paul*'s Time ? Do they think none were free from grofs Immorality ?

lity? Were there no Servants of GOD, no Believers in CHRIST? Yet the Apoſtle ſays *there is none righteous*, and he adds *no not one*, neither Infants not Adults; which ſhews that he ſpeaks of that original ſinful Stain that epidemical Diſeaſe of our Nature with which all are infected, and from which none are free.

The ſeventh Chapter is full of this Doctrine: ſo ver. 8. *Sin taking occaſion by the Commandment, wrought in me all manner of Concupiſcence.* If Man was in his primitive State of Purity and Holineſs, he would take occaſion by the divine Commandment to ſhew his Love and Obedience to GOD; but ſince he is apoſtatized from his original Creation, and hath contracted an Antipathy to God, the Law irritates and provokes the Corruption of his Heart, and makes it more boiſterous and predominant; yea, cauſes it to overflow juſt like a river ſtopt in its Courſe: This makes him ſay, *I had not known Sin but by the Law*, ver. 7. and *by the Law is the Knowledge of Sin*, ch. iii. ver. 20. When the divine Law is ſpread before a Sinner in its fulleſt Extent, Purity and Perfection, then he ſees what a filthy deteſtable Creature he is: the Law, as in a Glaſs, repreſents to him the Sinfulneſs and Deformity of his Heart, the Blindneſs of his Mind, the Perverſeneſs of his Will, and the Irregularity, Extravagance and Diſſoluteneſs of all his Affections. Hence he who was before *alive*, i. e. thought himſelf in a State of Grace and Salvation, *dies*, i. e. ſees in himſelf *the Sentence of Death*, is obliged to acknowledge Death is his Due, and is under

fearful

fearful Apprehenfions left all the Damnation of Hell fhould be revealed in his Soul *ver.* 9, and 2 *Cor.* i. 9. This inward Conviction of fin Perfons have when the Law of God is fet home upon their Hearts, and the inward fin of which they are then convinced is the Original Pollution whereof we fpeak; and when Men have this Experience of the Corruption of their Hearts, they will then know what this innate fpiritual Defilement is.

The Apoftle faith, ver. 18. *I know that in me (that is, in my Flefh) dwelleth no good Thing,*---This was the Cafe of the Apoftle; and this is the Cafe of every Man by Nature, *no Good* dwelleth in him, but on the contrary, all manner of Evil; there is no carnal Appetite in a Brute, no wicked Temper in a Devil, but Man hath a Degree of it in himfelf. Juftly therefore doth Bifhop Hall ftile an evil Man *half a Beaft and half a Devil.** This Corruption of Nature the Apoftle fpeaks of again ver 20. and calls it *the fin that dwelleth in him, the Law in his Members,* ver 23. and the *Flefh,* ver. 25. and the *old Man,* Eph. iv. 22. Coll. iii. 9.

The Apoftle *James* mentions this Depravity of the Soul chap. 1. ver. 14. calling it *Luft,* or *Defire* which is the very fame Appellation the Apoftle Paul gives it, Rom. vii. 7. *I had not known* Luft *or* Defire, *except the Law had faid, Thou fhalt not Covet.* There is in every unregenerate Heart a perpetual Bent and Incli-
nation

---

* See his Meditations, *Cent* ii.

nation to Evil, *a Defire* to commit Sin; and the Defire of fin is fin; it is fin in its Rife and Original; and this *Luft* or *Defire when it hath conceived, bringeth forth Sin*, James i. 15. Some deny that Concupifcence, or the Defire of fin, is fin, efpecially the Papifts. And I wifh none who call themfelves Proteftants were liable to Cenfure here: But whofoever they are that are thus criminal, how contrary they go to Scripture, the Texts above recited may fhew them; and how contrary they are to the Church of *England*, the conclufion of the Ninth Article may inform them: " Concupifcence and Luft " hath of itfelf the Nature of fin."

1 have infifted the longer upon this Head, becaufe it is the Hinge upon which the Controverfy turns, and the Centre of the whole Doctrine of Original Sin; forafmuch as it implies Adam's fin imputed, and infers a Liablenefs to God's eternal Wrath.* And this is a Truth of the higheft Importance. If you deny it, you do in Effect evacuate the Neceffity of the Gofpel-Revelation, and of Salvation by Christ: For if Children are born into the World pure and innocent, and have a natural Will and Power to obey the Will of God, then they may fave themfelves, and fo what Need have they of being beholden to Christ for Salvation? We fee therefore the Error and
Danger

---

* This is eafily explained; for the Original Defilement of our Nature is both a Sin and a Punifhment: when we take it in the latter Senfe, it implies the Tranflation of the Guilt of Adam's fin to us; and when in the former, it fhews us that we are Objects of the Divine Vengeance and deferve to fuffer eternal Mifery

Danger of the *Pelagian* Scheme; and hence we may learn what Judgment to form of thofe who efpoufe and vindicate it; they are not to be looked upon only as Impugners of a fingle Article of the Chriftian Faith, but as Under-miners and Subverters of the whole Evangelical Difpenfation.

And as this Doctrine is of great Weight and Moment, fo the Evidences of it are clear, co-pious, conclufive, demonftrative. It is demon-ftrated from the Scriptures; it is demon-ftrated from the State of Men's Hearts, and from the Debaucheries of their Lives. The whole World is full of it. The Weaknefs, the Sinfulnefs, the Miferies of the human Species, all confpire to prove it. Unawakened Sinners who are Dead in Trefpaffes and Sins, and deny it themfelves, are a glaring proof of the Truth of it in others. They by their Ignorance Per-verfenefs, Hypocrify and Beftiality, demon-ftrate the innate Turpitude of the Soul, and are miferable Inftances of the Truth of that Doctrine which they ftrive to oppofe. The Saints of God experience this Corruption in their own Hearts, and groan under the Plague and Burthen of it. If we rightly know ourfelves, if we fee all our own Vilenefs, Filthinefs and exceeding Sinfulnefs, we fhall be obliged to own, that we are very wicked, unholy, un-godly, abominable Wretches. And this will further appear (as Bifhop Wilkins obferves) " If we look upon *our own Natures* in the " Rage, Blafphemies, Bafenefs, Madnefs of " other Men's Lives: there being not any " kind

" kind of Evil, which either Man or Devil
" hath committed, but there are in our Na-
" tures the Principles and Inclinations to it ;
" the beſt of us being by Nature as bad as the
" worſt of Sinners." This is ſound Speech,
which cannot be condemned. The Author
ſpeaks like a Chriſtian, and he ſpeaks like a
Divine. And I could heartily wiſh all the Biſhops, Prieſts and Deacons in *England*, ſpoke
the ſame Language. If any reject this Doctrine, it cannot be for want of Evidence, but
for want of a Mind readily diſpoſed to receive
the Truth. Now if we had Time, and if I
was not afraid I had burdened the Reader already, how many uſeful Inferences might be
deduced from this Doctrine ? As

Firſt, Acknowledge it. By acknowledging
it, I do not barely mean receiving it as a Principle of Science or Philoſophical Speculation.
Alas ! you may thus receive it, and yet be never
the better. Many ſay they are Sinners, but
how few are convinced of the Miſery and Sinfulneſs of Sin ? How many have the Theory of
Original Sin in their Heads, who have not
the Experience thereof in their Hearts ? In our
Liturgy we confeſs that we " are grieved and
" *wearied* with the *Burden* of our Sins."* And
in another Place we acknowledge " The Re-
" membrance of our Sins is grievous unto us,
" the *Burden* of them is *intolerable*."§ Which
Places ſhew us, that the *Burden* of *Sin* is not
only to be confeſſed, but alſo to be felt by us.

D   Or

---

* Commination.   § Communion Service.

Or will you fay the *Burden* of Sin may be *intolerable*, and yet we have no feeling Senfe of it? This fhews as well the profound Ignorance as the horrid Impiety of thofe who ridicule the Doctrine of feeling the Burthen of Sin, and prefume to call it Cant and Enthufiafm. If Men never were *wearied* with the *Burden* of their Sins, never did feel them *intolerable*, nor defire fo to do; then fuch Prayers and fuch Confeffions will be fo far from doing them any real Service, that they will only bear Teftimony to their Hypocrify, and highly aggravate their Condemnation. Cry therefore to GOD, that he would make your Sins a *Burden too heavy for you**. Come unto JESUS *labouring and heavy laden*, and he will give you Reft. The Word in *Greek*, in *Mat.* xi. 28. fignifies *laden* as with a *Burden*. An infupportable Burden will crufh under the Perfon who bears it. Semblably Sin is a Burden infupportable, and will crufh us down to Hell, if JESUS doth not remove it from us, and give Reft to our Souls.

Secondly, Here fee the Folly of glorying in our Pedigree. We are all the corrupt Offspring of a corrupt Parent, *Adam*. Some boaft of their being of this great Family, and others of that; fome glory in being defcended from Kings and Princes; and others from Lords and Nobles. Alas! What Vanity is all this? Surely when People talk at this rate, they forget they all fprang from the fame Root, and are tainted from the Womb. The Prince and the Peafant, the
King

---

* Pfalm xxxviii. 4.

King and the Beggar are equal in this Refpect; they have all one common Father, *viz. Adam.* Trace your Pedigree from him, and you will have no reafon to glory, unlefs you will glory in your Shame. Look back to your proper Source and Original, and be afhamed and confounded at feeing what a polluted Sinner he was, and what a finful polluted Nature you have derived from him.

Thirdly, Let all your Actual Sins lead you back to the Original Corruption of your Nature. You perhaps lament this outward Sin, and the other: but do you fee the Root of all, the inbred Impurity of your Heart? What fignifies lopping off the Branches? Lay the Axe to the Root of the Tree. Confefs and lament the inward Depravity of your Soul, and be humbled before the LORD. Your outward Sins are but the Streams, the Fountain of all is your Original Corruption. "All that Pravity and Bafenefs, "which fills up every Part and Power about "us, are but Diffufions of our Original Cor- "ruption. What a World of Mifchief is there in "our feveral Parts? Our Wills, Affections, our "Tongues, Eyes: And yet all thefe are but as "little *Rivulets;* the *Fountain,* or rather the *Sea* "that feeds them is our corrupted Nature."*

Fourthly, We learn from hence, that all are equally corrupted; all are equally far gone from God; equally far fallen from Original Righteoufnefs; and equally funk into Original Sin. There is no Difference. All are alike by Na-

D 2

ture.

---

* *Wilkin's* Gift of Prayer.

ture. One is no better than another: Neither hath one Sinner any Reafon to glory over another. But then if all are equally corrupt, how comes it to pafs, that they do not all run into the fame outward Immoralities? Why do they not commit the fame grofs Enormities? The Reafon hereof is, becaufe Men have different bodily Conftitutions, different Educations, and different Temptations: They are under various Conftraints and Reftraints, and have different Degrees of Knowledge. If Men were all exactly in the fame Circumftances in every refpect, they would all difcover the fame Depravity of Heart, and commit equal outward Iniquity. But their different Circumftances, together with the Reftraints of God's Grace, and the Hand of his Providence, are Caufes why Men are not equally vitious outwardly. But all by Nature are alike degenerate, and inclined to Wickednefs.

Fifthly, Hence we fee the Neceffity of Regeneration. Is it poffible for Men in their Natural Eftate, to enter into the Kingdom of Heaven? Can unregenerate Sinners enjoy the Pleafures of that high and holy Place? Do you think that a Creature, full of the depraved Appetites of a Brute, and the malignant Difpofitions of a Devil, is fit to dwell with God in Glory? Therefore befeech God to create your Heart anew, that you may be fit to fee his Face. Never reft till a Second Birth hath paffed upon your Soul. What fignifies the Firft Birth, unlefs you experience a Second? You had better never have been born at all, than not to be born again. Pray to God therefore,

fore, that you may be born of his Spirit, and be reinstated in his Favour.

Sixthly and *Laftly*, Have you any thing beside Nature in you? Have you any Supernatural Grace in your Heart? Do you find any change in you? Are you different from what you was? Have you paffed from Darknefs to Light? Do you live the Life of Faith? Are old Things paft away? And are all Things become new in your Soul? Rejoice, and give God all the Glory. Do not infult other Sinners. Remember if you differ, 'tis the Grace of God that makes you to differ. Therefore be humble, be mean and abject in your own Eyes, and fay with the Apoftle, *By the Grace of God I am what I am.*

III. All Men are juftly liable to the Torments of Hell for ever, as a Confequence of Original Sin. This may feem a harfh Saying; but it is true, as I will make appear at once. Every the leaft Sin you can mention deferves Hell: Only allow then, that Original Sin is Sin, and it will follow, that Hell is the due Defert thereof. This is clear, and (if I was to fay no more) a fufficient Proof of our Propofition. I once, indeed, difcourfed with a Man who gave it as his Opinion, that Men would not be condemned at the Day of Judgment for Original Sin. I believe there are many of his Mind, if they would fpeak the Truth. But St. *John* declares, that *the Blood of* JESUS CHRIST *cleanfeth from all Sin*, which implies, that without an Intereft in his Blood, Men are

cleanfed

cleanfe from no Sin, neither Actual nor Original. St. *Paul* faith, *Heb.* ix. 22. *Without shedding of Blood*, i. e. the *Blood* of CHRIST there *is no Remiffion*, no Forgivenefs of Sin, either Actual or Original; confequently all who are found Unbelievers at the laft Day, will be condemned for both of them.

Some Divines there are of an acute Genius and philofophick Turn of Mind, who affirm that we only loft our Immortality in *Adam*, and fo (if there had been no Redeemer provided) fhould have died and perifhed like the Brutes, without arriving to any Future State, either of Happinefs or Mifery. Now if the Reader is of a candid and ingenuous Difpofition, the following Quotations from the Homilies will convince him of the Error and Falfhood of this Suppofition.

" We are by Nature the 'Children of GOD's
" Wrath, but we are not able to make our-
" felves the Children and Inheritors of GOD's
" Glory," fays the Homily on the Mifery of Mankind. GOD's Glory here denotes the eternal Fruition of him in Heaven, and confequently his Wrath, which is here oppofed to it, muft mean the Suffering of Eternal Torments in Hell, which is due to us for our *Original* or *Birth-Sin*; and therefore in the foregoing Part of this Homily we are called
" Children of the Wrath of GOD, when we
" *be born.*

In the fecond Sermon on the Paffion of our Saviour, the Church bewails our Apoftacy in *Adam*, in thefe Words, " O LORD, what had
" *Adam*,

·" Adam, or any other Perſon, deſerved at God's
" Hand, that he ſhould give us his Son? We are
" all miſerable Perſons, ſinful Perſons *damna-*
" *ble Perſons*, juſtly driven out of Paradiſe, juſtly
" excluded from Heaven, *juſtly condemned to*
" *Hell*." You ſee here as conſidered in Adam,
we are not barely called mortal Perſons, but
ſinful, yea, *damnable Perſons, i. e.* Perſons, de-
ſerving everlaſting *Damnation*. We are not ſaid
barely to loſe our Immortality, and to be condemned to a State of Inſenſibility or Non-exiſt-
ence, but to be juſtly condemned to *Hell Fire*.

The Homily on the Nativity of Jesus
Christ tells us, that " before Christ's com-
" ing into the World, *All men univerſally in*
" *Adam*, were nothing elſe but a wicked and
" crooked Generation, rotten and corrupt
" Trees, ſtony Ground, full of Brambles and
" Briars, loſt Sheep, prodigal Sons, naughty and
" unprofitable Servants, unrighteous Stewards,
" Workers of Iniquity, the Brood of Adders,
" blind Guides, ſitting in darkneſs and in the
" Shadow of Death: To be ſhort, nothing elſe
" but Children of Perdition and *Inheritors of*
" *Hell*." I have ſet this Paſſage before the
Reader, that he may ſee what opprobrious
Names and Characters our Chuch gives fallen
Man: ſuch as *a wicked and crooked Genera-*
tion, rotten and corrupt Trees, &c. &c. What a
Heap of diſhonourable Titles are here confer-
red upon the rebellious Creature! What a
Variety of Expreſſions are here made uſe of, to
deſcribe the Miſery and Sinfulneſs of Man in his
- apoſtate

apoſtate State! This I have taken notice of before.* This looks as if our Reformers were at a Loſs to find out Names bad enough for the degenerate Race of Mankind. And this is directly contrary to the Practice of ſome Men, who are ſo laviſh of their Encomiums on human Nature, as if they thought they could never ſay enough to diſplay its Dignity and Excellence. If any of the eſtabliſhed Church do this, let them read their Homilies, and then they will know better. Laſtly, does not this Paſlage clearly teach us, that *all Men univerſally in* Adam did not loſe their Immortality, and become periſhable in Soul and Body, but that they were, by his Tranſgreſſion, made Children of Perdition, and *Inheritors of Hell-fire?*

In the ſame Homily the Church makes her Lamentation in theſe Words, " Oh! what a " miſerable and woeful State was this, that the " Sin of one Man ſhould deſtroy and condemn " all Men."---This I mentioned under the firſt Head, to ſhew that Adam's firſt Tranſgreſſion was charged upon all his Seed natural. But now obſerve the Penal Conſequence hereof, which we have deſcribed in the Words immediately following; " that nothing in the " World might be looked for but only Pangs " of Death and *Pains of Hell.*" Is not this ſomething widely different from the bare Loſs of Immortality? Can you poſſibly reconcile our being expoſed to the *Pains of Hell,* with the ſole Forfeiture of our Immortality? And

ſoon

---

foon after we are faid not barely to fall from
Immortality to Mortality, or from Exiftence to
Non-exiftence, but " from Heaven to Hell".
A few Pages after, *Adam* is called " a Fire-
" brand of Hell, and a Bond-flave to the De-
" vil." And afterwards it is added, " Neither
" he, nor any of his, had any Right or Inte-
" reft at all in the Kingdom of Heaven; but
" were become plain Reprobates and Caft-
" aways, being perpetually *damned to the ever-*
" *lafting Pains of Hell-fire*"---How fhocking
is this! and yet it is true; our own Church
vouches it; and hence we learn, that finful
Adam, and all his finful Progeny, juftly deferve to be caft into *Hell-fire*. The ninth Article attefts the fame Truth; for having defcribed the innate moral Defilement of our Nature,
it immediately adds, " In every Perfon born
" into this World it deferveth GOD's Wrath
" and Damnation." All this fhews the Judgment of our Church, and may abundantly fatisfy us that our original Lapfe and Degeneracy
in *Adam* did not barely entail bodily Death or
Non-entity upon us, but did even render us obnoxious to the torments of Hell for ever.

I fhall clofe this Head with the following
Scriptures: Rom. v. 18. *By the Offence of one,*
Judgment came upon all Men to Condemnation.
Whether the Greek be tranflated *by the Of-*
fence of one, as in the Text, or *by one Of-*
fence, as in the Margin, the Confequence will
be the fame, namely, that by one *Offence* of
one *Man*, viz. *Adam*, all Men incurred the Defert of eternal *Condemnation*. 2dly, As the *Of-*

E

fence

fence of one here ſtands oppoſed to the *Righte-ouſneſs of one*, viz. CHRIST, it follows, that as the one is imputed for *Juſtification of Life*, ſo is the other for *Condemnation* to everlaſting Death or Miſery. So alſo, ver. 16. *The Judgment was by one to Condemnation.**

In the 21ſt Verſe the Apoſtle ſaith, *Sin hath reigned unto Death*. And by *Sin*, he here means *Adam's* ſinful Act, in eating the forbidden Fruit, which is by a judicial Appointment of GOD reckoned to all his Poſterity, and ſo reigns unto *Death*, viz. unto that Death which is oppoſed unto *eternal Life*, mentioned in the next Clauſe and that is eternal Death or Hell, which is called *Death*, Rom. vi. 23. James i. 15. John viii. 51. This is alſo ſtiled the *ſecond Death*, Rev. xxi. 8. This Death GOD threatened our firſt Parents with : *In the Day that thou eateſt thereof thou ſhalt ſurely die*, Gen. ii. 17. where by *Death*, GOD intended all that the Scripture includes in that Term, and eſpecially the ſuffering of endleſs Puniſhments in another Life, which the Word *Death* ſignifies in the Places abovecited, and which the Verb *die* imports, Ezek. xviii. 20. John vi. 50.---xi. 26. Rom. viii: 13. True therefore is that of St. *Auguſtine*; when it is aſked, with what Death God threatened our firſt Parents, if they tranſgreſſed his Command, and

did

---

* The Greek Word denotes the eternal Sufferings which await the Wicked in a future Life. In this Senſe the Word is uſed, Rom. viii. 1. and the Greek Verb bears this Signification, Mark xvi. 16.

did not continue in their Obedience? whether Death of the Soul, or of the Body, or of the whole Man, or that which is called the second Death? The Anfwer is, All thefe.

Rom. viii. 7. *The carnal Mind* (and that is the Mind of every Man by Nature) *is Enmity againft GOD.* . If it had been only an Enemy, then poffibly it might have been reconciled; but being *Enmity* in the abftract, it muft be in its own Nature irreconcilable to God; and fo informs us that this malevolent Principle muft be extirpated, and a Principle of Love to God implanted, before our Souls can be holy or happy. Natural Men have an *Enmity* againft the Being and Sovereignty of God, againft his holy Nature and his holy Law; they hate the Gofpel of his Son; the Doctrines of his Grace, and the Work of his Spirit upon the Heart. This we need not go far to fee. And they are fo totally ignorant of God, fo infinitely diftant from him, and fo diametrically oppofite to him, that this fame Apoftle calls them *Atheifts*, Eph. ii. 12. But what follows? *To be carnally minded is Death*, Rom. viii. 6. *The Minding of the Flefh*, is the inherent Depravation of our Nature, and is a proper Expreffion to denote Original Sin; therefore we fee this Phrafe is made ufe of for that Purpofe in the Ninth Article of our Church: and Death here being oppofed to *Life* and *Peace*, muft mean eternal Death, as I before noted. This Text therefore is a full Proof that Hell is the Defert of Original Sin.

The

The greateſt Text is ſtill behind, a Text which contains the whole Doctrine, and which therefore I reſerve to the laſt; it is *Eph.* ii. 3. *Among whom we all had our Converſation in Times paſt in the Luſts of our Fleſh, fulfilling the Deſires of the Fleſh and of the Mind; and were by Nature the Children of Wrath even as others.* The Apoſtle here reminds the Believers at *Epheſus* of their State before their Calling and Converſion to the Faith of CHRIST; and he does not think it ſufficient to admoniſh them only of their outward evil Converſation, expreſſed by *fulfilling* the Deſires of the Fleſh and of the Mind, but he tells them likewiſe of their Original Depravation, and thereupon calls them *Children of Wrath*; which anſwers to that of *Peter*, who calls natural Men, *Children of a Curſe**. Such are all Men in their natural State, as the Apoſtle informs us, by ſaying, in the firſt Perſon, *We all were, by Nature, Children of Wrath, even as others.* By *Wrath*, the Apoſtle here means GOD's Eternal *Wrath*: And ſince we are here ſaid to be, *by Nature, Children of Wrath*, this implies, that we are *by Nature* Sinners, for GOD's Wrath is due to none but Sinners, and for nothing but Sin: We are therefore *by Nature* Sinners: And how can this be any otherwiſe than by having the Sin of *Adam* imputed to us, and a defiled Nature communicated to us? Upon this Account therefore we naturally fall under the curſe of GOD, and deſerve to feel his infinite Wrath and fiery Indignation for ever. So that this Text plainly holds forth both the Guilt and Puniſhment of Original Sin.

Now

Now since this Place is so clear a Proof of our Point, we must expect that our Adversaries of the *Socinian* and *Pelagian* Persuasion will do all they can to wrest it out of our Hands. Various Methods are used to pervert it; and 'tis with extreme Difficulty our Opposers evade the Force of it. Let us then examine some of their Artifices and Subterfuges whereby they labour to avoid it. And some there are who by *Nature* understand acquired Habit, which, say they, is Second *Nature*, and therefore may not unfitly be called by that Name. But, *first*, though Habit and Custom are called *Second Nature*, does it follow that Nature is no more than acquired Habit or Custom? *2dly*, This Interpretation of the Word would make the Apostle guilty of Tautology. Observe, he had before told them of their actual and habitual Sins, in these Words, *fulfilling the Desires of the Flesh and of the Mind*; and therefore for him to have mentioned it over again, would have been needless and superfluous. A discerning Eye cannot but take notice how gradually the Apostle proceeds from speaking of their wicked Lives and Actions, to lead them to the Fountain of all, the original Corruption of the Heart, *ver.* 2, 3. *3dly*, The Scripture uses the Greek Word, to signify our Birth, *Gal.* ii. 15. we who are *Jews by Nature*, *i. e.* born such: Again, *Rom.* ii. 14. the *Gentiles* do *by Nature* the Things contained in the Law. Since the Word *Nature*, in these Places, denotes our Birth or Nativity, why should it not be so understood in the Text before us ? What Reason can possibly be assigned for giving the Word another

E 3

Turn

Turn, unlefs it be the inveterate Prejudice of Men againft the Doctrine we are defending?

Again, others labour to confine this Text to the *Gentile* World; but this will be no eafy Matter, becaufe of the general, yea, univerfal Terms the infpired Apoftle here makes ufe of, *we all*, plainly comprehending himfelf and all Mankind, both *Jews* and *Gentiles*. To this it is objected, that in the 1, 2, 5, 8, and 11th Verfes, the divine Writer fpeaks in the fecond Perfon; and from thence they conclude, that in this third Verfe there is only an ordinary Enallage of Perfons, the Firft is put for the Second: and when the Apoftle fays *we*, he means *ye*. But that there is no fuch Enallage of Perfons as is pretended, the following Confiderations fully demonftrate. *Firft*, The Apoftle defignedly includes himfelf, as is his conftant Way when he would humble himfelf upon a Review of his State before Converfion, and extol the Riches of GOD's Grace in CHRIST JESUS. Thus *Tit.* iii. 3. *We ourfelves alfo were fometimes foolifh, difobedient.* -- And, 1 *Cor.* xv. 9. he calls himfelf *the leaft of the Apoftles*, and *lefs than the leaft of all Saints*, Eph. iii. 8. and *the Chief of Sinners*, 1 Tim. i. 15. Why then fhould we think the Apoftle excludes himfelf in the Place under Confideration? Or rather have we not abundant Reafon to think he fpeaks in the firft Perfon on purpofe to include himfelf therein? *Secondly*, In the firft Verfe of this Chapter the Apoftle fpeaks in the fecond Perfon; and *you* hath he quickned who were *dead in Trefpaffes and Sins*: But then, in the

fifth

fifth Verſe he ſays, even when *we were dead in Sins.* Here you ſee is an Exchange from the ſecond Perſon to the firſt: And what Account can be given of this, unleſs the Apoſtle thereby intended to ſhew that he in his natural State was *dead in Sins* as well as they, and ſo was quickened by the ſame divine Power that quickened them? *Thirdly,* Pleaſe to obſerve in the three firſt Verſes he deſcribes the Condition of the *Epheſians,* and all Men by Nature; and then to the End of the Chapter ſets forth the State of Grace: In the latter he plainly reckons himſelf, *v.* 4, 5, 10. and this implies, that he once was in the former. Thus we ſee the Cavils of our Adverſaries are null and void; and this Text ſhews us, that all Mankind are originally corrupted; and ſo long as it remains in the Bible, will be an undeniable Teſtimony of the Truth of the Doctrine of Original Sin. This is the Sin of which the Apoſtle complains, Rom. vii. 21. *Evil is preſent with me,* it *lieth near me,* it ſticks cloſe to me, and I can't be rid of it. This Sin cleaves to us, it adheres to our Hearts, it ſticks as cloſe to us as our Skin to our Fleſh, or our Fleſh to our Bones. This Sin is wrapt up in us, it is deeply rooted in our Natures, and ſo ſtrongly faſtened to our Souls, that nothing but the Almighty Power of God can diſentangle us from it. Of this Sin *Jeremiah* ſpeaks, chap. x. ver. 14. *Every Man is brutiſh in his Knowledge.* Of this Sin *Solomon* was deeply convinced, when he cried out, *Surely I am more brutiſh than any Man, and have not the Underſtanding of a Man,* Prov.

E 4

xxx.

xxx. 2. And if he who was the wisest Man made such a Complaint, how much more Reason have we to bewail our native Ignorance and *Brutishness?* The late Archbishop* seems sensible of this when he says, "They (*i. e.* " our first Parents) by this first Transgression, " did not only lose for themselves the Image " and Favour of God, but withal deprived their " Posterity of that blessed Estate, *Rom.* iii. 23. " and plunged them into the contrary, *Rom.* v. " 12. bringing Damnation upon themselves and " us all." And another learned Prelate† clearly delivers this Doctrine in these Words " This " Original Sin hath been propagated to us " both by Imputation and real Communica- " tion. *1st.* By Imputation of Adam's parti- " cular Transgression, in eating the forbidden " Fruit; for we were legally Parties in that " Covenant which was at first made with him, " therefore cannot but expect to be liable to " the Guilt which followed upon the Breach " of it, *Rom.* v. 12. *2dly.* By real Communi- " cation of evil Concupiscence and Deprava- " tion of our Natures, which was the Conse- " quence of the first Rebellion: We were all of " us naturally in our first Parents, as the " Streams in the Fountain, or the Branches in " the Root and therefore must needs partake " of the same corrupted Nature with them " *Job* xiv. 4,--xv. 14. This might justly make " us more loathsome and abominable in God's " Eyes than either Toads or Vipers, or any " other

---

* Usher.　　　　† Bishop Wilkins.

" other the moſt venomous, hurtful Creatures
" are in ours; and for this alone he might juſtly
" cut us off and condemn us, tho' it were mere-
" ly for the Prevention of that Miſchief and
" Enmity againſt him which the very Principles
" of our Natures are infected with " I might
ſay a great deal more. We have abundant Te-
ſtimonies on our Side, both human and divine,
but I think I have fulfill'd my firſt Undertaking.
I have largely explained the Doctrine of Original Sin, and clearly ſhewn that Adam's Sin is
imputed to us, that a ſpiritual Contamination of
Nature is inherent in us, and that hereupon we
are juſtly liable to God's eternal Wrath. Some
Men cannot bear to hear of this Doctrine, becauſe it ſtains all the Pride of human Glory,
and debaſes Man, that excellent creature, as
they call him; yea, this Doctrine reſembles
carnal Men to Brutes and Devils, ſeeing they
are naturally tinctured with all the ſenſual Inclinations of the one, and all the malignant
Qualities of the other. Hence it is that this
Doctrine is generally diſreliſhed by the proud
Philoſopher and the ſelf-righteous Moraliſt.
But convicted Sinners feel the Truth of it in
their Hearts. And believe me, that is the beſt
Divinity which lays the Creature loweſt, and
exalts CHRIST higheſt. None ſavingly know
the Lord Jesus, but thoſe who are in ſome
degree acquainted with the inward Corruption
of their Hearts. If the Reader is wounded
with an experimental Senſe of his indwelling
Pollution and Sinfulneſs, he will gladly hear,
and greedily embrace the free Salvation of
CHRIST

CHRIST JESUS. But *they that are whole need not a Physician.* They that have no sensible Experience of their lost Estate by nature, neither see the Necessity, nor know the Value of a Saviour.

Upon the whole we may learn, *First*, to disclaim all Pretensions to the Merit of Heaven. We are Sinners by Nature as well as by Practice, and we deserve nothing but Hell. When we have done all we can, our natural Righteousness will never merit Heaven. Consequently the supererogatory Works of the *Papists*, and the Self-Righteousness of *Socinians*, *Pelagians* and *Semipelagians*, falls to the Ground. 'Tis true, proud Nature is not willing to acknowledge she deserves Hell. It is a very great conviction of the Spirit, when Persons are enabled sincerely to make this Confession. Many, indeed, formally say, they deserve Hell, who do not consider what Hell is. Yet none go to Heaven, But those who first see they deserve Hell; and none are saved but those who own they deserve to be damned. Are you convinced of this? Do you know you deserve Hell? Do you seriously acknowledge Damnation is your due, if GOD was to deal with you in strict Justice? Happy are they who have this Knowledge of themselves and their own Demerit. This is the first Step to eternal Salvation. If therefore GOD by his SPIRIT hath shew'd you your miserable Condition by Nature, he will surely shew you his Free, Rich, Sovereign Salvation by Grace.

Secondly,

Secondly, We cannot but observe, what a Parallel there is between our Apostacy in Adam, and our Restoration by CHRIST. As on the one hand, we have Sin Imputed, Sin inherent, and deserve Everlasting Damnation; so on the other, we have Righteousness Imputed, Righteousness Inherent, and are entitled to Everlasting Salvation. These are both of them great and wonderful Mysteries; and they mutually explain and illustrate each other; The greater Knowledge you have of the one, the greater Knowledge you will have of the other; and the experimental Knowledge of both is best. If a Man sees himself in the First Adam without seeing himself in the Second, 'tis enough to drive him to Despair and Distraction; and to make him perfectly miserable. But when a Person sees himself in the Second Adam, CHRIST JESUS, it makes his Heart rejoice; and such a Soul is truly Happy, unspeakably Happy, eternally Happy.

THE

CHAP. II.

Of JUSTIFICATION *by* FAITH.

INDEED it would grieve me to fpeak of the Ruin of Mankind, without pointing out the Way of their Recovery. It would be infinitely better for Man not to know his Difeafe, than not to know the Remedy. Having then in the foregoing Chapter, declared the deplorable State of Man by Nature, as he lies under the Guilt and Curfe of Original Sin, I now come to treat of his Salvation by CHRIST JESUS, and to difcourfe of Juftification by Faith alone. I take unfpeakable pleafure and Satisfaction in fpeaking upon this Subject, and I could dilate upon the Theme for ever. I had a great love for this Doctrine long before I felt the Power and Efficacy of it upon my own Heart, but fince I have tafted its Sweetnefs and Excellency, it is become the Life of my Soul, the Joy of my Heart, and the Support and Comfort of my Spirit. My delight and Glory is in proclaiming this Evangelical Truth; and I wifh I could hear it preached in all the Churches in *England*. I know, indeed, it is an arduous Undertaking for fuch a Stripling as I to attempt to handle this grand and important Article of our Religion. I know

my

my own Weakneſs, and truſt in the Lord
for Strength; I depend upon his Aſſiſtance;
through his Grace ſtrengthening me, I can do
all Things. And that I may ſet this Doctrine
before the Reader in the cleareſt Light I can,
I chooſe to ſtate it in the five following Propoſitions, each of which (if Gᴏᴅ enables me) I
will undertake to make good from the Homilies and Articles of the Church of *England*:

    I. Men can do no good Works acceptable to
       Gᴏᴅ before Faith and Juſtification.

    II. Juſtifying Faith is the Gift of Gᴏᴅ.

    III. Juſtification is by Faith only.

    IV. Works have *no Part* in our Juſtification.

    V. Good Works follow after Juſtification,
       and are the Fruits of Juſtifying Faith.

    I. I am *firſt* to ſhew, that Men can do no
good Works acceptable to Gᴏᴅ before Faith
and Juſtification. And this is more than once
aſſerted in the Homily of good Works, where
we meet with this Paſſage, " Faith giveth Life
" to the Soul, and they be as much dead to
" Gᴏᴅ that lack Faith, as they be to the
" World, whoſe Bodies lack Souls. Without
" Faith, all that is done of us is but *Dead be-*
" *fore* Gᴏᴅ, altho' the Work ſeem never ſo
" gay and glorious before Men; even as the
" Picture graven or painted, is but a dead Re-
preſenta-

" prefentation of the Thing itfelf, and is with-
" out Life or any manner of moving: fo be
" the works of all unfaithful Perfons.---They
" be but the *Shadows* and *Shews* of lively and
" good Things, and not good and lively
" Things indeed---Without Faith no Work
" is good before God". Thefe Words are
clear, and need no Commentary to explain
them. All Works without Faith, are here
faid to be *Dead*, juft as a Picture is but a dead
Reprefentation of the Original. The fame
Doctrine is afterwards confirmed and exempli-
fied by the following Inftance, " If a Heathen
" Man clothe the Naked, feed the Hungry,
" and do fuch other like Works: yet becaufe
" he doeth them not in Faith, for the Ho-
" nour and Love of God, they be but *Dead*,
" vain and fruitlefs Works to him."---Again,
it is faid in the fame Homily, " Faith of itfelf
" is full of good Works, and nothing is Good
" without Faith. And for a Similitude he
" [*Auguftine*] faith, that they which glifter
" and fhine in Good Works, without Faith in
" God, be like *Dead* Men which have goodly
" and precious Tombs, and yet it availeth
" them nothing---He that doth good Deeds,
" yet without Faith, he hath no Life." Perfons may be outwardly Moral and Virtuous,
they may appear very Good and Righteous,
and yet have no living Faith in the Lord Jesus. This is a common Cafe. Men abound
in Works feemingly good when yet they themfelves are Infidels in their Hearts. Hence
all their Good Works, for want of Faith in
the

the Blood of CHRIST, are *Dead* before GOD, and will no more profit their Souls than gilded Sepulchres profit dead Bodies.

The Thirteenth Article is much to our Purpofe; it runs thus:

XIII. *Of Works before Juftification.*

" Works done before the Grace of CHRIST,
" and the Infpiration of his SPIRIT, are not
" pleafant to GOD, forafmuch as they fpring
" not of Faith in JESUS CHRIST, neither do
" they make Men *meet to receive Grace,* or
" (as the School Authors fay) deferve Grace
" of Congruity; yea rather, for that they are
" not done as GOD hath willed and command-
" ed them to be done, we doubt not but they
" have the *Nature* of Sin." We fee here
what Eftimate our Church makes of Works
done before Faith and Juftification: They
have not only the Form or Appearance, but
even the very *Nature* of Sin. " All the Works
" of *Unbelievers* and *Natural* Men (faith Bi-
" fhop *Sanderfon*) are not only ftained with
" Sin, (for fo are the beft Works of the Faith-
" ful too) but alfo are *really* and *truly* Sins."*
Hence the popifh Doctrine of Grace of Congruity, or Men's making themfelves *meet to
receive Grace,* is juftly condemned. Indeed
I could wifh none but *Papifts* held the faid
Doctrine. But, alas! there is Popery enough
without going to *Rome* for it. Yet I would
obferve

------

* Sixth Sermon.

obferve, this Article which condemns the Grace of Congruity of the *Papifts*, does equally condemn the preparatory Conditions of the *Socinians* and *Remonftrants*. What a Folly is it to talk of, or to fuppofe in fallen Man, Conditions previous to his Juftification? They who talk at this rate, know not what they fay, nor whereof they affirm. In a natural Man there is no *Meetnefs*, but a *Meetnefs* to Sin, and a *Meetnefs* to be damned. They who know themfelves, know this. And there are no Conditions prerequifite to Juftification, but what GOD by his SPIRIT is pleafed to work in Men's Hearts. None are *meet* to receive Grace, till GOD makes them fo. None are *meet* to obey the Gofpel, till GOD implants in their Souls a Principle of Faith and Evangelical Obedience. Before this is done, there is no *Meetnefs* in the Creature, no Difpofition to any thing fpiritually Good; neither are any of our Works acceptable and well-pleafing in the fight of Almighty GOD. This is the Doctrine of the Church of *England*, and they are all Diffenters from her Articles and Homilies that affert the contrary.

And as this Doctrine is agreeable to the Conftitution of our Church, fo is it exactly confonant with the Holy Scriptures. Thus faith *Solomon*, Prov. xv. 8. *The Sacrifice of the Wicked is an Abomination to the* LORD. All Unbelievers are wicked Perfons; how fober and upright foever their lives may be, their Hearts are wicked and impious. And while they are in this State, all their *Sacrifices i. e.* their religious

ous Performances, are not barely unacceptable, but abominable, yea an *Abomination* (in the Abſtract) *unto the* LORD. The ſame thing is again aſſerted *Ch.* xxi. *v.* 27. which plainly ſhews us the Judgment of *Solomon* in this matter. And hence we learn, that all the Works of thoſe who have no ſaving Faith in CHRIST are odious and abhorred of Almighty GOD. We may obſerve *Sacrifice* is here oppoſed to *Prayer* in the next Clauſe, for when the *Jews* offered *Sacrifice* they generally joined *Prayer* with it. This Text therefore teaches us, that both the *Prayers* and the *Sacrifices* of the *Wicked* are equally diſpleaſing in the ſight of GOD. Some make an ill uſe of this Text, and from hence take Occaſion, to omit *Prayer*; for ſay they, the *Prayer of the Wicked is an Abomination to the Lord*, and therefore we think it better not to pray at all. Thus the Devil deludes them. Such Perſons ought to conſider, *Firſt*, It is not the deſign of the inſpired Writer to deter Men from *Prayer*, but only to warn them againſt *praying* with their Hearts full of Impenitency and Infidelity. The Uſe therefore we are to make of this Text, is not to omit praying at all, but to approach the Lord in an acceptable manner; which we can do no otherwiſe, than by drawing near to the Throne of his Grace through Faith in his dear Son, and *lifting up holy Hands* in Prayer *without Wrath* and *Doubting*. 1 Tim. ii. 8. *Secondly*, the *Omiſſion of Prayer* is a Sin of itſelf, and in its own Nature, whereas the *Prayer of the Wicked* is not a Sin in itſelf, but only in reſpect of the

F

Form

Form or Manner of performing it, viz. becaufe Evangelical Faith is wanting. Altho' therefore the *Prayer* of the *Wicked* is an *Abomination* to the Lord, yet their *Omiffion of Prayer* is a much greater *Abomination.* The Wicked then had much better pray as well as they can, than not pray at all. *Thirdly,* 'Tis true indeed, if Men pray againft Sin in general, or any one fin in particular, and yet indulge themfelves in the wilful and habitual practice of it; what Hypocrify is all this! To be fure fuch Prayers muft be very loathfome and deteftable in the Eyes of the Almighty: But then if Perfons are awakened to a Senfe of their Wickednefs, if they groan under the Burthen of it, and defire to be delivered from it, will you fay that their *Prayers* are an *Abomination* to the Lord? This can never be, elfe what is the meaning of that Promife in Ifaiah, *Seek ye the Lord while he may be found, call ye upon him while he is near; let the wicked forfake his Way, and the Unrighteous Man his Thoughts; and let him return unto the Lord, and he will have Mercy upon him, and to our God, for he will abundantly pardon him.* This fhews how groundlefs this Cavil is. And the Truth of all is, Men are willing to omit Prayer, and fo the Devil and their own wicked Hearts furnifh them with many Pleas and Pretences to excufe themfelves.

Our Saviour delivers this Doctrine, *John* xiv. 6. *No Man cometh unto the Father but by me.* Our Perfons and our Performances are both accepted of God upon the fame Foundation;

but

but our Perfons are not accepted without Faith
in Chrift, neither therefore are our Performances. This Text then is a plain Proof,
that none of our Good Works are pleafing to
God, till we have Faith in his Son Chrift
Jefus our Lord.

The Apoftle *Paul,* in many Places, afferts
this Truth. Thus *Rom.* viii. 8. *So then they
that are in the Flefh cannot pleafe God.* Flefh
here denotes the fame as the *minding of the
Flefh,* ver. 6. *i. e.* the unregenerate State of
Man. All who are in this State *cannot pleafe*
God, and the Reafon is, becaufe they have no
Faith in the Mediator; for, as St. *John* faith,
*Whofoever believeth that Jefus is the Chrift is
born of God,* 1 John v. 1. So on the contrary,
thofe who are not born of God do not believe.
Therefore Unregenerate and Unbelievers, are
Terms convertible; and therefore of thefe latter, as well as the former, the Apoftle affirms,
that they *cannot pleafe* God; he does not fay,
they cannot fo eafily, they cannot fo exactly,
they cannot fo perfectly; but he fpeaks fimply
and abfolutely, they *cannot*; to let us know
they cannot pleafe him in any Meafure or Degree. Let them do what they will or can,
ftill fo long as Unbelief is in their Hearts, this
poifons all their Services, and makes their beft
Works unacceptable and offenfive to Almighty
God.

So again *Ch.* xiv. *ver.* 23. *Whatfoever is
not of Faith is Sin.* Whatfoever Work or Action does not fpring *out of Faith,* as the Fruit

F 2

out

out of the Tree, is Sin, and fo confequently muft be difpleafing to our heavenly Father. 'Tis true the holy Apoftle delivers this Sentence particularly, concerning eating divers or all kinds of Meats, which fome weak Chriftians lately converted from *Judaifm* fcrupled: The Divine Teacher therefore here admonifhes fuch fcrupulous Perfons to abftain, informing them, that fince they queftioned the Lawfulnefs of it, it would be Sin in them to eat: altho' to others who had no Doubt nor Scruple concerning it, it would be no Sin at all, *ver.* 2--23 But then we are alfo to obferve that the Apoftle lays this down as a general Maxim in Chriftian Divinity, and accordingly we are to take it in a large Senfe; and fo it teacheth us, that all our Works without Faith are nothing Worth; they are finful, yea, Sin itfelf, faith the Apoftle. And I remember the Church of *England* in one of her Homilies* makes this Ufe and Application of this Text.

The fame infallible Author fpeaks the fame Language, *Heb.* xi. 6. *But without Faith it is impoffible to pleafe him*, viz. God. The Apoftle, in the Words foregoing, had teftified that *Enoch pleafed GOD*; whence it inevitably follows, that he muft have been a Believer in Chrift, for *without Faith* in him 'tis abfolutely *impoffible to pleafe GOD.* And as *Enoch* could not pleafe God without Faith, fo neither can any other Perfon. This therefore is univerfally

---

* Of Good Works.

verfally true, that none of our Services, how fpecious or perfect foever they may feem, can pleafe God, if they are not done in the Faith of Chrift. And thus I think I have faid enough to prove and eftablifh my firft Propofition. This and the forementioned Texts evidently declare, that no Good Works, acceptable to God, can poffibly be done by us, before we believe in the Saviour, and are juftified.

From what hath been faid we infer,

I. The Neceffity of Faith in the Redeemer.

II. The utter Impoffibility of Juftification by Works.

I. How neceffary is Faith in the Redeemer? Neither our Perfons nor our Services are accepted of God without it. How earneftly then fhould we feek after this Grace? How unwearied fhould we be in the Purfuit of it? All the Good Works you do are difpleafing to God, unlefs they fpring from a living Principle of Faith in Chrift Jefus our Lord. Never therefore give any Reft to your Soul till you find this gracious Principle wrought in you. Cry Day and Night to God to implant it in your Heart. It is Faith in Chrift which recommends both our Perfons and our Performances to the Acceptance of our heavenly Father, and without this neither the Works of Heathen Philofophers nor Chriftian Profeffors are well-pleafing in his Eye. *Gentiles, Jews*

and Chriſtians, ſtand upon the ſame Foundation in this Reſpect; they all equally ſtand in
need of, and are equally beholden to the Merits
of Chriſt to intereſt them in the divine Favour. Are you therefore profeſs'd Chriſtians?
ſtill I muſt preſs and exhort and beſeech you
to believe in the Lord Jeſus Chriſt, or elſe
you cannot be ſaved. You may be ready to
think with yourſelves, do not Chriſtians believe
in Chriſt? How elſe are they Chriſtians?
And in what an extravagant Way doth this
Man talk, when he exhorts Chriſtians to believe in Chriſt? If he exhorted Heathens
to believe in Chriſt, we ſhould not ſo much
wonder at it; but to exhort Chriſtians to believe in Chriſt, ſeems to us quite needleſs
and ſuperfluous, yea, inconſiſtent and contra-
dictious. This is a common Objection; and
'tis true indeed, if Perſons do not believe in
Chriſt, they are no Chriſtians: But then how
many paſs for Chriſtians who have no vital
Faith in the Blood of Chriſt, yea, perhaps,
maliciouſly oppoſe the Doctrine of true evangelical Faith, and ridicule all Chriſtian Experience? Alas! all are not *Iſrael* that are of *Iſrael.* All are not chriſtians that take to themſelves the Name and Profeſſion of Chriſtianity.
Many ('tis to be feared) call themſelves Chriſtians, who yet know no more of Saving Faith
in Chriſt than *Jews, Turks,* Papiſts or Pa-
gans. Indeed 'tis an eaſy Matter for Men to
ſay they believe in Chriſt, but then 'tis not
ſo ſoon done as ſaid. Let me exhort thee
therefore, dear Reader, to enquire how 'tis
with

with thy own Soul.   Thou mayeſt have heard
of Jeſus Chriſt with *the hearing of the Ear*,
but hath the *Eye** of thy Faith *ſeen him?* Haſt
thou beheld his Fulneſs and All-ſufficiency?
Haſt thou had a View of his incomparable Excellency? Haſt thou felt in thy Heart the abſolute Neceſſity of juſt ſuch a Saviour as he is?
If thou haſt not, aſſure thyſelf that thou art
yet in Sin and Unbelief, and haſt no ſaving
Acquaintance with the dear Immanuel.   I now
therefore call upon all Chriſtians : I command
you all, in the Name of the Lord Jeſus
Chriſt, *Examine yourſelves whether you be in
the Faith*, 2 Cor. xiii. 5.

But how ſtands the Caſe if Perſons are not
only nominally but really Believers in Chriſt?
Is it reaſonable and expedient to exhort ſuch to
believe in his Name? What think you? Is
it adviſable to follow our Saviour's Example,
or is it not? If it is, obſerve what he ſays to
his Diſciples, *John* xiv. r. *Ye believe in GOD,
believe alſo in me.*   Our Lord's Diſciples were
Believers at this Time, and yet you ſee he exhorts them to believe in him, which ſhews
that it is highly, yea, infinitely reaſonable to
call upon Believers to believe in Chriſt.   And
what think you of the *Epheſians* and *Theſſalonians*, to whom St. *Paul* directed three of
his Epiſtles? I preſume you will allow they
were Chriſtians; and yet you may obſerve, the
ſacred Writer exhorts the former to take *the
Shield of Faith*, and the latter to put on *the*
F 4 *Breaſt-*

---

* *Job* xlii. 5.

*Breaſt-plate of faith**.   The Evangeliſt *John*
puts this Matter beyond Doubt, 1 *John* v. 13.
*Theſe Things have I written unto you that believe
on the Name of the Son of GOD, that you may
know that ye have eternal Life, and that ye may
believe on the Name of the Son of GOD.*   The
holy Apoſtle here doth not write to Heathens,
but to Chriſtians; he doth not write to Unbelievers, but to *Believers*; and for what Purpoſe? Why, the inſpired Author himſelf tells
us, that they may *believe on the Name of the
Son of GOD.*   All this ſhews, that 'tis necef-
ſary to exhort not only Heathens and Infidels,
but even Chriſtians, to *believe* in Chriſt.
The Reaſon of this is eaſily aſſigned; for
Faith is a progreſſive Grace, and (if it is of a
right Sort) is continually upon the Increaſe,
and makes perpetual Advances towards the
Maturity of a full Aſſurance.   All who are
true Believers find the Uſe and Influence of
ſuch Exhortations, to ſtrengthen and perfect
their Faith; they cannot reſt in their preſent
Attainments, but are continually purſuing after
greater Meaſures of this heavenly Grace.   Let
us all then forget the Things that are behind,
and reach forth unto thoſe which are before, if
*we may apprehend that for which we are appre-
hended of Chriſt Jeſus,* Phil. iii. 12, 13.

II. From hence we infer the Impoſſibility of
Juſtification by Works.   This is plain and ob-
vious; for if we can do no Works acceptable

---

able to God before our Juſtification, how then can we be juſtified by our Works? This is utterly impoſſible. If we were to be juſtified by our good Works, they muſt of Neceſſity precede our Juſtification, which they do not, and conſequently we are not juſtified by them. My late Lord of St. *Aſaph* plainly ſaw the Force of this Way of arguing, and therefore in his private Thoughts he bears a noble Teſtimony on our ſide. " 'Tis a Matter of Admi-" ration to me, how any one that pretends to " the Uſe of his Reaſon, can imagine that he " ſhould be accepted before God for what " comes from himſelf. For how is it poſſible " that I ſhould be juſtified by good Works, " when I can do no good Works at all before " I be firſt juſtified ? My Works cannot be " accepted as good before my Perſon be ſo ; " nor can my perſon be accepted of God till " ingrafted into Christ, before which en-" grafting into the true Vine 'tis impoſſible I " ſhould bring forth good Fruit; for *the Plow-*" *ing of the Wicked is Sin,* ſays *Solomon* ; yea, " *the Sacrifices of the Wicked are an Abomina-*" *tion to the LORD,* Prov. xxi. 4.---xv. 8." Thus ſpeaks this judicious Writer, this Phœnix of the *Britiſh* Divines, as he is called ; and he hath the Scriptures, and the XIIIth Article of the Church of *England,* to countenance him herein, as I have before ſhew'd.

And if the above Argumentation be allowed, then who ſees not that this is a previous Proof of our third and fourth Propoſitions ?

And

And truly I know no poffible Way of evading the Force of this, unlefs our Adverfaries have Recourfe to that Variety of Juftifications which they have invented, which is an Artifice they frequently make ufe of juft to blind their own Eyes, and to obfcure Divine Truths. Accordingly you will often obferve them making a Diftinction between the Juftification of Heathens and the juftification of Chriftians, between Juftification at Baptifm, or at the Time of Believing, and Juftification at the Day of Judgment. But what mean thefe groundlefs Diftinctions? Have they any Foundation in Scripture? *Firft*, The Scripture mentions but one Way of Juftification both for Heathens and Chriftians, and that is by Faith, *feeing it is one GOD who fhall juftify the Circumcifion by Faith, and Uncircumcifion through Faith*, Rom. iii. 30. *Secondly*, The Scripture fpeaks of but one Time of Juftification, and that is when Perfons believe in CHRIST; fo *Acts* xiii. 39. And *every Believer in him is juftified*. And our Saviour faith, *He that believeth on me hath everlafting Life*. Which fhews that when Souls believe in JESUS, they are inftantly and forthwith juftified. We fee then that Juftification is a Privilege conferred on believers while they are in this prefent World. As to Juftification at the Day of Judgment, it is nothing elfe but GOD's folemn Declaration, and open Acceptance of thofe whom he hath in this Life juftified. GOD will then accept none who were not juftified before they departed hence. Of this declarative juftification, faith our Lord,

I will

I will confefs, i. e. publickly own and approve of thofe who *have confeffed me before Men.---Then fhall the Righteous fhine forth as the Sun in the Kingdom of their Father,* Matt. x. 32.--- xiii. 43.

II. Juftifying Faith is the Gift of God. This Propofition contains two Particulars. Accordingly in explaining it, we fhall, *Firft,* Enquire what Faith is. *Secondly,* we fhall fhew that it is the Gift of God.

Firft, What is Faith? And the fhorteft and withal the fureft Way to know this is to confult the Holy Scriptures. There we are informed, that *Faith is the fubftance of Things hoped for, the evidence of Things not feen.* This is a general Defcription of Faith.. Faith is here defcribed by two of its effential Parts or Properties. *Firft,* It is *the fubftance of Things hoped for.---*Faith is the Foundation of Hope. We muft believe the Truth of a Promife before we can hope for its Accomplifhment. Hope therefore immediately follows Faith. Faith and Hope are nearly related. Faith brings near to us thofe Things which are the Objects of our Hope; it gives us a prefent Poffeffion and Enjoyment of them, and gives them a prefent being and Subfiftence in us, and is therefore fitly and properly called the *fubftance of Things hoped for.* The Greek Word is fometimes*

tranf-

---

* 2 Cor. ix. 4. Heb iii. 14.

tranflated *Confidence*, as fignifying that full Affurance which Faith give us of our obtaining
the full Fruition of thofe Things for which we
hope, and which we partly poffefs at prefent.
Secondly, Faith *is the Evidence of Things not
feen*. It gives us a View of the invifible Glories of another World. It is a fpiritual Optic,
whereby we difcern thofe Things which are
concealed from the Eyes of our Body, and
which are unfeen by the Eye of Natural Reafon. Faith is the *Evidence* or *Demonftration*
of thefe Things; it fo illuminates and magni-
fies them, and gives us fuch a near Profpect of
them, and fuch a clear infight into them, as
leaves no Doubt upon our Minds of their Truth
and Reality. This is an account of Faith at
large, and comprifes in it as well an hiftorical
Affent to revealed Truths, as a faving Acquaintance with Jefus the Mediator.

But then juflifying Faith, or Faith as it
efpecially refers to Chrift, and hath his Merits and Righteoufuefs for its object, is varioufly
expreffed and reprefented in Holy Scripture.
Sometimes this Faith is fignified by *coming* to
Chrift. So faith our bleffed Lord; *Come
unto me all ye that labour*,---And *he that cometh
to me fhall never hunger, and he that believeth
on me fhall never thirft*, John vi. 35. The
latter Claufe explains the former, and lets us
know that *coming* to Chrift is as much as *believing* in him. Sinners, by Nature, are at an
infinite Diftance from God: they have loft all
Com-

Communion with him, and are become entire Strangers to him. *We all like Sheep have gone astray,*---but by Faith we return unto Jesus *the Shepherd and Bishop of our Souls.*---And *by* him *we have Access by one* Spirit *unto* God *the Father.* Isaiah liii. 6. 1 Pet. ii 25. Eph. ii. 18.

Saving Faith is sometimes meant by *leaning* upon Christ. The Church is said to come up from the Wilderness *leaning upon her Beloved,* Cant. viii. 5. *Leaning* implies our own Weakness and Inability. A Person leans upon a Staff or Pillar when he is weak, just ready to faint, and unable to support himself. In like Manner when a Sinner feels his own Weakness, when he is oppressed with the insupportable Weight of Sin, and finds himself just ready to sink under it, then he leans upon Christ, is supported by him, and derives spiritual strength and Refreshment from him.

Sometimes the Word *Rest* is made use of to denote living Faith in Christ. *Rest in the* Lord, saith the Psalmist, Psal. xxxvii. 7, and our Saviour promises to give *Rest* to those who come unto him Matth. xi. 28. As the weary Mariner finds Rest in the Haven, or as the weary Traveller rests when he gets home, so the weary Sinner hath Rest for his Soul when he believes in Christ.

Sometimes this Faith is intended by *Staying.* Thus God commands those *who walk in Darkness, to trust in the Name of the LORD, and stay upon their GOD,* Isa. l. 10. And the *Remnant of Israel* are described as *staying upon the*
LORD,

LORD, *the Holy One of Ifrael in Truth*, Ifa. x. 20. So again, *chap.* xxvi. *ver.* 3. *Thou wilt keep him in perfect Peace whofe Mind is ftayed on thee; becaufe he trufteth in thee.* This Text teacheth us, that *Staying* is equivalent to *Trufting, i. e.* Believing. Man in this World is like a Ship at Sea. An Unbeliever is like a Ship, in a tempeftuous Ocean, without Ballaft or Anchor. A Believer is a Ship at Stays: Faith is the Cable, and Chrift is the *Anchor fure and ftedfaft*, Heb. vi. 19. And although Winds blow hard and Billows run high, yet they fhall never be able to drive him from his Anchor, nor fink him in the Sea of Perdition.

In fome Places of Scripture, the Word *Roll* expreffeth that Act of Faith which is juftifying. *He trufted in the* LORD, faith *David*, *Pfal.* xxii. 8. or, as 'tis in the Margin, *He rolled himfelf on the* LORD. So alfo, *Pfal.* xxxvii. 5. *Commit thy Way unto the* LORD. Or, according to the *Hebrew, Roll thy Way on the* LORD. *Rolling on the* LORD, is believing or trufting in him; and fince the Scripture ufes this Expreffion, we cannot doubt of the Significancy and Propriety of it. And if *rolling on the* LORD, i. e. *rolling* on GOD the Father, be a proper Expreffion, why not *rolling* on GOD the Son? Many pious Divines therefore have made ufe of the Phrafe, *rolling on* Chrift, to denote Saving Faith in him. And thofe who are experimentally acquainted with Chrift, know the Fitnefs and Suitablenefs of this Expreffion

to

to fpecify their Reliance upon Chrift, to defcribe their cafting their Souls entirely upon
him, and entrufting the whole Affair of their
Salvation in his Hand.   Notwithftanding this,
fome Perfons cannot bear this Way of fpeaking,
they look upon it as no better than Cant and
Enthufiafm, and ridicule and deride all who
make ufe of it.   But Men will fpeak Evil of
Things they know not.   Hereby they fhew
their Ignorance, both of the Scriptures, and
alfo of the Power of God.   Thus the Infidels
in *David*'s Time reproached him, *Pfalm* xxii.
8. and thus the Scribes and Elders mock'd and
reviled our Saviour, *Matth.* xxvii. 43, fo that
we fee ancient and modern Scoffers agree.
The Mockers of our Day fymbolize with the
Mockers of old, they go Hand in Hand, they
ufe the very fame Taunts and Jeers, and difcover the fame Infidelity and Depravity of
Heart.   If Chrift himfelf was thus derided,
why fhould his Followers expect any better
Treatment?   Is the Servant above his Mafter?
or the Difciple above his Lord?   If therefore
they have thus hated and maligned the Mafter
of the Houfe, how much more thofe of his
Houfhold? If they fhot out fharp Arrows, even
bitter Words, at the Lord Jefus himfelf, how
can you expect to efcape them? Or why fhould
you think much of bearing thofe *cruel Mock-*
ings which Chrift Jefus endured before you,
and for your Sake?   And with refpect to the
Adverfaries, they perhaps may think they only
laugh at a few Cant-Terms and odd Expreffions
of fome poor, filly, whimfical Enthufiafts:

But

But this is bad enough, feeing thefe Terms and Expreffions are found in Scripture, as I have before fhewed. But the whole Truth of the Matter is, thefe profane Scoffers do not ridicule Words and Phrafes only, but they deride and banter the Things fignified thereby; and therefore they are highly criminal, and (if they repent not) will bring upon themfelves fwift Deftruction.

Receiving Chrift is another Scriptural Denotation of faving Faith, Thus John i. 12. *But as many as received him to them gave he Power to become the Sons of God, even to them that believe in his Name*: So that we fee *receiving Chrift* is *believing* in him; therefore, faith the Apoftle, Col. ii. 6. *as ye have received the* Lord Jefus.---Hence we hear of *laying hold upon the Hope fet before us*, Heb. vi. 18. and of *holding faft that which we have received*, Rev. iii. 3. All which fignifies our Reception of Chrift. This Reception of Chrift is the Life of Faith. Thereby a Soul applies and appropriates the Lord Chrift to himfelf, and can with *Thomas*, call him *my* Lord *and my* God, or fay with the Apoftle *Paul, he loved me and gave himfelf for me*. A true Believer receives Chrift, and poffeffes him as his own Right and Property, Poffeffion is the Foundation of all Happinefs. Poffeffion fweetens all Bleffings to us, whether Temporal or Eternal. When a Worldling takes a Survey of large Tracts of Ground, when he fees great Sums of Money, or cafts his Eyes on fine Bays of Building, if he can fay, All this is mine, how

is his carnal heart delighted! and with what fenfible Pleafure is his earthly Mind affected! It is
juft fo in fpiritual Things.   When a Soul, by
the Eye of Faith, fees the unfearchable Riches
of Chrift, when he hath the heavenly *Ca-
naan* laid before him as in a Map ; and when
he beholds a Building of God Eternal in the
Heavens, if he can fay (and fay upon fure
Grounds) all this is mine ; how wonderfully is
the Soul tranfported! and what folid Joy does
a Chriftian feel at fuch a Time! 'Tis the Poffeffion of thefe Things that endears them unto
him, and they give him infinitely greater Happinefs and Satisfaction, than all the Pleafures
and Profits of this World could poffibly afford.

Thus I have given you the Scriptural Account of Faith ; and this I hope will fatisfy
you : If it will not, I know not what will.
You perhaps may be for a Faith of a more Ma-
thematical Exactnefs, you may defire a more
logical Definition of this Grace.   But beware
(I befeech you) left you miftake the Shadow
for the Subftance, and reft in the Definition,
inftead of the Thing itfelf.   You may turn
over Volumes of Theological Writings, and
you will find different Divines give different
Definitions of Faith, and every one thinks his
own the beft.   God is not confin'd to Rules of
Logick.   He does not delight to entertain us
with Philofophical Definitions.   He is infinitely
above all.   And he gives Defcriptions of Things
according to his infinite Wifdom.   Whatfoever right Conceptions we have of juftifying
Faith, we muft borrow from his holy Word:
G
And

And there we find this Grace defcribed by *coming* to, *receiving* of, *leaning, refting, ftaying* and rolling upon Chrift.

After all, a Perfon will beft know what Faith is, when he is poffeffed of it. You may give a Man born blind as many Definitions of Light as you pleafe, yet he will never know what Light is, 'till his Eyes are opened, and he fees it. Juft fo you may give an Unbeliever as many Defcriptions of Faith as you pleafe or can, yet he will never know what Faith is, till he hath it in his Heart. Doth any one therefore enquire what Faith is? Let him believe on the Lord Jefus Chrift, and then he will know what Faith is, and never till then. The Experience of the Thing beft informs us of the Nature of it. If the Reader hath not yet had this Experience, I come now to tell him how and where he may attain it; for,

Secondly, Faith is the Gift of God. This was the fecond Thing to be proved. And this is clearly demonftrated from the Homilies and Liturgies of the Church of *England*.

The Homily on Prayer directs us, " firft of " all to crave fuch Things as properly belong " to our Salvation, as the Gift of Repentance " the *Gift of Faith*.

The Homily on the Mifery of Man tells us, " we have neither *Faith*, Charity, Hope, Pa- " tience, Chaftity, nor any thing elfe that good " is, but of God, and therefore thefe Virtues " be called there *(viz. Gal.* v.*) the fruits of* " *the Holy Ghoft*, and not the Fruits of Man." According to this, *Faith* is not the Produce of

Man's

Man's Free-will, or natural Power, but the *Fruit and Produce of the Holy Ghost.* And this is rightly reduc'd from the Mifery of Man in his lapfed Eftate; for as a Natural Man hath not in himfelf Love to God, Humility, Purity of Heart, or any other Grace, fo neither hath he the Grace of Faith. And all the Allegations from Scripture or Reafon, that prove Man is deftitute of any other Chriftian Grace or Virtue, will equally prove that he is deftitute of this alfo.

Accordingly in the Homily of the Salvation of Mankind we are told, that " three Things " muft go together in our Juftification, — " and the third is a *true and lively Faith* in " the Merits of Jefus Chrift, which yet is " not ours, but by God's *working in us.*" If our Faith is fuch as we work in ourfelves, and not fuch as God by his Spirit *works in us;* then ours is not a *true* and *lively,* but a falfe and dead Faith. Some allow that Faith is the Gift of God, but then by Faith they mean the Objects of Faith, *viz.* Chrift, the Scriptures and all Divine Revelation. But this Paffage fpeaks of a Faith of God's *working in us,* which you fee is not fo properly applicable to the Objects of Faith, as to the Grace or Principle of Faith in the Heart.

.. The Homily for Rogation Week exhorts to " hear what is teftified firft of *the Gift of Faith,* " the firft Entry into a Chriftian Life, without " which no Man can pleafe God." In the Margin *Eph.* ii. 8. is referr'd to, which we fhall have Occafion to confider afterwards.

G 2

The

.The Liturgy is full of this Doctrine. In one Collect * it is said, " Almighty and " Everlasting God, give unto us the *In-* " creaſe of Faith*, Hope and Charity, &c. If the *Increaſe of Faith* be God's Gift, then ſo is the firſt Seed and Principle therof for the ſame Reaſon. Accordingly we find the Church returning Thanks to God in this Manner: " We give thee humble Thanks " that thou haſt vouchſafed to call us to the " Knowledge of thy Grace and *Faith* in " Thee : ‡ " And it would be endleſs to mention all the Paſſages in the Liturgy to this Purpoſe. I only juſt take Notice, that as Faith, ſo likewiſe *Repentance* is the Gift of God. The Homily on Repentance ſays, " He " (Christ) was exalted to give Repentance " and Remiſſion of Sins unto *Iſrael*."——— " We muſt beware and take heed that we do " in no wiſe think in our Hearts, imagine, " or believe that we are able to *repent* aright, " or to turn effectually unto the Lord by " our own Might and Strength."———" To " *repent* is a good Gift of God."———And in the Liturgy, " That it may pleaſe thee to *give* " us true *Repentance*," This is agreeable to Scripture†: And this may ſerve to correct the Error of thoſe who tell Men Repentance is in their own Power, and they may repent when they will.

---

* Fourteenth Sunday after Trinity.
‡ Office of Baptiſm.
† Acts v. 31. xi. 18. 2 Tim. ii. 25. &c. &c.

But

But to return.   The Scriptures are clear in this Point.   Our Saviour faith to *Peter, Matt.* xvi. 17.   *Bleſſed art thou Simon Barjona, for Fleſh and Blood hath not revealed it unto thee, but my Father which is in Heaven.* Peter is pronounced *bleſſed,* becauſe he had not a human but a divine Faith wrought in his Soul; not *Fleſh* and *Blood, i. e.* neither his own Reaſon and natural Underſtanding, nor yet the Inſtruction or Argumentation of others; but the *Father* only revealed it unto him, that CHRIST *was the Son of the living* GOD, ver. 16.   We are not to look upon this as an extraordinary Revelation.   This Revelation is common to all true Chriſtians; and unleſs the ſame *heavenly* Power reveals Chriſt in our Hearts, we ſhall never believe to any ſaving Purpoſe.   And God works this Grace of Faith in his Children by the Influence of the HOLY GHOST, who is therefore called *the* SPIRIT *of Faith,* 2 Cor. iv. 13.   Agreeable to which the Apoſtle *Paul* tells us, that no Man can ſay JESUS *is the* LORD *but by the Holy Ghoſt,* 1 Cor. xii. 3. which ſhews that the eternal Spirit is the Efficient of juſtifying Faith.

In *John* vi. 44. our Saviour declares the utter Inability of Man to believe of himſelf; *No Man can come to me, except the Father which hath ſent me draw him.*——And therefore in the next Verſe he very ſeaſonably adds, *Every Man therefore that hath heard and hath learned of the Father cometh unto me, i. e. believeth in me.*   They, and they only,

who

who are drawn of the Father, who *hear* and *learn* of him, believe in Chrift. Our Lord therefore calls Faith *the Work of* God, ver. 29. and the Apoftle *Paul* ftiles it *the Faith of the Operation of* God, *Col.* ii. 12. Hence we are faid to *believe according to the working of his mighty Power, Eph.* i. 19. The fame Power that *raifed* Christ *from the Dead,* ver. 20.

St. *Paul* in enumerating the Gifts of the Spirit, 1 *Cor.* xii. 9. faith, *To another Faith by the fame Spirit*; where by *Faith* fome underftand a Power to work Miracles: But *firft,* there is no Neceffity of taking *Faith* here in this Senfe; becaufe *working of Miracles* is mentioned juft after: *Secondly,* If a *Faith* that would enable us to work outward Miracles be the Gift of God, much more is juftifying *Faith*; for that Faith which juftifies the Soul is as great, if not greater Energy than which would qualify us to work miraculous Cures on the Bodies of Men.

John the Baptift informs us, that *A Man can receive nothing, except it be given him from above, John.* iii. 27. And the Apoftle *James* preaches the fame Doctrine; *Every good and perfect Gift is from above,* chap. i. ver. 17. Faith is a *good and perfect Gift,* and therefore that is from above. And can a Man *receive nothing, except it be given him from Above?* How then fhall he *receive* Faith, unlefs he have it from thence? To this we may adjoin the Teftimony of the Apoftle *Paul, Phil.* i. 29. *Unto you it is given in the Behalf*

Behalf of Christ, *not only to believe on him, but also to suffer for his Sake.* The Apostle in the foregoing Verse, is encouraging the *Philippians* under Trials and Afflictions, and he seasonably reminds them of God's having *given* them Faith; which is designed to direct them to look to the same God who *gave* them this Belief, for the Preservation and Consummation of it. The same infallible Divine faith to the *Ephesians, By grace ye are saved through Faith; and that not of yourselves, it is the Gift of* God, Eph. ii. 8. In inculcating the Doctrine of Salvation by Grace, he asserts it to be by Faith, as the instrumental Means thereof: Now, lest the *Ephesians* should surmise they had this Faith in or from themselves, he informs them it is the Gift of God, that so he may cut off all Occasion of boasting. Indeed it is this Doctrine only that excludes all Boasting; for if we could believe of ourselves, we should have whereof to glory; but since we cannot believe of ourselves, the Creature is humbled; and since we are obliged to come to God, and receive the *Gift of Faith gratis* at his Hands, we must (if we will glory) glory only in the free Grace of God in Christ Jesus our Lord.

And here I might appeal to Experience; for what mean these Complaints of Unbelief which we hear from awakened Souls? Do they not shew that it is not in Man's natural Will or Power to believe? Yea, do not convicted Sinners feel in their Hearts that they cannot believe? I ask you therefore, are you

a Be-a Believer in Chrift? If you are, I refer you no further than to your own Experience to convince you that Faith is the Gift of God. Do you not remember the Time when you did not believe? Do you not remember the Time when you could not believe? Do you not remember the Time when God firft gave the Gift of Faith to your difquieted Soul?

The main Queftion therefore is, Have you received the Gift of Faith? Are you a Believer in Chrift? Do not deceive yourfelf. Do not think yourfelf a Chriftian before you are fo. You may repeat all the Articles of your Creed, you may believe the Scriptures and all the Truths therein contained; you may be a Member of an Orthodox Church, where found Doctrine is preached and the Sacraments are duly adminiftered: you may practife the Ceremonies of Religion, and yield an external Obedience to the moral Precepts of the Gofpel, and yet have no living Faith in your Heart. All this you may do, yea, and as much more, and all the while be only an almoft Chriftian. Thus far and a great deal further an Infidel may go. Let me ferioufly afk you then, have you *a fure truft and Confidence in* God's *merciful Promifes to be faved from everlafting Damnation by* Chrift? This is the Defcription our Church* gives of Faith and if you have not this Faith in you, if you do not find a *fure Truft* in God, a firm *Confidence* in Chrift, I fear you have but little, if any Faith at all.

---

* Homily of Salvation.

Search

Search therefore into your Heart; examine narrowly into yourſelf; never be ſatisfied till you know the Truth of your State: See whether you are a Believer or an Unbeliever. If you are an Unbeliever, I do not flatter you, I tell you your Doom at once, or rather Chriſt himſelf tells it you, Mark xvi. 16. *He that believeth not ſhall be damned.* You may think this hard; and be ready to cry out, " Is not " this cruel? you have before told us it is not " in the Power of Man to believe, and now " you aſſert, that Man is *damned* for not be- " lieving. What is Man *damned* for not do- " ing that which he hath no Power to do?" I anſwer, though a Man hath not a natural Power to believe, let him go to God and aſk Faith; and God will give it him. Inſtead therefore of diſputing about your Inability to believe, inſtead of inventing Pleas and Excuſes to ſkreen you in Unbelief, come to God fully convinced of your own Impotency, and God will give you the Gift of ſaving Faith. Otherwiſe you are inexcuſable, and your Damnation is juſt. But, Reader, may I hope better Things of you? Have you received this Gift? Hath God given you to believe in the Name of his eternal and only begotten Son? Then with how many *Cords of Love* hath the Lord encompaſſed your Soul? And how many Obligations of Gratitude, Obedience, and Joyfulneſs are incumbent upon you? Therefore,

Firſt, Give God all the Glory. Look back and ſee how lately you were dead in Sin, and buried in Unbelief. Then you groaned by rea-

H ·

ſon

fon of the Infidelity of your Heart, and you could no more believe than you could remove the Mountains. How comes it to pafs, that you now believe? Whence is it that the Scene is thus changed? Whence is it that your State is fo much better'd? Who wrought this heavenly Alteration in you? Hath not the Lord himfelf done this marvellous Thing? Hath not his own Right-hand and his holy Arm gotten himfelf the Victory? Therefore *not unto us O Lord, not unto us, but unto thy Name give the Glory.* And if God hath given you this Gift he hath made you an infinitely greater Prefent than if he had given you all the Riches of *India*, or all the Treafures of *Egypt*. The Gifts of Nature and Providence may fail, or be taken from you; but the Gift of Faith fhall never be taken from you. It is an immortal Seed that knows no Decay: it is a permanent Principle that endures for ever. Therefore blefs God who gave it you, love him, thank him, praife him, delight in him, and rejoice before him continually. And praife and blefs the Son equally with the Father. Altho' this Faith is a free Gift to you, yet it coft Jefus Chrift dear; he fhed his own Heart's Blood to purchafe it for you. When he afcended up on high *he led Captivity captive, and received Gifts for Men,* and amongft the reft the Gift of Faith. This he diftributes to his People; and if you have it, he gave it you. Chrift by his Blood bought it for you. Chrift by his Spirit wrought it in you. Therefore be fure

praife

praife Jesus Christ and his Spirit for ever.

Secondly, Praife God with your Life as well as your Lip: Live to his Praife. Evidence your Faith by your good Works. Faith is a very prolifick Grace: and if its deeply rooted in your Heart, it will produce Obedience in your Life. *Faith without Works is Dead.* If you do no good Works, you are no Chriftian; but if you produce evil Works what are you then? You are a Difgrace to your Religion, you are worfe than a Heathen. What fignifies profefling Chriftianity, while you walk as the *Gentiles*, which know not God? Or why do you pretend to be a Believer in Chrift, while you live in fin? Your practice gives the Lie to your Profeffion, and if you go on thus, you will in the End receive everlafting Damnation. Either make no Profeffion or elfe live up to it. The former of thefe I would have you by no Means embrace. All that remains therefore is, to evince the Truth and Sincerity of your Profeffion, by the Purity of your Heart, and the Piety of your Converfation.

Thirdly, Look to God for the Increafe of Faith. The greateft Chriftian will yet find fomething wanting. The ftrongeft Believer, if he is fenfible of his remaining Unbelief, will feel the Need of perpetual Additions to his Faith. None can fay I am perfect in myfelf, and want no more. Now we have no more Power to increafe our Faith than to work it in ourfelves at firft. We muft be beholden to the fame God, who gave us the firft Grace, to give

us

us all future Acceffions and Augmentations thereof. Do you therefore complain that your Faith is weak? Do you find a great deal of Unbelief, and but little, very little Faith in you? Is your Faith as fmall as a Grain of Muftard Seed? Is your Faith like a Spark cover'd with Afhes, fcarcely difcernable? Then let your continual Cry be, LORD *increafe my Faith*; LORD *I believe, help my Unbelief*. And affure yourfelf, that the fame God who hath given you the firft Degree of Faith, will give all other Degrees neceffary to Salvation. What he hath already given you is only an Earneft of more. And

Laftly, Faith will foon be turned into Sight. Now we know but in Part, but when that which is perfect is come, then that which is in Part fhall be done away. Rejoice therefore in hope of the Glory which fhall be revealed. This Veil of Flefh now intercepts God from our View; but when this Veil is removed, when this Curtain is undraw'd, then fhall we have a full view of God, then fhall we fee him Face to Face, and know him even as we are known. Faith will then be turned into Sight: Hope will be fwallowed up in Enjoyment: and Love and Joy will flourifh and increafe for ever. Therefore be conftant and endure to the End. Wait for the glorious Appearance of the LORD JESUS CHRIST, whom having not feen you love; in whom, tho' now you fee him not, yet *believing*, you rejoice with Joy unfpeakable and full of Glory.

But

But I am senfible I muft attend to the Complaint of a weak Chriftian, " Ah, (fays fome
" poor diftreffed Soul) this is a great Happinefs
" indeed, for thofe who believe---but for
" my Part, I am an Unbeliever, and therefore
" I have neither Lot nor Portion in this Mat-
" ter. I have no Faith. I cannot believe.
" Unbelief like a Mountain preffes upon my
" Heart; and I cannot get rid of it. I cannot
" come to Chrift; I wifh I could: But oh!
" I have no Power. You may invite me to
" come to Chrift as long as you pleafe, you
" may call upon me till your Tongue cleaves
" to the Roof of your Mouth; your Labour
" is in vain, you fpend your Strength for
" nought; I can no more believe, than I
" can reach Heaven with my Hand." Well,
hath God given you this Conviction? Then
happy is it for you. Do you feel the Hardnefs
of your Heart? Do you find an Emptinefs in
your Soul? Do you fee yourfelf full of Unbelief? Hath God by his Spirit revealed thefe
Things to you? Then affure yourfelf the Lord
would not have fhewed you all thefe Things,
if he had intended to deftroy you. It is the
Way of God, firft to convince Sinners of Unbelief, and then to take it away, and confer
faving Faith upon them. None ever believed
but he was firft convinced of Unbelief. To
fee and feel your Unbelief is therefore the firft
Step to believing in the Lord Jefus. A Natural Man, if he leads a good, fober, moral
Life, thinks himfelf in a fair Way for Heaven,
and never doubts of his Salvation. A Perfon

                    who

who is awakened to a Senfe of his Sinfulnefs, who fees the Impurity of his Heart, and the Impiety of his Life, then begins to be concerned about his Salvation; he queftions whether Chrift will fave him or not; yea, he is inclined to defpair, he is ready to think the Lord will never fave fuch a Sinner as he is. You fee then the Difference: The carnal Moralift never doubts of his Salvation; the convicted Sinner ftands upon the Point of Defperation: The one buoys himfelf up with groundlefs Prefumption; the other is fenfible of his Sin and Danger and is in great Diftrefs. Now there is more Hope of a Soul under a *Weak* or *Little Faith**, than of one who is afleep in a carnal Security.

Again; Do you complain you cannot come to the Lord Jefus? Then the Lord Jefus will kindly come to you? Do you fay you cannot believe? Then Chrift himfelf will enable you to believe. The tender Jefus fees your Mifery and Helpleffnefs, he Sympathizes with you, and longs to be gracious unto you. Hath he convinced you of Sin? He will alfo convince you of his Righteoufnefs. The Son of God knows your inability to believe, he fees you want Faith. This Grace he hath purchafed for you by his Blood, and he will work it in you by his Spirit. The Bleffing is in fure Hands, and you need not fear receiving it. God, who freely *juftifieth the Ungodly*, doth freely give them juftifying Faith. Jefus Chrift

never

---

* Matth. vi. 30. Rom. xiv. 1.

never loft, Jefus Chrift never will lofe one Soul of his People for want of giving them that Faith which is neceffary to their Juftification : And though your Soul may be at prefent in great Darknefs, Sorrow and Vexation, yet be not afraid, neither be difmay'd; humbly hope, and patiently wait for Salvation from the Lord. Soon will thefe Clouds pafs off; foon will your Heavinefs be turned into Joy. A great Calm generally follows a great Storm, and great Confufion generally goes before great Peace. The more fhaken you are now, the more eftablifhed you fhall be hereafter. The *Things that are fhaken,* viz. Self-confidence, Hypocrify, Unbelief, Lukewarmnefs and Formal Religion fhall be removed, that the Things *which cannot be fhaken,* viz. Righteoufnefs, Peace, and Joy in the Holy Ghost *may remain,* Heb. xii. 27. Your *Confolations* fhall infinitely abound over all your *Tribulations,* 2 Cor. i. 4, 5. The Lord Jefus will remove all Impediments that lie in your Way :- He will folve all Difficulties, anfwer all your Objections, fcatter all your Doubts and Fears, and fill you with the Fulnefs of the Bleffing of the Gofpel of Peace.

III. I come now, in the *Third* Place, to fhew, that Juftification is by Faith only. The opinion of *Luther* on this fubject is fo well known, that it is not neceffary to mention it. Though I know *Luther's* Judgment is of little Efteem among fome People; and others who have a great Value for the Doctrine and Writ-

H 4

ings

ings of that great Man of God may be ready to aſk, If *Luther*'s Judgment be allow'd, what will become of the Church of *England?* I anſwer, The Articles and Homilies are the Standard of the Doctrines profeſſed by any Church; the Doctrine of free Juſtification is clearly contained in the Articles and Homilies of the Church of *England*, and therefore ſhe is found in this Point, and will never fall by the Judgment of *Luther*. Yet I would add, *Luther*'s Sentiment is a juſt Reproof of thoſe who ſubſcribe to orthodox Articles, and yet preach contrary Doctrines.

Before I fully enter upon this Head, I think it may not be improper to deſcribe the Privilege of Juſtification at large. Juſtification therefore conſiſts of three Things; 1. In the Forgiveneſs of Sins. 2. In the Imputation of Chriſt's Righteouſneſs. And 3. In our receiving a Right and Title to eternal Life.

Firſt, Juſtification conſiſts in the Forgiveneſs of Sins. The Word *juſtify* is made uſe of by Lawyers, and Civilians, and hath an eſpecial Reference to the Proceedings of Courts of Judicature. A Perſon is ſaid to be juſtified when he is acquitted by the Judge from all the Accuſations that were alledged againſt him. To be juſtified, therefore, is to be cleared, abſolved, or pronounced innocent. The Word *Juſtify* bears this Senſe in Holy Scripture. It is ſaid, Exod. xxiii. 7. *The Righteous and the Innocent ſlay thou not, for I will not juſtify the Wicked.* God dehorts from Murder, and eſpecially from the Murder of the *Righteous and In-*
nocent ·

nocent ; and the Reafon he affigns for it is this,
I will not *juftify*, i. e. abfolve, acquit, or pronounce guiltlefs, thofe who are thus criminal.
So in Deut. xxv. 1. *If there be a Controverfy
between Men, and they come into Judgment that
the Judges may judge them, then fhall they juftify the Righteous, and condemn the Wicked.*
Since here is Mention of a *Controverfy*, of
Judges and of *coming into Judgment*, there can
remain no Doubt upon our Minds that thefe
Words have a Refpect to judicial Proceedings,
at which it is both the Command of GOD,
and the Duty of good Magiftrates, to *juftify*,
that is, to clear and difcharge the *Righteous*,
and *condemn* the Guilty. Befides, *juftify* is
here oppofed to *condemn*; as in Ifa. l. 8, 9. and
Rom. viii. 33, for *Juftification* and *Condemnation*
are both judicial Acts, and are paffed upon
different Perfons occafionally. But I think I
have faid enough to fhew that the Term *juftify*
is of forenfick Ufe and Signification, and that it
is ufed in this Senfe in the facred Writings.
Now then obferve how well this Explication of
the Word fuits our Purpofe. We are all Criminals, all Malefactors, all Rebels againft the
moft High GOD: We have all broken the
divine Law; we ftand arraigned at the awful
Bar of GOD's infinite Juftice; our Mouths
are ftopped, and we have nothing to plead but
Guilty, Guilty. We are all become guilty before GOD, we are all guilty of Death, even
eternal Death; and GOD, the great GOD,
the Judge of Heaven and Earth, would

pronounce

pronounce a Sentence of Hell and Damnation upon us, did not the precious Blood of Christ interpofe, pacify the Divine Wrath, and prevent the eternal ruin of our Souls. The dearly beloved and only begotten Son of GOD was made a Curfe for us, and therefore we efcape the Wrath and Curfe of GOD for ever, and inftead of a Sentence of Condemnation, we receive a Sentence of Juftification from our Almighty Judge. Hereupon all our Sins are forgiven; they fhall be no more remembered againft us. All our Sins, both of Omiffion and Commiffion, the Iniquities of our Hearts, and the Obliquities of our Lives; all our Offences in Thought, Word, and Deed; all our Treipaffes againft God, our Neighbours, and ourfelves; all our crimes how numerous foever, how aggravated foever: In fhort, all our Tranfgreffions, both paft, prefent, and future, are freely pardoned, are utterly blotted out in the Blood of Chrift, and we are looked upon as innocent in the Sight of God, as if we had never committed any Sin at all. What a glorious Privilege then is Juftification? Sinner, doth not thy Heart leap for Joy at hearing of it? Is not thy Soul tranfported at the News? Are not all thy Powers within thee ready to break out in the Praifes of God for fending thee fuch glad Tidings? And yet this is not all: For,

Secondly, Juftification confifts in the Imputation of Chrift's Righteoufnefs to us. To *juftify*, is to reckon, repute, or efteem righteous. Thus Matt. xi. 19. *Wifdom is juftified*

of

of her Children. True Religion and Godlines are condemned, and deemed Madnes and Enthusiasm by the Children of this Generation; but *Wisdom* and her Ways are approved of, and counted juft and righteous by the Children of God, who are born of his Spirit, and partake of his Nature. Again, Rom. iii. 4. *That thou mightest be justified in thy Sayings, and mightest overcome when thou art judged.* Wicked Men are often finding Fault with the Divine Difpenfations; they cenfure the Tranfactions of God's Providence, they traduce the Methods of his Grace, and in innumerable Inftances calumniate and condemn the Divine Oeconomy. But when all Things come to be cleared up (as at the Day of Judgment) God will be *juftified*, i. e. he will be acknowledged and pronounced righteous, even by his Adverfaries; they who audacioufly blamed the Adminiftrations of the Moft High, will then take Shame unto themfelves, and openly declare that God is righteous in all his Ways, and holy in all his Works. And Chrift is faid to be *juftified in Spirit*, 1 Tim. iii, 16. that is, he was approved and accepted as a righteous Perfon, and he was pronounced fuch by the Holy Ghoft, Matt. iii. 17. To *juftify* therefore, is not only to abfolve from Sin, but alfo to account or efteem righteous. In this Senfe the Word is taken in Holy Scripture, and efpecially in the Writings of St. Paul. God in Juftification, not only pardons our Sins, but alfo looks upon us as perfectly righteous: He imputes

putes his Son's Righteousnes unto us, and reckons us righteous upon that Account. Here therefore appear the Riches of Divine Grace. We are all unrighteous and ungodly Sinners, we are rebellious, disobedient, ill-deserving and Hell deserving Wretches: We have no Righteousnes of our own to recommend us to God. Our Good Works are full of Sin, and all our *Righteousnesses* are as filthy Rags ; they are as a very unclean Thing, and do not, cannot merit the Divine Favour. The Lord sees us in this miserable Condition, he takes Pity on us in this last Extremity. The God of all Grace, the Lord of infinite Compassion gives us the Righteousnes of his only begotten and most dearly beloved Son JESUS CHRIST; he places it to our Account, and reputes us obedient in that Obedience which Jesus the Mediator performed in our Stead. Therefore by the all-sufficient Righteousnes of our Saviour's Life, as well as by the infinitely meritorious Satisfaction of his Death, are Sinners justified in the Sight of Almighty God.

I know indeed there are some who assert, that Remission of Sins and Justification are one and the same Thing, and that to be justified is no more than to have our sins forgiven. That Remission of sins is a Part of Justification I deny not; but then it is not the Whole. Justification includes in it the Forgivenes of sins; but then Forgivenes of sins is not all that is intended by Justification. The Scripture makes a plain distinction between these two, and teaches us that this latter is somewhat more

than

than the former. Thus Acts xiii. 38. *Thro' this Man is preached unto you the Forgiveness of Sins.* And then *v.* 39. the Apostle adds, *And by him all that believe are justified.* Which shews us, that Justification is a greater Privilege, an higher act of Grace than the bare *Remission of Sins,* even because it includes in it the Imputation of Christ's Righteousness to our Souls. The same Apostle, in *Rom.* iv. 6. informs us, that David describeth the Blessedness of the Man to whom God *imputeth Righteousness* without Works. And ver. 8. *Blessed is the Man to whom the Lord will not impute Sin.* Whence we learn, that Justification consists as in the *Non-imputation of Sin,* so also in the *Imputation of* the Redeemer's *Righteousness* to us. Accordingly the same infallible Penman (who well knew how to make proper Distinctions, and to state all Points of Divinity clearly, and especially this of Justification, which seems to be his Master-piece) speaks of the *Non-imputation of Trespasses,* 2 Cor. v. 19. and then tells us *We are made the Righteousness of G O D in him;* ver. 21. If therefore we believe the Scriptures, we must allow that Justification comprises in it both the Forgiveness of Sins and the Imputation of Christ's Righteousness or active Obedience unto us. How unscriptural, yea, how anti-scriptural then is the Opinion of those who exclude Christ's Righteousness from our Justification? The Foundation of this mistake is, such Persons do not believe any such Thing as Christ's Righteousness imputed, and therefore they diminish and curtail

the

the doctrine of Juftification, in order to make it fquare with their Hypothefis. But all who truly know themfelves will find the infufficiency of their own Righteoufnefs, will fee the Neceffity of Chrift's Righteoufnefs and will be fo far from oppofing this Doctrine, that they will rejoice in it, and blefs God for it.

Thirdly, Juftification confifts in our receiving a Right and Title to eternal Life. If you will not allow this to be a conftituent Part of Juftification, but rather an Effect and Confequence thereof you may ufe your Liberty, we fhall not differ about this Matter. All that I affert is, we are *all by Nature Children of Wrath*, i. e. of Hell; and if *Children* then Heirs; fo that all are Heirs of Hell by Nature. This is clear. All have finned againft God, and all deferve eternal Damnation for their Sins. When God created Adam at firft he gave him a Right and Title to eternal Happinefs. This he retained fo long as he continued in a State of Innocency and Perfection; but when he finned againft God, he loft all Title to Life and Glory, and merited eternal Mifery and Condemnation; and all his Pofterity through his Difobedience, forfeited their Title to Heaven, and became entitled to Death and Hell. But O the Depth of the Riches both of the Wifdom and Goodnefs of God! That Title to Heavenly Happinefs, which we loft in the *Firft Adam*, is reftored to us in the *Second*; and this is conveyed to us at the Time of our Juftification, which makes the Apoftle fay, Being *juftified* by his Grace, we are made *Heirs*, i. e. receive a

Right

Right and Title to *Eternal Life*, Tit. iii 7.
A *juſtified* Perſon therefore you ſee is an *Heir* of
Heaven: His Title is good, his Right inde-
feaſible, his Inheritance is ſecure, and nothing
in Earth or Hell ſhall be able to alienate it from
him, or deprive him of it.   Thus I have ſhewn
you what Juſtification is and wherein it conſiſts.   Many in deſcribing this bleſſed Privilege,
are apt to mangle and depreciate it, and ſo they
deprive God of a great deal of Glory, and his
Children of a great deal of Comfort.   I have
endeavoured to ſet it before the Reader in the
faireſt and cleareſt Light I poſſibly could: And
though few explain it ſo largely as I have done,
yet I find Biſhop *Downame*, in his Treatiſe of
Juſtification, makes it to conſiſt in three
Particulars I have mentioned.   After he hath
mentioned Remiſſion of Sins as one Part of Juſtification, he hath theſe Words: " God *im-*
" *puteth* unto every Believer the *Righteouſneſs*
" of the Mediator Jeſus Chriſt, as if it were
" properly their own and performed by them,
" that being clothed therewith, they may
" be *perfectly righteous* in God's Sight and
" ſo obtain a *Right* unto everlaſting *Life* and
" *Happineſs.*"
The Author or efficient Cauſe of our Juſti-
cation is God.   He it is that confers this un-
ſpeakable Privilege upon us; therefore he is
called *the Juſtifier of him that believeth in JE-*
SUS. Rom. iii. 26.   He is ſaid *to juſtify the*
Ungodly, Rom. iv. 5.   *It is God that juſtifieth,*
Rom. viii. 33.   Hence he is ſaid *to recon-*
cile the World unto himſelf, 2 Cor. v. 19. And
indeed

indeed who can forgive fins but God alone? Who can juftify Souls but only the moft high God? This is his peculiar Prerogative; and the inftrumental Caufe or Means on our Part is Faith, which we are now to fhew. And here I might tranfcribe the whole Homily on the Salvation of Man, for it is all to our Purpofe; but this I refer the Reader to at his Leifure. I fhall only juft mention one or two Paffages; for when I come to the next Propofition, that will be a full Proof and Eftablifhment of this.

The Homily aforefaid hath thefe Words: " St. Paul declareth here nothing upon the " Behalf of Man concerning his Juftification; " but *only a true and lively Faith*,--and yet " that Faith doth not fhut out Repentance, " Hope, Love, Dread and the Fear of God, " to be joined with Faith in every Man that is " juftified, but it fhutteth them out from the " Office of juftifying." Though all other Graces are in the Soul at the fame Time Faith is, yet it is the Prerogative of Faith only to juftify. So afterwards. " This Sentence that " we be *juftified by Faith only*, is not fo meant " of them, that the faid *juftifying Faith* is " alone in Man without true Repentance; " Hope, Charity, Dread, and the Fear of God, " at any Time and Seafon." Though Faith only juftifies, yet juftifying Faith is not feparate from Repentance, Hope, Love, and other Fruits of the Spirit. It is the proper Office of Faith to juftify, for Faith is the Grace that is juft fuited for this Purpofe. As the Eye is fitted for Seeing, or the Hand for Acting, fo

is

is Faith exactly fitted for Juftifying, *i. e.* for feeing Chrift, and taking hold of him for Strength and Righteoufnefs : But as neither the Eye fees, nor the Hand acts feparate from the Body (for deftroy the Subject or Organ, and its Act is alfo deftroyed) fo neither does Faith juftify feparate from other Graces (for then it would not be true living Faith) yet it alone juftifies; the Office of Juftification is its peculiar Privilege, and the other Divine Principles in the Heart have no fhare in this Affair.   In fhort, though Faith and all other Chriftian Virtues and Graces are in the Heart at the Time of our Juftification, yet thofe other Virtues and Graces have no Hand in our Juftification, but Juftification is the Office and Prerogative of Faith alone.

In the third Part of this Homily it is faid, *We be juftified by Faith only*; which is thus explained: " We put our Faith in Chrift, that " we be juftified by him only, that we be jufti- " fied by God's free Mercy, and the Merits of " our Saviour Chrift only, and by no Virtue " or good Works of our own that is in us, or " that we can be able to have or to do for " to deferve the fame; Chrift himfelf only be- " ing the Caufe meritorious thereof."   Here our own Works and Virtues are excluded, and Chrift afferted to be the meritorious Caufe of our Juftification.   What then becomes of the Opinion of thofe who extol the Merit of Works, and affign them a Part in our Juftification? Some are willing to make an Evafion here: " We (fay they) hold that Works are a Con-

·I

" dition,

" dition, but not a meritorious Condition of
" our Juſtification." But if Woiks are not
meritorious, how can they be any Condition
at all of our Juſtification? I leave this Difficulty for our Adverſaries to explain.

In the ſecond Part of this Homily, the Teſ-
timonies of *Hilary*, *Baſil*, and *Ambroſe*, are
produced; and *Origen*, *Chryſoſtom*, *Cyprian*, *Auguſtine*, *Proſper*, *Oecumenius*, *Proclus*, *Bernar-
dus*, and *Anſelm*, are mentioned as Advocates
and Eſpouſers of this Doɛtrine of Free Juſtification, which is deſigned on Purpoſe to ſhew
the Concurrence of *Greek* and *Latin* Fathers
in this important and everlaſting Truth.

I muſt juſt mention the Eleventh Article,
which is clear and explicit on our Side: It
is entitled,

Of the Juſtification of Man.

" We are accounted righteous before God,
" only for the Merit of our Lord and Saviour
" Jᴇsᴜs Cʜʀɪsᴛ, by Faith, and not for our
" own Works or Deſervings. Wherefore that
" we are *juſtified by Faith only*, is a moſt
" wholeſome Doɛtrine, and very full of Com-
" fort, as more largely is expreſſed in the Homi-
" ly of *Juſtification*." The Doɛtrine of Juſtification by Faith only, is here ſo clearly delivered, and ſo poſitively aſſerted, that one would
think nothing but corrupt Nature, an evil Heart
of Unbelief, Prejudice, or worldly Intereſt,
could incline Men to underſtand this Article
in any other Senſe, or conſtrain them to put a
double

double Meaning upon it. Our Reformers here call it a wholefome Doctrine, and very full of Comfort; and all who experience it, find it fo; although thofe who do not experience it, do not know either the Wholefomenefs or Comfort of it. Many People have the Doctrine of Juftification by Faith in their Heads; but yet are very miferable for want of having it in their Hearts. When Souls firft come acquainted with this Doctrine, it generally gives them a great deal of Pleafure and Delight. When the Apoftles firft faw our Saviour after his Refurrection, they *believed not for Joy, and wondered*, Luke xxiv. 41. And Peter's deliverance out of Prifon was fo unexpected that he did not think it real, but imagined he *had feen a Vifion*, Acts xii. And when the Lord turned again the Captivity of *Zion*, the returning Captives were like thofe that *dream*, Pfal. cxxvi. 1. So when a free Saviour firft manifefts himfelf to Sinners in Diftrefs, they are fo overjoyed, that they know not how to believe the Manifeftation to be real; they think the News too good to be true; they are ready to fear they are in a *Dream*, or fee a *Vifion*, and too often fufpect 'tis all a Delufion. This may feem Foolifhnefs to carnal People, yet I am fatisfied 'tis agreeable to the Experience of many of God's dear Children.

The facred Writings are full of this Doctrine. To produce all the Texts wherein it is mentioned would be endlefs. I fhall fet fome of them before the Reader. Our Saviour speaking to *Nicodemus*, fays, that *GOD fo loved the*

 World,

World, that he gave his only begotten Son, that whosoever believeth in him should not perish but have everlasting Life. So that *everlasting Life* is the Attainment not of him that does Good Works, and depends upon them for Salvation, but of him that *believes* in the *only begotten Son of God.* Our Saviour therefore here preaches the Doctrine of Justification by Faith in his Blood. And this he very seasonably informs *Nicodemus* of; for he, being a *Pharisee* and Dependant on his own Righteousness, was in all Probability as ignorant of the Doctrine of Justification by Faith as of that of Regeneration; (and yet how many in our Day are as ignorant of both those as *Nicodemus* was?) Our blessed Lord therefore having instructed him in the One, verses 3, 4, *&c.* here instructs him in the Other; and may the same heavenly Instructor instruct us all in both these Truths, God's appointing this way of Justification, and his giving his Son for this Purpose, are both the Effects of his superlative and ineffable Love. *GOD so loved the World!* How do these Words exercise the skill of Critics, Expositors and Orators! How do they all labour to fathom the mysterious Depths of Divine Love signified thereby! And yet how far short do all their Explications and Illustrations fall of the Glory of the Thing itself! *Sic Deus dilexit,* (saith Bishop *Sanderson*) *So GOD loved the World.* But how much that *So* containeth, no Tongue or Wit of Man can reach. Nothing expresseth it better to the Life than the Work itself doth. That the Word should be made

Flesh

Flesh, that the Holy One of God should be made Sin, that God blessed for ever should be made a Curse, that the Lord of Life and Glory should suffer an inglorious Death, and pour out his own most precious Blood to ransom such worthless, thankless, graceless Traitors as we were, that had so desperately made ourselves away, and that into the Hands of his deadliest Enemy, and that upon such poor and unworthy Conditions. Oh Altitude! Love incomprehensible! It swalloweth up the Sense and Understanding of Men and Angels, fitter to be admired and adored with Silence, than blemished with any of our weak Expressions.§

Our Saviour delivers the same Doctrine to the *Jews,* John v. 24. *Verily, verily I say unto you, he that heareth my Word, and believeth on him that sent me, hath everlasting Life.*-- Here, as before, they, and they only, are entitled to eternal Life, who have Faith in God, and in his Son Jesus Christ. Indeed, if it was otherwise, what Comfort could we have ? Seeing our own inward Experience (if we are Christians in Truth and Reality) must thoroughly convince us, that if our Salvation depended upon any Thing in us, or any Thing to be done by us, we could then have no Hope of ever being saved at all. And observe, our Lord says, *believeth on him that sent me,* thereby pointing us to God the Father, as the ultimate Object of Justifying Faith. So also

---

§ Seventh Sermon *ad Aulam.*

I 3

the

the Apoſtle, GOD *was in* CHRIST *reconciling the World unto himſelf,* 2 Cor. v. 19. And, *Rom.* iv. 5. the Sinner is directed to believe *on him that juſtifieth the Ungodly.* And who is that but God the Father? We ſee therefore that Juſtifying Faith ultimately terminates in him: And this is very rational and intelligible; for, if you believe in Chriſt, I would aſk, Under what Character do you believe in him? Is it not as he is a Mediator? Now a Mediator is not a Mediator of one, but of two Parties: Now we are the One, and God the Father is the Other, and therefore our Faith muſt ultimately terminate in him. God the Father is the Party offended, and we are the Party offending; Jeſus Chriſt is the Reconciler, and *through him we have Acceſs by one Spirit unto the Father, Eph.* ii. 18. If we are in Chriſt, the Father loves us as much as the Son. Chriſtians are often apt to look upon God the Son as their Friend, and God the Father as their Enemy; but why ſo? The Bleſſed Jeſus tells his Diſciples, and in them all Believers, *the Father himſelf loveth you, John* xvi. 27.

The Writings of St. *Paul* are richly ſtor'd with this Evangelical Truth. In his Epiſtle to the *Romans,* he ſpends at leaſt ſix or ſeven Chapters upon this Head; and the whole Scope and Tenor of the Epiſtle to the *Galatians* is to eſtabliſh this important Point. In both theſe Epiſtles this Divine Verity ſhines forth with the brighteſt Evidence, and I remember, when I

was

was firſt let into this Doctrine, I was never
eaſy, but when I was looking into one or other
of them.   How ſtrongly and clearly does the
Apoſtle aſſert this Doctrine in the Third to the
Romans?   He concludes negatively, *ver.* 20.
*Therefore by the Deeds of the Law ſhall no Fleſh
be juſtified in his Sight*;   and then poſitively,
ver. 28. *Therefore we conclude, that a Man is
juſtified by Faith without the Deeds of the Law.*
What Argument can be more convincing?
What Concluſion more juſt and valid?   The
Deeds of the Law are here abſolutely excluded,
and *Faith* in Chriſt aſſerted to be the only
Way of Juſtification before God.   " Yes (ſay
" ſome) *the Deeds of the Law* are here exclu-
" ded, but of what Law?   Not the Moral, but
" Ceremonial;   and the Works of this latter
" we readily allow have no Share in our Juſti-
" fication."   This is a common Evaſion, but
(I think) as groundleſs as it is frequent.   That
the Apoſtle here by *Law*, means the moral
Law, and ſo excludes the Works done in conformity thereto from our Juſtification, the following Reaſons may fully evince.   *Firſt*, the
Holy Apoſtle ſpeaks of a *Law* the flagrant Violation of which he had been charging upon the
Jew, ver. 10,---18.   And this can be no other
than the moral Law, as the Crimes there ſpe-
cified evidently ſhew.   *Secondly*, he ſpeaks of
a Law, whereby not only the *Jews*, but alſo
the *Gentiles* were obliged, and for breaking
which *both* Jews *and* Gentiles *were become
guilty before God*, ver. 9, 19. but the Ceremonial Law never reached the *Gentiles*, and there-

I 4

fore

fore the Moral muſt be here intended. *Third-ly*, he ſpeaks of a Law whereby is the Knowledge of Sin, which therefore muſt be the Moral, *Rom.* vii. 7, *Fourthly*, the Apoſtle excludes a Law, the Excluſion of which excludes *Boaſting*, ver. 27. Now what are Men more ready to boaſt of than their Morality? And would you have *Boaſting* excluded? But how can this be, unleſs moral Duties are excluded from having a Hand in our Juſtification? This therefore is what the Apoſtle does in this Place. *Fifthly*, the Apoſtle ſpeaks of a Law which we *eſtabliſh by Faith*, ver. 31. But will you ſay, this is the Ceremonial? It certainly is the Moral, which you ſee upon all theſe Accounts is ſhut out from the Office of juſtifying us before God.

To this add, *Gal.* iii. 11. *No Man is juſtified by the Law in the Sight of God.* Here alſo the Apoſtle ſpeaks of the Moral Law, as is plain : *Firſt*, Becauſe the Law here ſpoken of is ſuch as promiſes Life to the Obſervers of it, *ver.* 12. which is not the Property of the Ceremonial Law, but of the Moral, *Rom.* x. 5. *Lev.* xviii. 5. *Ezek.* xx. 11, 13. *Luke* x. 18. *Secondly*, the Law here meant *curſes all who do not continue in all* the Commands thereof *to do them*, ver. 10. which therefore is the Moral, *Deut.* xxvii. 26. *Thirdly*, the Law here mentioned, is that from the *Curſe* whereof Chriſt *hath redeemed us*, ver. 13. but we were never under a *Curſe* for breaking the Ceremonial Law. All this may convince us, that as the

Law

Law of Rites and Ceremonies, fo alfo the Law
of Moral Precepts is excluded from our Juftification; and as we cannot be juftified by our
Conformity to the one, fo neither can we be
juftified by our Conformity to the other. "We
" are not juftified by ourfelves, nor by our
" own Wifdom, nor Underftanding, nor Pi-
" ety, nor Works which we have done in the
" Holinefs of our Hearts; but by Faith, by
" which Almighty God hath juftified all from
" the Beginning.

Rom. v. 1. *Therefore being juftified by Faith,*
we have Peace with God through our Lord
Jefus Chrift. The illative Particle therefore
informs us, that thefe Words are a Conclufion built upon Premifes foregoing; and
if we look back to fee upon what this In-
ference is grounded, we fhall find the Apoftle hath proved his Point from the Prophets,
chap. i. ver. 2, 17. and chap. iii. 21. from
the Catholick Corruption of Mankind, *i. e.*
both of the *Jewifh* and *Gentile* World, chap.
i. 20, 21. *&c.* Chap. iii. 9. 19. and from the
Inftance of *Abraham* chap. iv. Whence we
fee how reafonable and well grounded a Conclufion this is, and what an important *there-*
fore is here inferted. When the Apoftle afferts, that we are *juftified by Faith*, he would
thereby inform us, that Faith is the Inftrument of our Juftification. He doth not fay, as
if Faith was the efficient Caufe of our Juftification, (for that we have before proved to
be God) but which I take to be equivalent to

Rom.

Rom. iii. 30. which denotes Inftrumentality, and fo lets us know, that Faith performs the Office of an Inftrument in our Juftification. " That Juftification is attributed to Faith, as " the Inftrumental Caufe, is evident; for it is " the proper Act of Faith to receive Remiffion " of Sins, Acts xxvi. 18. to receive the Gift " of Righteoufnefs, Rom. v. 17. to receive " Chrift in the Promife, as the Gift of the " Father, John i. 12. iv. 10." And this is the only Way of obtaining *Peace* with God, being *juftified by Faith we have Peace with God.* If you feek to be juftified by Works, you will never obtain *Peace* with God. All who make the Experiment find the Truth of this Affertion. And Perfons who labour Years or fcores of Years under the Law, are conftrained at laft to flee to Chrift by Faith and fo they procure *Peace* with God. They, and they only, who are juftified by Faith, receive this Bleffing, for the Work of Righteoufnefs fhall be *Peace,* and the *Effect of Righteoufnefs i. e.* of Chrift's Righteoufnefs imputed by God, and applieth by Faith, *is Quietnefs and Affurance for ever.* *Ifa.* xxxii. 17.

Rom. ix. 33. *Behold I lay in* Sion *a ftumbling Stone and Rock of Offence, and whofoever believeth on him fhall not be afhamed.* Chrift is here called a *Stumbling Stone,* and a *Rock of Offence*: And this the Apoftle fpeaks as an Accomplifhment of the Prophecy of *Ifaiah* chap. viii. ver. 14. The *Jews* ftumbled and fell upon this *Stumbling Stone,* they fplit upon this *Rock*

of

of Offence, and were shipwreck'd into the Gulph of eternal Perdition. And is not this Scripture this Day fulfilled in our Ears? How many stumble at the Doctrine of Faith in Christ, and that too, because they *seek* Righteousness *by the Works of the Law?* Are not the Words of *Simeon* fulfilled? Is not Christ and his Gospel a Sign that is spoken against? Is not this Child set for the *Fall* as well as the rising again of many in *Israel?* But as this Text contains a Word of Terror for self-righteous Infidels, so also it affords a Word of Comfort for humble Believers. *Whosoever believeth on him* (saith the Apostle) *shall not be ashamed.* The weakest Sinner, who truly *believes* in Christ, shall not be disappointed of his Hope, he shall find Peace with God, and shall never be *ashamed* of his Confidence in Christ; such a one will never be *ashamed* of professing Christ and his Cause publickly, he will not be *ashamed* to stand before Christ in Judgment; neither shall he be put to everlasting *Shame* and Contempt.

Rom. x. 10. *With the Heart Man believeth unto Righteousness.* So that *Faith* in Christ is the only Way of obtaining a justifying *Righteousness,* and it is not a Faith of the Head, *i. e.* of the Understanding only, but of the *Heart, i. e.* of the Will and Affections that avails to this Purpose. True, living, justifying Faith is seated in the *Heart;* and unless we have this Faith, all our intellectual Assents will profit us nothing; God will never accept us

with-

without this, how refin'd foever we may be in our Conceptions, lofty in our Speculations, or deep in our Penetration. When a Soul truly humbled under a Senfe of his own Sin, Mifery and Indigence comes to the Lord Jefus; the Saviour of Sinners receives that Soul, and juftifies him freely. Faith is an Act of Humility, and Self-dereliction, a Holy Defpair of any Thing in ourfelves, and a going to Chrift, a receiving, a looking towards him, and his All-fufficiency *: This is the Faith which the Scriptures fo much recommend, and without it 'tis impoffible to be faved. This is the only Way of our Acceptance with God, and Juftification in his Sight. This the Epiftle to the *Romans* largely and fully declares; and therefore Natural Men, who are Enemies to this Doctrine, have a great Antipathy to this Part of Holy Writ. I remember I once read an Author, who advifed young Beginners in Religion, not to read the eleven firft Chapters of this Epiftle. This was an Artifice of his. He was a profefs'd Adverfary to the Doctrine of Juftification by Faith, and he ufed this Method to keep Perfons from coming to the Knowledge of that Truth. However, I follow'd his Advice for a while; but had I done fo much longer, fuch a blind Teacher as he, and fuch a blind Scholar as I, might both have dropt into the Ditch of Hell together.

I might now quote the whole Epiftle to the *Galatians*. It is all to our Purpofe, and as

----

* Bifhop *Reynolds*.

clearly

clearly contains the Doctrine of Free Juftification, as that to the Romans. I would therefore have the Reader perufe it carefully. Left
I fhould feem tedious, I fhall only mention
one Place which is clear and explicit, and may
fatisfy all ingenuous Minds of the Truth of this
Doctrine. Pleafe therefore to confult chap. ii.
ver. 15 16. *We who are Jews by Nature, and
not Sinners of the Gentiles knowing that a
Man is not juftified by the Works of the Law,
but by the Faith of Jefus Chrift, even we
have believed in Jefus Chrift, that we might
be juftified by the Faith of Chrift, and not by
the Works of the Law; for by the Works of the
Law fhall no Flefh be juftified.* How earneft
the Apoftle here is! The Works of the Law
are here thrice exprefsly fhut out from our Juftification, and Faith in Chrift as often afferted
to be the only Way of our Juftification before God. Surely thefe Words muft convince
People, if they are not paft Conviction. The
Greek Particles are not underftood exclufively,
as all allow, Rev. xxi. 27. but are alfo rendered
by an Exclufive, as in Mark xiii. 32. No
one knows but the Father, which in Matth.
xxiv. 36. is thus exprefsed, no one knows but
the Father alone. Wherefore this expreffion
that *a Man is not juftified by the Works of
the Law but by the Faith of Chrift,* is equivalent to this exclufive Propofition, that a
*Man is not juftified by Works but by Faith
only.* This is fair arguing; and yet what
Pity it is that fome Men, yea, and thofe of a
good natural Genius too, cannot fee into it?

But

But it is not a good natural Genius without the Spirit of God, that will enable Men savingly to understand Divine Truths. Observe further, the Apostle says, *We who are Jews by Nature, and not Sinners of the* Gentiles, *&c.* So in like Manner we who are Christians by Nature, and not Sinners of the Heathen World; we who have been born within the Pale of the Christian Church, who have been educated in the Doctrines of the Gospel, and have attended all the Ordinances of Religion, even we renounce all our Merits and Good Works and are as much beholden to the Free Grace of God for our Justification as Heathens, or Infidels or the vilest Sinners in the World. Some cry out, " Yes, we allow that Heathens, and such " as never before heard of Christ, are justified " by Faith only; but professed Christians, who " have heard the Sound of the Gospel must " not expect to be justified in this Manner, " they must do Good Works, and thereby " they will find Favour and Acceptance with " God." Indeed I would not discourage any from doing Good Works, but at the same Time I would not have Men, whether Christians or Heathens, depend upon them for Salvation; for if they do, they will find themselves miserably disappointed. All our moral Deportment will never recommend us to God. When Men have done all they can, they must not build their Hopes of Salvation upon their Performances; they must disclaim their own Righteousness teoufnefs, and ftand upon a level with Publicans and Harlots, and the grofleft Offenders for Juftification before God.   The Moral and Immoral, the Sober Man and the Debauchee are all juftified in the fame Way, viz. by Faith in Chrift Jefus.   Our moft refined Morality is not good enough to fave us, but juft bad enough to damn us, if God fhould enter into Judgment with us for it.

I might add many more Places * from this Epiftle, but I proceed to fhew

IV. *Fourthly*, That Good Works have *no Part* in our Juftification.   Few, if any, are fo grofly ignorant as to affert, that we are juftified wholly by Works, but then they join Faith and Works together, and will have thefe latter to bear *a Part* in our Juftification. Now I will evince the contrary.   And this I chufe to make a diftinct Propofition of, becaufe it is the Centre of the whole Debate, and being once decided, may juftly put an End to all future Difputes about this Matter.   The Homily on the Salvation of Mankind, fays, " our " Juftification doth come freely by the *meer* " *Mercy* of God, and of fo Free and Great " Mercy, that whereas all the World was not " able of themfelves to pay *any Part* towards " their Ranfom, it pleafed our heavenly Fa- " ther of his *Infinite Mercy*, without any our

----

* See chap. iii. ver, 8, 11, 22. chap. iv. ver. 26, 28, 31. chap. v. ver. 1, 4, 6.

Defert

" Defert or Deferving, to prepare for us to the
" moft precious Jewels of Chrift's Body and
" Blood," Now how do they depreciate and
undervalue God's Free and Infinite Mercy,
who fay that Good Works have a Part in our
Juftification! I would here have it obferv'd,
that our Church doth not fay the whole
World was not able to pay the *Whole*, but
the World was not able to pay *any Part* towards their Ranfom. But if our Good Works
have *a Part* in our Juftification, then I think
we are able to pay *a Part*, and that a very
confiderable one too, towards our Ranfom; yet
our Church afferts, that we are not able to
pay *any Part* towards it. Now how will
our Adverfaries be able to evade this? Some
fay, that Works done in our Natural Eftate
have *no Part* in our Juftification; but that
Works done in the Grace and Spirit of Chrift
have. The Anfwer to which is ready; for we
have not the Grace and Spirit of Chrift in
us, 'till we are firft juftified, how then can
Works proceeding from thence have *a Part*
in our Juftification? So that you fee our
Evangelical Obedience cannot juftify us before God, becaufe this doth not precede, but
follow our Juftification.

The Homily on the Mifery of Mankind
bids us " know our own Works, of what
" Imperfection they be, and then we fhall
" not ftand foolifhly and arrogantly in our
" own Conceits nor challenge any Part of
" Juftification by our Merits or Works."

Here

Here not only *Merits* (which our Adverfaries feem ready to difclaim) but alfo *Works* (though they fhould be fuppofed to have no *Merit* in them) are excluded from juftifying us, yea, from having *any Part* in our Juftification. And from this Paffage we learn, that 'tis Men's Ignorance of themfelves and their Performances that leads them into this Miftake; for if they knew the Imperfection of their Works, they would never be fo foolifh and arrogant as to build their Hopes of Salvation upon fo fandy a Foundation. Where then is the Self-jufticiary? What becomes of the Man who trufts to his own Righteoufnefs for Salvation? Tell me, O thou felf-righteous Sinner, which of thy Works doft thou think fo good that thou may'ft fafely depend upon it for Salvation? I only challenge thee to mention one. But if thou can'ft not truft to any one Good Work taken feparately, how can'ft thou truft to the whole Sum of thy Works collectively? Does not the fame Sin and Imperfection that taints one fingle Action, diffufe itfelf through the whole Circuit of thy Obedience? How much foever therefore thou may'ft have boafted of thy good Deeds hitherto, yet when thou feeft the Corruption of thy Heart, and the Deficiency of thy beft Righteoufnefs, thou wilt be neceffitated to renounce all, and to depend on Jefus alone for Pardon of Sin, Peace with God, and eternal Salvation.

The fecond Part of the Homily of Salvation hath thefe Words: " Juftification is not the

K

Office

" Office of Man, but of God; for Man cannot
" make himself righteous by his own Works,
" neither *in Part* nor in the *Whole*; for that
" were the greatest Arrogancy and Presumption
" of Man, that Antichrist could set up against
" God, to affirm that Man might, by his own
" Works, take away and purge his own Sins,
" and so justify himself." Here we are expressly told, that we are not justified by Works either *in Part*, or in the *Whole*. What Words can be plainer? And how black does this Passage look upon those who preach Justification by Faith in such a Manner, as to make Good Works a necessary Condition of our being justified in the Sight of God! Do not such Preachers forget their Homilies? Yea, do they not forget their Liturgies?

For even there it is said, " We put not our " Trust in *any Thing* that *we* do*." Now how can we say we put not our Trust in *any Thing* we do, if we Trust in Part to our own Works for our Justification? Elsewhere‡ we profess, " We lean *only* upon the Hope of " thy Heavenly Grace." How can we make such a Declaration as this, if we lean partly to our own Works, and partly to the Divine Grace? Is it not evident then that Good Works have no Part in our Justification? Have I not clearly shewed that this is the Judgment of the Church of *England?* Have I not made good my Proposition? Is it not as clear as any Demonstration in Mathematics? Why then do

---

* Collect for Sexagesima
‡ Fifth Sunday after Epiphany.

you

you fcruple giving your Affent to it? Why do you feek after Cavils and Evafions, in order to avoid it? Are you afraid of being deceived by the plain Senfe of Words? Why then do you fufpend your Judgment? Why are you fo backward in giving your Verdict in fo clear a Cafe? Therefore if you are a Member or Minifter of the Church of *England*, approve yourfelf fuch by receiving and preaching the Doctrine which fhe recommends unto you. Surely you have more Confcience than to deny this to be her Doctrine, fo long as you have thefe Extracts from the Homilies in your Eye.

The Scriptures are clear and explicit in this Point. Rom. iv. 4. *To him that worketh is the Reward not reckoned of Grace, but of Debt.* Juftification is by Grace, and therefore Works have no Hand in it: If our Juftification was by Works, then it would not be of *Grace*, but of *Debt*. This is what the Apoftle afferts in the Words of the Text, *To him that worketh is the Reward not reckoned of Grace, but of Debt:* This the Apoftle lays down as a Pofition univerfally true, and equally applicable in all Cafes. If we work for Life, and acquire it by our Works, then the *Reward,* i. e. Eternal Glory, is not a *Grace*, or Free Gift, which God gives us, but a *Debt* which he owes us. The Servant who works for Hire muft have his Wages, after he hath done his Work; and he doth not look upon his Wages as a Gift or gratuitous Donation, but as a juft Debt which his Mafter is obliged to pay him. This exactly reprefents the Cafe; and hence it follows, that all Works,

whe-

whether Ritual, Moral, or Evangelical, are excluded from the Office of juftifying us before God, feeing the Reward would be equally *of Debt*, whether we fhould fuppofe it to be conferr'd in Confequence of any or of all of thefe. And hence too it eafily appears that Works can have no Part in our Juftification; for juft as far as you allow our Good Works to bear Part therein, fo far you make the Reward to be *of Debt*, and not *of Grace*! but the Reward is wholly of *Grace*, it is not of *Debt* in the leaft Meafure or Degree, and therefore Works can have no Hand at all in procuring it.

The Apoftle argues nearly in the fame Manner, *chap.* iv. *ver.* 16. and *chap.* xi. *ver.* 6. *Therefore it is of Faith, that it might be by Grace.—And if by Grace, then it is no more of Works; otherwife Grace is no more Grace: But if it be of Works, then it is no more Grace; otherwife Work is no more Work.* The Incompatibility of *Grace* and *Works* in Point of Juftification is here fet before us. 'Tis true indeed this latter Text is deliver'd concerning Eternal Election; but fince that, as well as our Juftification is of *Grace*, thefe Words are applicable to either or to both thefe. The former Text informs us, that Juftification is *by Grace*, thro' Faith, as the means or Inftrument thereof; from the Latter we learn, that *Works* and *Grace*, are two irreconcileable Oppofites in the Affair of our Juftification: From both together therefore we infer, that *Works* are abfolutely excluded from our Juftification. To make a Mixture or Compofition of *Grace* and *Works* in the Office

of

of our Juſtification (as ſome attempt to do) is in Effect to deſtroy their very Nature. In vain therefore do Men think thus to compromiſe the Matter. Juſtification is wholly *by Grace*, or wholly *by Works*. If you deny that 'tis wholly *by Grace*, you do implicitly aſſert that 'tis wholly *by Works*. What ſignifies trifling? The Covenant is either a Covenant *of Grace*, or *of Works*. If you ſay that *Works* have a Part therein, (whether more or leſs it matters not) you immediately turn it into a Covenant of Works; for *Majus & Minus non mutant ſpeciem*, as Logicians ſay: If therefore you are ſtiff and peremptory, and will have Works to be ſharers with Grace in the great Buſineſs of Juſtification, you may talk of Grace if you pleaſe, but you are ſtill under the Covenant of Works; and while you thus reaſon and diſpute, you plainly ſhew that you know no other Way of Salvation but by *the Law of Works*.

The Epiſtle to the Galatians, is full of this Doctrine; chap v. ver. 3 the inſpired Author ſaith, *I teſtify again to every Man that is circumciſed, that he is a Debtor to do the whole Law.* By *Law* here is meant the Moral *Law*; as *Matth.* xxii. 36.---xxiii. 23. *Luke* x. 26. *John* vii. 19. *Rom.* iii. 31.---vii. 7. *Gal.* v. 14. Or rather the *whole Law* includes both the Moral and Ceremonial. Here therefore the Apoſtle acquaints the Judaizing Chriſtians that if they obſerved Circumciſion or any other Moſaic Rite, in expectation of being juſtified thereby, they were neceſſarily obliged to keep the *whole Law*, both Ritual and Moral, or elſe they

would

would miss of their Aim. So if Christians observe the Ordinance of Baptism, or the Lord's Supper, or any other divine Institution, with a Dependence thereon for Justification, they must fulfil the *whole Law* perfectly, or else they are undone for ever. So then what think you? Can you fully obey all the Commands of the Divine Law? If you cannot, why are you so unwilling to renounce your slight Performances? Is it not safer to trust to Christ's Obedience than to our own Works for Salvation? Or are you obstinate? And had you rather trust to your own Good Works (as you call them) and be damned, than to Christ's Merits and be saved?

Eph. ii. 8. 9. *For by* Grace *ye are saved,--- not of* Works *left any Man should boast. Boasting* is here absolutely excluded, as in Rom. iii. 27. But how could this be, if Works had a Part in our Justification? If any one Good Work bore Part therein, there would be Room for our boasting of that. Thus if *Abraham,* by offering his Son, had in any Measure procured his Justification, he would have gloried of that notable Act of Faith: But what saith the Scripture? *He hath not whereof to glory before* God, Rom. iv. 2. The same is true of all the Faithful; they have nothing whereof to glory before God. *Boasting* is excluded, not in Part, but entirely; and therefore Works are not partially, but totally excluded from our Justification. Now I have mentioned the Instance of *Abraham,* I am apprehensive some may object from *James* ii. 21. that *Abraham* was justified by Works. It may be sufficient to reply, that St.

James

James fpeaks of Juftification not abfolutely, but relatively. In the former Senfe, *Abraham* was juftified about thirty Years before he offered his Son, as is evident by comparing Gen. xv. 6. with xxii. 12. and in the latter, he was juftified, *i. e.* declaratively juftified, or evidenced to be in a juftified State by this Action among others, to wit, his offering up his Son *Ifaac.* But then this declarative Juftification does not at all militate againft the Doctrine of Free Juftification by Faith only ; neither will it in any ways anfwer our Adverfaries Purpofe ; for we hold, as well as they, that Faith and Juftification are manifefted and approved by Obedience and Good Works.

Although this Doctrine is fo clear, yet how many Arts and Devices do Men ufe in order to avoid it ! Some hold the Doctrine of Juftification by Faith, but then they make Good Works a Part of Juftifying Faith? How irrational and prepofterous a Scheme of Religion is this ! Are Faith and Works the fame thing ? Or are Works a Part of Juftifying Faith? What faith the Apoftle? *To him that worketh not, but believeth,* Rom. iv. 5. Here you fee that *working* is contradiftinguifhed from, and even oppofed to (I mean in refpect of Juftification) *believing.* And *Faith* and *Works* are diftinguifhed, Rom. iii. 27. Eph. ii. 8, 9. How then (if you will fubmit to the Judgment of an Apoftle) can you make Works a Part of Faith, or fay that Faith and Works are one and the fame thing? Befides, to maintain Juftification by Faith, and then make Works

a Part

a Part of Faith, is no other in Effect than to hold Juftification by Works, or at leaft by Faith and Works conjoin'd, which is the very Doctrine of the Papifts, and is both Antifcriptural and Antichriftian. Again, in the laft Place, Faith is the Caufe, Good Works the Effect: Faith is the Tree, Good Works are the Fruit. Now, will you fay that the Caufe and Effect, the Tree and its Fruit are one and the fame Thing? Why then do you labour to confound Faith and Works? To confound and mingle Caufes with their Effects is counted very bungling and injudicious in Philofophy. Is it not much more unfkilful as well as unfafe to do fo in Theology? I would alfo add, Does not Men's ufing fuch fallacious Methods to defend their Opinion, fhew that their Caufe is weak, and give us Reafon to fufpect, that the Light of Truth fhines into their Confciences with fo glaring an Evidence, that with all their Sophiftry, they are fcarcely able to withftand Conviction?

When we affirm that we are juftified by Faith, we do not mean that Faith merits or deferves our Juftification at God's Hands. Faith hath no more Merit in it than any other Grace: How fhould it, when itfelf is the Gift of God? And can we merit any Thing of God by that which we receive from him? What therefore our Saviour faith of Works, Luke xvii. 10. we may fay of Faith, *When ye fhall have done all thofe Things which are commanded you, fay, We are unprofitable Servants, we have done that which was our Duty to do.*

So

So fimilarly, when we have believed all thofe Things which God hath commanded us to believe, we are unprofitable Servants, we have believed that which it was our Duty to believe. Accordingly our Church tells us, " We muft " renounce the Merit of all our faid Virtues, " of Faith, Hope, Charity, and all other " Virtues and good Deeds, which we either " have done, fhall do, or can do, as Things " that be far too weak and infufficient, and " imperfect, to deferve remiffion of our Sins " and our Juftification*." The meritorious Caufe of our Juftification is, the Active and Paffive Obedience of the LORD JESUS CHRIST. Faith is only the Inftrument whereby we apply his precious Blood and his perfect Righteoufnefs to our own Hearts, and fo are juftified before God. But as in other Evangelical Truths, fo in this, the Experience of it will beft acquaint us with the Nature of it: And when Men know it favingly, there will not be fo much difputing about it. The Application is the beft Explication of it. It is a Doctrine very fweet and full of Comfort. Sinners, what fay you? If I was to preach Juftification by Works to you, would not this drive you to Defpair? Would not one go away faying, " Well, " if this Doctrine be true, I can never hope to " be juftified, becaufe I have never done any " one good Work in all my Life? Would not another go hence complaining, " This Doc- " trine is Death to me; my Works are wicked " from my Youth up, and therefore I muft

L

unavoid-

---

* Homily on Salvation.

" unavoidably be damned?" Indeed if Juftification was by Works, no Flefh could be faved. They therefore who preach fuch a Doctrine, are truly and properly Preachers of Damnation. They that are under the *Law*, are under the *Curfe*, Gal. iii. 10. and all are damned who truft to their own good Works for Salvation. But now, behold I bring you glad Tidings of great Joy! I publifh Salvation by Chrift, and Juftification by Faith only. How ought you to rejoice in fo falutary a Doctrine? How can you ever enough blefs God, for bringing the Gofpel of his Grace to your Ears? And O! may the Lord God, the Father of Mercies, the God of all Comforts, grant that the Word of Reconciliation may reach your Hearts. O! that there was fuch an Heart in you that you would believe on the Lord Jefus Chrift. Jefus. Chrift loves, Jefus Chrift faves all univerfally who believe in his Name. Come to him, and he will never caft you out. All Believers are faved, but all Unbelievers are damned. Do you deferve Damnation in yourfelves? Yet Chrift hath merited eternal Salvation for you. Here is a Meffage of Comfort for you; *In him you have Redemption, even the Forgivenefs of your Sins. He is your Peace, and by him All that believe are Juftified.* Sinners, Rebels, Criminals, Malefactors, Apoftates, and Perfecutors, believe on the Lord Jefus and you fhall be faved. Come unto Jefus by Faith, and he will freely pardon all your Sins, from firft to laft, and fully inftate you in the Favour of that God, in whofe Pleafure is Life, Life

fpiritual,

ſpiritual, Life celeſtial, and Life eternal. And O! ye Chriſtleſs Wretches, do you conſider what it is to be in an unjuſtified State? Do you know that the Wrath of God abideth on you? Do you ſee the Vitals of God's Wrath hanging over your Heads, and juſt ready to be poured out upon your Hearts? Are you ſenſible what great Plagues remain for the Ungodly? Do you remember that he that believeth not ſhall be damned? And do you know, that all *Unbelievers ſhall have their Part in the Lake which burneth with Fire and Brimſtone?* Flee therefore from the Wrath to come.--- Eſcape for your Lives.--The Avenger of Blood is behind you; make haſte to the City of Refuge; reach out the Arm of Faith, lay hold on the dear Redeemer of the World, and he will ſkreen you from the Wrath of God, and deliver your Souls from going down to the Pit of Hell.

Again, are there not ſome here who are in a juſtified State? Have not ſeveral of you taſted that the Lord is gracious? Do you not enjoy a Peace of God which paſſeth all Underſtanding? Bleſſed, bleſſed are your Souls; happy are ye above all People that dwell on the Face of the Earth. How ſhall I addreſs you? How ſhall I congratulate your Felicity? You have free Remiſſion of all your Sins in the Blood of the Lamb, your Souls are inveſted with the Mediator's pure and ſpotleſs Righteouſneſs, and your Title to Heaven is good, you have an everlaſting Inheritance. Rejoice therefore in Chriſt Jeſus, and bleſſed be the Lord God of *Iſrael* from

this

this Time forth for evermore.—The Love of God is unchangable, the Purposes of his Grace are unalterable: God hath forgiven you your Sins, and he will never impute them unto you again; he hath given you Chrift's Righteoufnefs, and he will never take it from you. You are intitled to Heaven, and your gracious Father will never difinherit you; Being once juftified, you are juftified for ever, and fhall never (if I may fo fay) be unjuftified again. All the Powers on Earth or in Hell fhall never be able to fruftrate your Hopes, nor rob you of your Eftate in Glory. Therefore praife God continually, fpend your Lips and your Lives in finging of his Salvation. A Chriftian hath one Thing to do, and that is to fing the Praifes of God and his Son Jefus Chrift for ever. Therefore keep praifing God on Earth till at length you praife him in the Kingdom of Heaven. Look and long for that bleffed Time, and rejoice in Hope of the Glory that fhall be revealed. 'Tis true, while you are in this World, you muft not expect to be free from Temptations; the World will lay fnares for you, the deceitful lufts of your own Heart will plot againft you, and the Devil will fhoot his fiery Darts at you. Satan is the Troubler of the Ifrael of God; he loves to terrify thofe whom he cannot deftroy. He tempted our Lord Chrift to Prefumption, to diftruft of Divine Providence, to the Love of the World, yea, to fall down and worfhip him. Why then fhould you wonder if he tempts you to as great or greater Sins? Is the Difciple above

his

his Lord? If therefore the Devil was fo impudent as thus to tempt your Lord and Saviour, why are you furprized at his tempting you? You perhaps expected to go to Heaven without any Trouble or Vexation, but what faith the Scripture? *Through much Tribulation we muſt enter into the Kingdom of God.* Befides, Temptation is a Sign of our belonging to Chriſt, thus Luke xxii. 28. *Ye are they which have continued with me . in my Temptations.* Hence faith the Apoſtle James ch. i. ver. 2. *My Brethren count it all Joy when ye fall into divers Temptations.* Therefore be of good Courage. Fight in the Strength of Chriſt, and you are fure of conquering. Chriſt ſhall conquer for you, Chriſt ſhall conquer in you.; Chriſt ſhall give you Victory over all .your Temptations, how many foever they may be in Number, how mighty foever they may be in Power. *Laſtly*, ſhew your Gratitude to God by your Obedience. *Do we through Faith make void the Law? God forbid; yea, we eſtabliſh the Law.* Approve your Faith by your Good Works, otherwife it will appear, that you have no Faith at all. Are you juſtified? See then that ye are fanctified. Whomfoever God juſtifies, he doth alfo fanctify, unlefs therefore you are fanctified in fome Degree, in vain do you pretend to be juſtified. This will further appear when we come to ſhew

V. *Fifthly*, and *Laſtly*, That Juſtifying Faith produces Good Works after Juſtification. This will need the lefs Proof, becaufe few deny it.

L 3

Yet

Yet as I thought proper to let our Adverſaries know that we are no Enemies to Good Works I choſe profeſſedly to eſpouſe and openly vin- dicate this Poſition, in order to ſtop the Mouths of Gainſayers. The Difference be- tween us and our Adverſaries is this; they hold that Good Works go before our Juſtifica- tion, and have an Influence therein; we be- lieve that Good Works follow after our Juſti- fication, as the Fruits and conſequences there- of. The Homily of Salvation is clear to our Purpoſe, and calls juſtifying Faith " a true and " lively Faith, out of the which Faith ſpring " Good Works." And again, in the third Part of the ſame Homily, it is deſcribed thus, a " true and lively Faith in Chriſt, bringing " forth Good Works, and a Life according " to God's Commandments." A Perſon may have a dead Faith, and perform no Good Works; but if his Faith is lively it will as na- turally exert itſelf in Good Works, as a living Man performs vital Actions. Conſonant to this the concluſion of the ſaid Homily ſaith, " Theſe be the Fruits of true Faith, to do " Good, as much as lieth in us to every Man, " and above all Things, and in all Things to " advance the Glory of God."

In another Place of the ſaid Homily we are told, " the right and true Chriſtian Faith is " not only to believe that the Holy Scripture, " and all the foreſaid Articles of our Faith are " true: but alſo to have a *ſure Truſt* and *Con-* " *fidence* in God's merciful Promiſes to be ſav- " ed from everlaſting Damnation by Chriſt,
" whereof

" whereof doth follow a *loving* Heart to *obey*
" his Commandments." Faith is here firſt
deſcribed by a *ſure Truſt* and *Confidence* in
God, and then *Love* and *Obedience* are mentioned as conſequences thereof; which exactly
correſponds to that of the Apoſtle, *Gal.* v. 6.
*In Chriſt Jeſus neither Circumciſion availeth
any Thing nor Uncircumciſion, but Faith which
worketh by Love.* *Faith* and *Love* go together
in every converted Soul. They are Siſter
Graces and therefore are frequently joined together in the Apoſtolical Writings.* The
Love of God revealed to the Soul, kindles a
Flame of Sacred Love in the Soul,† and Love
is an effectual Motive to Obedience‡. The
whole Matter we find well ſumm'd up in our
Homily on Faith: " Such is the true Faith,
" that the Scripture doth ſo much commend,
" the which when it ſeeth and conſidereth
" what God hath done for us, it alſo moved
" through continual Aſſiſtance of the Spirit
" of God to ſerve and pleaſe him, to keep his
" Favour, to fear his Diſpleaſure, to continue
" his obedient Children, ſhewing Thankful-
" neſs again, by obſerving or keeping his
" Commandments, and that freely for true
" Love chiefly, and not for dread of Puniſh-
" ment, or Love of Temporal Reward, conſi-
" dering how clearly without Deſervings we
" have received his Mercy and Pardon freely."
L 4

Again,

---

* See 1 Theſſ. i. 3. iii. 6. Philem. 5. Eph. i. 15. 1 John
iii. 23. &c. &c.   † See 1 John iv. 19.
‡ 2 Cor. v. 14.

Again, the Homily of Salvation informs us thus, " nor when they fay, that we fhould be " juftified freely, do they mean that we " fhould or might afterward be *idle,* and that " nothing fhould be required on our Parts *af-* " *terwards.*" We are here taught not to be *idle* after Juftification. Good Works have here their proper Place affigned them; they do not go before but follow after our Juftification. This alfo the Homily on Fafting afferts in Terms very explicit, " Good Works go not " before in him which fhall afterward be " juftified, but Good Works do follow after, " when a Man is firft juftified." Can any Thing be plainer? And then the Reafon hereof is foon after affigned, " for that they are good " Declarations and Teftimonies of our Jufti- " fication."

There is a remarkable Paffage in the Homily of Good Works, which I fhall juft mention and fo conclude my Quotations from the Homilies: " Faith may not be naked, without " Good Works, for then it is no true Faith; " and when it is adjoined to Works, yet it is " *above the Works.*" How contrary is this to the Judgment of thofe who give Works the Preference to Faith? Our Church here ex-preffly afferts, that when Faith is adjoined to Works, yet it is *above* them.

Article XII. *Of Good Works.*

" Albeit that Good Works, which are the " Fruits of Faith and follow after Juftification,
cannot

" cannot put away our Sins, and endure the
" Severity of God's Judgment; yet are they
" pleaſing and acceptable to God in Chriſt,
" and do ſpring out neceſſarily of a true and
" lively Faith, inſomuch that by them a lively
" Faith may be as evidently known as a Tree
" diſcerned by the Fruit." This Article is very
clear and defecate, and is of itſelf a ſufficient
Proof of our Doctrine. As a good Tree brings
forth good Fruit, ſo a true, living, juſtifying
Faith produces Good Works. If a Tree yields
bad Fruit, that is an undeniable Evidence, that
the Tree itſelf is bad; ſo if thoſe who profeſs
to have Faith in Chriſt live wicked Lives, that
is a plain Demonſtration that their Profeſſion is vain, and their Faith dead, *Matt.* vii.
17. *Luke* vi. 43.

The Scriptures are clearly on our Side; they
in almoſt every Page inculcate the Neceſſity of
Good Works. He that runs may read; and
therefore I need not ſay much under this Head.
Our Lord inſtructs us in this Truth, *Matt.*
vii. 21. *Not every one that ſaith unto me Lord,
Lord, ſhall enter into the Kingdom of Heaven, but he that doeth the Will of my Father,
which is in Heaven*; where you ſee it is not
the formal Profeſſor, or the nominal Chriſtian,
but the *Doer* of the Divine *Will*, that is to
enter into the Kingdom of Heaven; in vain
therefore do you expect to go to Heaven when
you die, if you indulge yourſelf in Sin while
you live.

In

In *Luke* vi. 46. Our Saviour reproves some who profeſſed Faith in him, becauſe they were deficient in their Obedience, *why call ye me* Lord, Lord, (faith he) *and do not the Things which I ſay?* 'Tis not enough for Perſons to *call* Jeſus their Lord and their Saviour (as many do) and yet live in Indolence, Softneſs, and Worldly mindedneſs. If you call Jeſus your Lord, why do you not do the Things which he hath commanded? Why do ye not approve your Faith by your Obedience? How can you preſume to call Jeſus your Lord and your Saviour, while you live in the wilful omiſſion of Prayer, of reading the Divine Word, and of receiving the Lord's Supper? 1 *Cor.* xi. 20. What a ſtrange ſort of Religion is this? And yet what numbers are fallen into it? Such a Religion as this is juſt calculated to lull corrupt Nature aſleep upon a Pillow of Eaſe, and will only ſerve to convey Men's Souls ſmoothly to Hell. You perhaps may give a Sneer, and be ready to toſs this Paper by; yet I aſſure you again and again, that that Religion which allows People in the Omiſſion of any known *Commandment*, *John* xiv. 15. or in the Commiſſion of any known Sin, comes not from God, but from the Devil. And whatever Appearance of Sanctity the Profeſſors or Abettors of ſuch a Religion may wear, yet we are to look upon them as deluded; and we ought to avoid their Errors, and pray for their Perſons.

The Apoſtle *Paul* always inſiſts upon Good Works. His general Way is firſt to ſtate Doctrines

trines clearly, and then he exhorts to Good Works pathetically. He firſt eſtabliſhes Chriſtian Verities, and then inculcates Chriſtian Virtues and Graces. This is his Way in almoſt all his Epiſtles; and eſpecially in his Epiſtle to the *Romans*, where the grand Doctrine of Juſtification is handled at large; leſt any one ſhould look upon the ſaid Doctrine as deſtructive of Good Works and Obedience, how careful is the Apoſtle to prove the reverſe? Inſomuch that he ſpends the five laſt Chapters of that Epiſtle in exhorting to Chriſtian Holineſs in general, and to every Evangelical Duty in particular. And 'tis obſervable when he gives Inſtructions to Biſhops and Paſtors, how ſtrictly he charges them to preach up Good Works; thus, Tit. iii. 8. *This is a faithful Saying, and theſe Things I will that thou affirm conſtantly, that they which have believed in God, might be careful to maintain Good Works*: And then for an Encouragement he adds, *theſe Things are Good and Profitable unto Men.* And in his ſecond Epiſtle to Timothy, ch. ii. ver. 19, he ſaith, *let every one that nameth the Name of Chriſt depart from Iniquity,* And O! that all Preachers would follow the Apoſtle's Injunctions, by preaching up Good Works in their Sermons, and practiſing them in their Lives.

If we enquire of Matter of Fact, we ſhall find it every way anſwers our Purpoſe. Obſerve the Conduct of Primitive Chriſtians, obſerve the Behaviour of modern Believers, how do they all abound in Good Works? Hence they

they are ftiled in Scripture *a peculiar People zealous of Good Works.* As foon as *Zaccheus* had *received* the Lord Jefus, you find him difpofed to Acts of Juftice and Charity, *Luke* xix. 6, 8. No fooner was *Lydia baptized* into Chrift, but fhe was given into Hofpitality and Beneficence, *Acts* xiv. 15. And in the fame Chapter we may obferve how full of Tendernefs and Compaffion the Jailer was after he *believed in God:* This is vifible from his wafhing the Apoftles Stripes, his bringing them into his Houfe, and fetting Meat before them, *ver.* 33, 34. When the Apoftle *Paul* was converted, his cry was, Lord, *what wilt thou have me to do?* He was defirous to *do* fomething for God. And this is the Language of every true Chriftian; having tafted the Love of God, they are eager to *do* the Will of God. To enumerate all the Examples of Chriftian Piety and Virtue would be endlefs. The Scriptures are full of them, and fo is Church Hiftory. And if you want Inftances of the Power and Efficacy of Faith, read the Eleventh to the *Hebrews:* There you will fee the Glory of his Grace difplayed in the eminent Tranfactions and exemplary Sufferings of many Chriftian Worthies. There you will meet with a Cloud of Witneffes, to illuftrate and confirm the Doctrine we are defending. And now what remains but to exhort you, dear Reader, to be one of that Number, and in your own Life to fhew forth the Fruitfulnefs and Excellency of Juftifying Faith?

Are

Are you then in a juftified State? And, indeed, if you are not in a State of Juftification, you muft be in a State of Damnation; for there is no Medium.   If you are not juftified, you are condemned already*: If you are not faved you muft be damned.   Do you then believe in Chrift? Let the Piety of your Converfation evince the Sincerity of your Profeffion. The Doctrine of Juftification by Faith only hath no Tendency to deftroy Good Works. Altho' we are juftified freely without Works, yet Good Works follow after Juftification, and are the genuine Effects of Juftifying Faith. The Grace of God that bringeth Salvation, teacheth us to deny Ungodlinefs and worldly Lufts, and to live foberly, righteoufly and godly, in this prefent World.   The free Love of God in Chrift, is an irrefiftible Conftraint to Obedience.   What? fhall we continue in Sin, that Grace may abound? Shall we do Evil becaufe God hath done us Good? "Shall "we ceafe from Good Works and relinquifh "Charity? May the Lord never fuffer this to "befal us, but let us haften to perform every "Good Work with Diligence and Alacrity." Only follow the Advice of this Apoftolical Father, and then what will become of *Antimonianifm?* Are thofe who hold free Juftification chargeable with it? Or does the Doctrine I have been defending countenance it? Is this Doctrine an Antithefis to Good Works? They are the worft *Antinomians* who are *Antinomians*

-----

* John iii. 18.

tinomians in Life. What signifies Men's disput-ing for Good Works, if they do not practise them? You may quarrel all your Life-time about Good Works and be damned at last for not performing them. What a Shame is it, that generally those who are most zealous in contending for Good Works, are most careless and indifferent in doing them? When Men ask this Question, what signifies doing Good Works, unless we are justified by them? we might be apt to imagine, that such Persons who expect to be justified by their Works should excel and abound therein; but how strange is it! The direct contrary appears in Fact. We may observe those who are most litigious and disputatious for Works having a Hand in their Justification, are most negligent of them in their Conversation. But what Hypocrisy is this? Is not this mocking God and dissembling with a double Heart? And how dreadful will the Condition of those be, who boast so much of their Virtuous Actions and Moral Righteousness, if they are found wanting---if while they are so contentious for the Theory they are deficient in Practice?

It is often objected, that those who believe Justification by Faith, frequently live wicked Lives, and from thence Men are ready to con-clude, that their Doctrine is false. But how inconclusive an Argument is this? Is a good Doctrine to be condemned for the Wickedness of those who profess it? The best Things may be abused. The Doctrine of Justification by

Faith

Faith only, does not tend to promote Impiety and Licentiousness, and if any pervert it to such Purposes, 'tis not the Fault of the Doctrine, but of its Abettors. The evil Conversation of those who hold this Doctrine does not in the least defile the Doctrine itself. Yet what a Pity is it that so wholsome a Truth should suffer so much from the corrupt Lives of those who profess it? And how deplorable must their Case be, who hold so heavenly a Truth in such hellish Unrighteousness? What Ingratitude is this to God? What Cruelty to Jesus Christ? Such Persons crucify the Son of God afresh, and put him to open Shame. Oh! how is the Lamb of God wounded in the House of his pretended Friends? They, like *Judas*, betray their Master with a Kiss; and under the Appearance of Friendship cut their Saviour to the Heart, as *Joab* slew *Abner*. These bring more Dishonour upon Christ and his Gospel, and hinder the Progress of the Word of God more than the most inveterate open Enemies, and the bitterest Persecutors. Do you consider this, ye formal Hypocrites, who have the Truth in your Understandings, but no Life in your Hearts? Will you make Christ the Minister of Sin? Will you turn his Grace into Lasciviousness? What then do you expect for your Portion, but everlasting Damnation? Do you think to reconcile Christ and Belial? Or do you imagine you may live in Sin here, and go to Heaven hereafter? If you flatter yourselves with such vain Conceits, if you buoy yourselves up with such

false

falſe Hopes, you may be ſure, that an evil Heart hath deluded you, and Sin hath blind‑ed you. Why then do ye call Chriſt your Maſter? The Devil is your Maſter, and Hell will be your Wages. Repent therefore of your Spiritual Fornication, otherwiſe God *will caſt you into a Bed,* and all *them that com‑mit Adultery with you into great Tribulation** ; *great Tribulation, greater* than can be ex‑preſſed, *greater* than can be conceived; and what ſort of *a Bed* do you think this is which God here threatens to caſt you into? Now perhaps you ſleep upon *a Bed* of Down or Feathers, but how will you do to ſleep upon *a Bed* of Fire and Brimſtone? Now per‑haps you ſtretch yourſelves every Night and every Morning upon *a Bed* of Eaſe, how can you bear to ſtretch yourſelves in Hell‑fire? Now you lay down your weary Heads upon a ſoft Pillow, but then hot burning Coals will be your Pillow for ever. Inſtead of lying in Sheets of fine twined Linen, you will lie in Sheets of Fire and Brimſtone; Hell‑flames will cloath you on every Side; they will ſtick as cloſe to you as your Skin to your Fleſh, or your Fleſh to your Bones. This will be the Condemnation of all thoſe who *profeſs* to know God, but in *Works* deny him, who are Abominable and Diſobedient, and unto every *Good Work reprobate,* Tit. i. 16. A great Profeſſion without a ſuitable Converſation, will only procure you a greater Damnation.

There‑

---

* Rev. ii. 22.

Therefore awake, ye sleepy Virgins; up, and be doing: Shew your Faith by your Works. There is no true Religion without Good Works. There may be Works seemingly Good where there is no true Religion. Good Works are not the Causes, but the Fruits and Effects of True Religion; and where True Religion is, these will naturally follow. Do not deceive yourselves; if you will not follow after Holiness, if you are not conversant in Good Works, I tell you, you are not in a State of Justification, but in a State of Condemnation; and what Conceptions soever you may form, or how clearly soever you may discourse of Justification by Faith only, yet if you sleep in Sin here, you will awake in Hell hereafter. There is no going to Heaven but in a way of Holiness, *Heb*. xii. 14   If you have Faith to walk therein, you will be saved; but if you are unholy, you will never be admitted to see God, but you will be excluded the Divine Presence, and shut up in eternal Misery.

M

CHAP.

CHAP. III.

OF THE

HOLY SPIRIT.

THE Holy Spirit is the Third Person in the sacred TRINITY, who is God over all, blessed for evermore. The Godhead consists of Three Persons, the Father, the Son, and the Holy Spirit, and these Three are one in Essence, their Glory is equal, their Existence eternal. The Holy Ghost is endued with the Attributes of Infinity and Eternity; he is Omnipotent, Omniscient, Omnipresent, Immutable and Incomprehensible; he is Infinite in Goodness, in Justice, in Truth, in Purity and Holiness, and every Perfection. In short, he is God of God, Light of Light, very God of very God; he proceedeth from the Father and the Son, and with the Father and the Son he is worshipped and glorified.

When our Lord Jesus Christ was just upon leaving his Disciples, he commissioned them *to baptize in the Name of the Father, and of the Son, and of the Holy Ghost*, Matth. xxviii. 20. So St. Paul salutes the *Corinthians* with praying, that *the Grace of our* LORD

Jesus

JESUS CHRIST, *the Love of* GOD, *and the Communion of the* HOLY GHOST, *may be with them,* 2 Cor. xiii. 14. All which evidently proves, that the Holy Ghoſt is GOD as well as the Father and the Son; to which Truth the Evangeliſt *John* bears a clear and indubitable Teſtimony, 1 Epiſt. ch. v. ver. 7. *There are Three that bear Record in Heaven, the Father, the Word and the Holy Ghoſt, and theſe Three are One.* The Divinity of the Holy Ghoſt, is alſo aſſerted in many other Places of holy Scripture: Thus Matth. xii. 31, 32. *The Blaſphemy againſt the Holy Ghoſt ſhall not be forgiven unto Men, neither in this World, neither in the World to come.* The Holy Ghoſt muſt be ſtrictly and properly God, or elſe the Sin againſt him would not be of ſo heinous a Nature and abſolutely unpardonable. In Acts v. 3. ſaith Peter to Ananias, *Why hath Satan filled thine Heart to lie to the Holy Ghoſt?* And ver. 4. he adds, *thou haſt not lied unto Man, but unto God:* Which plainly ſhews us, that the Holy Ghoſt is true and very God; which alſo is further confirmed by the Judgment which overtook Ananias upon his Commiſſion of this Sin. *he fell down and gave up the Ghoſt,* ver. 5. The Apoſtle Paul ſwears by the Holy Spirit, 1 Cor. xv. 31. *I proteſt by your rejoicing.* Now we cannot ſuppoſe he ſwears by the Perſons *rejoicing,* much leſs by *Joy,* conſidered as a Quality in them; he muſt therefore ſwear by the Holy Ghoſt, who was the Author of their Joy, and ſwearing is an Acknowledgment of

M 2

the

the Perfon by whom we fwear to be the True
GOD*.   The Apoftle therefore, by fwearing
by the Holy Ghoft, lets us know that he is
the true and eternal God.   The Spirit is faid
to fearch the deep Things of God. 1. Cor. ii. 10.
which he could not do unlefs he himfelf was
equal to God in Wifdom and Knowledge.
But what fignifies multiplying Arguments?
We have faid enough to prove the Godhead of
the Holy Ghoft.   We now therefore proceed
to fhew,

I. That the Holy Ghoft dwells in the
   Hearts of all True Believers.

II. That the Illumination of the Spirit is
    neceffary to a right and faving Knowledge
    of the Holy Scriptures.

III. That the comfortable Influences of the
    Holy Ghoft are really *Felt* by thofe Souls
    to whom they are communicated.

I. The Firft of thefe Propofitions is not fo
generally denied as the Two laft, and therefore fome may be inclined to think I need not
long infift upon it.   However, I intend to give
the Reader full and fufficient Proof of each of
thefe Heads, if the Lord enables me.   The
Homily on Reading the holy Scriptures faith,
" He that keepeth the Word of Chrift is
                                    " promifed

---

* See Deut. vi. 13. Pf. lxiii. 11.   Ifa. lxv. 16,

" promifed the Love and Favour of God, and
" that he fhall be the *Dwelling-place or Temple*
" *of the bleſſed Trinity.*" Here the Indwelling
of the Spirit is afferted, when he that keepeth Chriſt's Word is called the *Dwelling-place*
or *Temple of the bleſſed Trinity.* Becauſe the
Holy Ghoſt being one in Subſtance with the
Father and the Son, where 'he is they are
alſo ; ſo the whole *Trinity* dwells in a believing Soul, *John* xiv. 23.

In the third Part of the Homily for *Rogation
Week* we are thus exhorted ; " Let us therefore
" meekly call upon that bountiful Spirit, the
" Holy Ghoſt, which proceedeth from our Fa-
" ther of Mercy, and from our Mediator Chriſt,
" that he would affiſt us and *infpire* us with his
" Prefence,—for without his lively and fecret
" *Infpiration* can we not ſo much as ſpeak the
" Name of our Mediator." Here *expreſs* Mention is made of the *Infpiration* of the Spirit,
as there is alſo in the XIIIth Article ; " Works
" done before the Grace of Chriſt, and the *In-*
" *fpiration* of his Spirit, are not pleaſant to
" God." And 'tis obfervable, as in the Homily above cited, we are ſtirred up to pray that
the Holy Ghoſt would affiſt us, and *infpire*
us with his Prefence ; ſo the Liturgies are full
of *Infpiration*, and Petitions for that Purpoſe.
Thus in the Prayer of Chriſt's Church-militant,
we find the Supplicants " befeeching God to
" *infpire* continually the univerfal Church with
M 3   " the

" the Spirit of Truth, Unity and Concord."
And in the Collect for the *Fifth Sunday* after
Eafter, " Grant to us thy humble Servants, that
" by thy holy *Infpiration* we may think thofe
" Things that be good."   And in another
Place,* " Cleanfe the Thoughts of our Hearts
" by the *Infpiration* of thy Holy Spirit, that we
" may perfectly love thee, *&c.*" Now then,
what think you? Do you believe the Church
holds the Doctrine of the *Infpiration* of the
Spirit, or not? I have fet thefe Paffages before you on purpofe to convince you that fhe
doth. What fhall we fay then to thofe who
are ready to rave and gnafh their Teeth at Perfons who lay Claim to *Infpiration?* Do not fuch
People contradict the Articles and Homilies and
Liturgies of the Church of *England?* And what
a fhocking Thing is it for Minifters to offer up
fuch Petitions in their Prayers, and then preach
againft *Infpiration* as foon as they get into the
Pulpit! Do not fuch Men, while they deny and
oppofe the *Infpiration* of the Spirit of God,
prove that they are infpired with a contrary
Spirit? It is in vain here to reply, We only
fpeak againft the miraculous and extraordinary
Infpiration of the Spirit: For who is there pretends to this miraculous and extraordinary *Infpiration?* I know none that make any fuch
Pretenfions. I entreat you therefore, do not
make this Pretence of denying *miraculous Infpiration* a Cloak for oppofing *all Infpiration* whatfoever. Do you believe the Articles and Liturgies
of the eftablifhed Church? If you do, why do

you

you difrelifh the Term *Infpiration?* And why are you offended at thofe who preach this Doc-trine, and experience it in their-Hearts? Do you think our Church, in the Places I have quoted, means *extraordinary Infpiration,* i. e. Power to work Miracles? But and if the com-mon Influence and *Infpiration* of the Holy Ghoft is hereby intended, why fhould you de-ride, much lefs defpife or malign thofe who receive this divine Afflatus? Ought you not rather to acknowledge your Want of it, and to wait upon God in Prayer, and the Ufe of all other Means, that you alfo may ob-tain it?

The Liturgy in feveral other Places, holds forth this Doctrine: Thus in the Prayer for the King, " Replenifh him with the Grace of thy " Holy Spirit." In that for the Royal Family; " Endue them with thy Holy Spirit," In the Collect for *Quinquagefima Sunday;* " Send thy " Holy Ghoft, and pour into our Hearts that " moft excellent Gift of Charity." And in the Office of Confirmation; " *Fill* them, O Lord, " with the Spirit of thy holy Fear." Where you fee the Bifhop prays, that the Perfons con-firmed may be endued, yea *filled* with the Spirit. So St. Paul prays for the *Ephefians,* that they may *be filled with all the Fulnefs of GOD,* Eph. iii. 19. He doth not pray that they may be *filled with GOD,* or *with the Ful-nefs of GOD,* but *with all the Fulnefs of.GOD.* Who can tell how much thefe Words contain? And yet the Apoftle offers up this Petition for the general Bulk of Believers in the *Ephefian*

M 4

Church;

Church; and this Prayer had its effect, the Event was accordingly, if we will believe *Ignatius*, who in his Epiftle to the *Ephefians*, faith, " Let us therefore do all Things, as hav-
" ing him dwelling in us, that we may be his
" Temples, and he may be in us our own
" God." And in another Epiftle, viz. that to the *Magnefians*, he hath thefe Words; " Know-
" ing that you are full of God, I briefly ex-
" hort you." To which we may adjoin that Paffage of *Clement* the *Roman:* " A full Effufion
" of the Holy Ghoft was upon all." And yet fome Men of Senfe and Learning efteem thofe Expreffions, *Full of* God, and *Full of the* Holy Ghoft, as oftentatious and enthufiaftical, notwithftanding they are countenanced by the Scriptures, and found in the Writings of Primitive Fathers. And Bifhop Hall defcribes the State of his Soul under the Influences of the Divine Spirit, as " Ready for God, yea, Full
" of God."

I now offer the following Texts of Scripture in Proof of what I have faid upon this Head. *John the Baptift*, who was to prepare the Way for our Lord's Coming, informs thofe who came to his Baptifm, that there was one coming after him, *viz.* Chrift, who fhould *baptize them with the Holy Ghoft and with Fire*, Matth. iii. 2. By being *baptifed with the Holy Ghoft*, is meant receiving him to regenerate and fanctify our Souls, both which are typified by Water Baptifm. And if the Conjunction *and* be here taken exegetically, the Senfe of the Words would be this, *He fhall baptize you with the Holy Ghoft, who*

for

for his illuminating, penetrating quickening
and refining Influences refembles *Fire*. Accordingly he is compared to *Fire*, Rev. iv. 5.
And when he defcended on the Apoftles, Acts
ii. 3. *There appeared unto them cloven Tongues
like as of Fire*; which was to denote the Power
and Efficacy of the Word preached, when the
Spirit of God attends it.

In John vii. 38. we find thefe Words, *He that
believeth on me, as the Scripture hath faid, out
of his Belly fhall flow Rivers of living Water*.
Our Saviour here gives us a Promife of the
Spirit under the Similitude of *Water*. As
Water cleanfes the Body from Filth and Dirt,
fo the Holy Ghoft purifies the Heart from the
Pollution of Sin: and as *Water* cools and refrefhes our Bodies when we are faint and weary,
fo the Spirit of God refrefhes and comforts our
Souls: Hence it is that the Eternal Spirit is
fo frequently exhibited to us in Scripture under the Figure and Refemblance of *Water*. God
calls himfelf *the Fountain of living Waters*, Jer.
ii. 13. for whofoever drinks this *Water lives* for
ever.   The Prophet *Ifaiah* invites *every one that
thirfteth to come to the Waters*, Ifa lv. 1. and fo
doth our Saviour, *Rev*. xxi. 6.--xxii. 17. St. *Paul*
mentions *fpiritual Drink*, 1 Cor. x. 4.--xii. 13.
This *fpiritual Drink*, this *living Water* is the
common Privilege of all Believers, which makes
the Evangelift add, *This fpake he of the Spirit,
which they that believe on him fhould receive*, ver.
39. And fo faith God, *Acts* ii. 17. *I will pour
out of my Spirit upon all Flefh*. i. e. upon all the
fallen Race who believe in Jefus Chrift.

The

The Angel who foretold the Birth of *John the Baptift*, faith, *he fhall be filled with the Holy Ghoft even from his Mother's Womb*, Luke i. 15. *Elizabeth* and *Zacharias* were both *filled with the Holy Ghoft*, ver. 41, 67. *Peter* was *filled with the Holy Ghoft*, Acts iv, 8. and *Paul*, Acts xiii. 9. *Stephen* is defcribed as *a Man full of Faith and of the Holy Ghoft*, Acts vi. 5. fo likewife is *Barnabas*, Acts xi. 24. You will be ready to object, Thefe are particular and extraordinary Inftances, and they are no Rule for us to go by: Though the Apoftles and fome others had fuch plenteous and plenary Vouchfafements of the Holy Spirit, we are not to expect the fame now. But why not? Have we not as much Need of the Holy Spirit as the Apoftles and firft Chriftians had? Is it not our Privilege upon whom the Ends of the World are come? Why then fhould we not afk for it, and expect to receive it at God's Hands? And I would advife Perfons to be cautious of confining the Spirit to primitive Times, left they confine Heaven to primitive Times, and fo mifs of it themfelves; for indeed there is no going to Heaven without receiving the Holy Spirit. Befides, what faith the Scripture? *The Difciples were filled with Joy and with the Holy Ghoft*, Acts xiii. 52. By the Difciples are here meant not only the Apoftles, Prophets and Evangelifts, but alfo the whole body of Believers in general. Was it then the Privilege of the Followers of Chrift to be filled with the Holy Ghoft in thofe Days? And is it not equally their Privilege now?

now? Who will undertake to prove the contrary? they will find it a difficult, yea, infuper-
able Tafk. The Apoftle Paul therefore with
good Reafon exhorts the faithful Souls at *Ephe-*
fus to be filled with the Spirit, Eph. v. 18. He
had before prayed that they might be filled with
all the Fulnefs of God, chap. iii. ver. 19. And
Oh! that this Prayer and this Exhortation may
have their Accomplifhment in the Hearts of
all thofe who are called Chriftians!

The fame Truth is afferted in divers other
Places of Scripture. The great Apoftle of the
Gentiles faith, *Gal.* iv. 6. *Becaufe ye are Sons,*
God hath fent forth the Spirit of his Son into your
Hearts, crying, Abba, Father. To which add,
Rom. viii. 15. *Ye have received the Spirit of*
Adoption, whereby we cry, Abba, Father. All
real Chriftians are Sons of God, both by Regeneration and Adoption; and as natural Children
have Freedom and Familiarity with their Parents, fo the Children of God have free Accefs
to and clofe Communion with their heavenly
Father. For this Purpofe God fends forth the
Spirit of his Son into their Hearts, not calling,
or faying, but (as *Luther* obferves) *crying,*
Abba, Father; for when they pray, they cry
unto God, Luke xviii. 7. Pfal. lxxvii. 1.---
lxxxviii. 1. a Spirit of Grace and Supplication
is poured out upon them. They find Enlargement of Heart, Liberty of Speech, and a Power
freely to lay open their minds to God.. The
Word *Abba* denotes that Love and Affection,
as well as that Simplicity and godly Sincerity
wherewith

wherewith the true Saints of God approach his Throne; therefore we find our Saviour addressing God the Father in this familiar and pathetic Language, *Abba, Father, all Things are possible unto thee,* Mark xiv. 36.

The indwelling of the Spirit is again mentioned, 1 *Cor.* iii 16. *Know ye not that ye are the Temple of God, and that the Spirit of God dwelleth in you?* And chap. vi. ver. 19. *What, know ye not that your Body is the Temple of the Holy Ghost which is in you, which ye have of God, and ye are not your own?* These Interrogatories are equivalent to positive Assertions, and teach us, that the Hearts of Believers are the Temples of the Holy Ghost. This the same divine Author directly affirms, 2 Cor. vi. 16. *Ye are the Temple of the living God; as God hath said; I will dwell in them, and walk in them. I will inhabit in them.* Which expression specifies the intimate Union and Communion there is between God and his People, their Hearts are his Habitation, and there he resides as in his holy Temple. And I take the Word *dwell* to admonish us of God's perpetual abiding with his People: He doth not turn in for a Night or a Day, as a way-faring Man, but when he once enters into their Hearts, there he abides for ever. Their Hearts are his Home. This Text hath of old been made use of to prove and establish our Doctrine. It was quoted by Ignatius the Martyr, in his Examination before Trajan, the Emperor. Trajan said ‘ Who is Theophorus?’ Ignatius answered,

‘ He

' He that hath Chrift in his Breaft.'---And a little after the Emperor faid, ' Have you there-' fore in you him that was crucified?' Ignatius anfwered, ' Yes: For it is written, I will dwell ' in them, and walk in them.' Whereupon Trajan pronounced Sentence of Death upon him, and ordered him to be torn to Pieces by wild Beafts. I think proper to mention this, that none may take part with Trajan in con-demning the Generation of the Righteous, in perfecuting thofe who have Chrift in their Breaft, and bear in them Jefus that was cru-cified. For how ready are fome People to tear others in Pieces, for no other Reafon but this, becaufe they acknowledge they have the Spirit of God dwelling in them? And yet we fee upon what ample Teftimony this Doctrine depends; it is fo clear from the Scriptures, and our own Articles and Homilies, that none but thofe who are wilfully blind can avoid feeing the Truth of it. The Apoftle and Evangelift *John* is as exprefs as the Apoftle *Paul* upon this Head; *he that keepeth his Com-mandments dwelleth in him and he in him,* 1 John iii. 24. and chap. iv. ver. 13. *hereby know we that we dwell in him and he in us, be-caufe he hath given us of his Spirit* and ver. 16. *he that dwelleth in Love, dwelleth in God, and God in him.*

It remains therefore now to propound St. *Paul's* Queftion, Acts xix. 2. *Have ye received the Holy Ghoft fince ye believed?* I fuppofe what I have faid may convince you of the Neceffity of receiving the Holy Ghoft, and I hope now you do not look upon this Doctrine as Enthufiafm or Delufion; how is it therefore with your Soul? Anfwer to God and your own Confcience. Have you received the Holy Ghoft, or have you not? If you have not, what is all your Religion worth? Do you think you have any true Religion in you? I tell you you have not. The Spirit of God is all in all in the Chriftian Religion: So much of the Spirit as you have in you, fo much true Religion you have. But *if a Man have not the Spirit of Chrift he is none of his, Rom.* viii. 9. Therefore never prefume to call yourfelf a Chriftian, till you have the Spirit of Chrift in your Heart. The principal Difference between heathen Morality and vital Chriftianity I take to be this, the one is the Effect of Natural Reafon refined, the other is the Work of the Holy Spirit in the Soul. Now you may call yourfelf a Chriftian, and be fo deem'd by others; but if you have not the Holy Spirit in you, all your Religion is like a Body without a Soul, *i. e.* dead; and your external Chriftianity is no better than heathen Morality, and fo will never procure your Admiffion into the Kingdom of Heaven. But further, if you have not the Spirit of God in you, then the Evil Spirit is in you. Ah! you will be apt to fay this is a hard Saying indeed, who can bear it? Tho' this Affertion may feem ftrange; yet it is true, and is thus demonftrated: The Holy Spirit and the Evil Spirit divide all Mankind

betwixt

betwixt them ; the Children of God are under the Influence of the one, and the Children of Difobedience are under the Power of the other; there is no Medium, and confequently, if you are not under the Influence and Agency of the Holy Spirit, the Infernal Spirit, *i. e.* the Devil, is in you. Perhaps you would be terrified and affrighted above meafure if the Devil was to appear to you outwardly, but I affure you if he bears Sway and Empire in your Heart, (as he moft certainly does, unlefs the Spirit of God be in you) he will do you infinitely more Mifchief there, than he could do by any outward vifible Appearance whatfoever. But you may be ready to reply, I am eafy and quiet, and do not perceive myfelf to be under *Satan*'s Power and Dominion: What then? Is your Condition the fafer, becaufe you do not perceive your Danger? If you was fenfible of your Danger, you would probably ufe fome Means for your Efcape. Your Lukewarmnefs, Indolence and Senfelefsnefs, your being at eafe in a carnal State, and your Indifference to the Things of God and Religion are Evidences to others of your being under the Guidance and Agency of the Evil Spirit, tho' you may not perceive it yourfelf. *The ftrong Man armed keepeth his Palace, and his Goods are in Peace, Luke* xi. 21. You therefore are in a falfe *Peace*, becaufe the *ftrong Man, i. e.* the God of this World, hath Poffeffion of your Heart. Your Danger therefore is not the lefs, but the greater by reafon of the Infenfibility of

your

your Condition. As for those who ridicule the Doctrine of the Spirit, and hate and revile those holy Souls in whom he dwells, the Case is evident; they are earthly, sensual, *devilish, having not the Spirit, Jam.* iii. 15. *Jude* 19. Ye Serpents, ye Generation of Vipers, how can ye escape the Damnation of Hell? Do not mistake me, I do not speak this as if I wish'd you in Hell, or as if it was impossible for you to escape Damnation. I only admonish you of your Danger, as our Saviour did the *Jews, Matt.* xxiii. 33. I tell you there is yet Mercy for you: I advise you therefore not to persist in the Error of your Way. Turn from the Path that leads to Destruction, be humbled for your Obstinacy in opposing Christ and his Spirit, and meekly call upon God to give you that Holy Spirit whom you have so long resisted, and so blindly contradicted and blasphemed.

But in the next Place, if you have received the Holy Ghost, what an infinite Honour what a glorious Privilege hath God conferred upon you! What a Wonder of Grace is it that God should in very Deed dwell with Men? Ye are *a Spiritual House, an holy Temple in the* LORD, *an Habitation of* GOD *through the Spirit,* 1 *Pet.* ii. 5. *Eph.* ii. 21, 22. How highly hath God favour'd you! And this he did not do for any Goodness, Merit or Excellency in you, but for his own Mercy's Sake. You are by Nature no better than others. If ye differ, it is the Grace of God that makes you to differ. Therefore glory not in yourselves; but glory

only

only in the unmerited Goodnefs of God, and his
Free Grace in Chrift Jefus our Lord. "I
" tafte much of God (faith *Ignatius*) but I mo-
" derate myfelf, left I fhould perifh in glorying."
I wifh all who have the Spirit of God in them
were of this holy Martyr's Mind.

The Spirit of God is Holy, and therefore
by way of Eminence called the Holy Ghoft.
He is infinitely Holy as God, and he reftores all
in whom he dwells to the Image and Likenefs
of God. It is he that purifies the Hearts of
God's People, and makes us Partakers of a holy,
heavenly and divine Nature. As foon as the
Apoftle *Paul* had inculcated the Doctrine of
God's dwelling in the Souls of his Children, he
immediately fubjoins this Exhortation, *wherefore come out from among them, and be ye feparate,
faith the Lord, and touch not the unclean Thing,*
2 *Cor.* vi. 16, 17. If the Holy Spirit refides in
you, he will make you holy; he will fubdue the
Power of Vanity and Corruption, and make you
pure in Heart : You will no longer live in a fer-
vile Subjection to Sin, but have Freedom from it,
and Dominion over it. The Lufts of the Flefh
will decay and die, all holy Defires will be quick-
en'd in you, and the Virtues and Graces of the
Spirit will flourifh and ripen in your Heart. The
Houfe of *Saul* will wax weaker and weaker, and
the Houfe of *David* ftronger and ftronger.
How is it then with thy foul ? Doft thou
feel thefe Effects wrought in thee? Art thou
holy in Heart? Doft thou avoid every Appearance of Evil? Doft thou fupprefs the

firſt ſtirrings of Sin in thy Soul? Doſt thou live in no ſecret Sin? Doſt thou indulge in no unclean Thought? Art thou as careful to avoid ſinning againſt God in private, as if the whole World ſaw thee? In ſhort, haſt thou an inward and irreconcileable hatred of all Sin, and an eager panting, hungring and thirſting after all Degrees of Holineſs? Do not labour to ſhift off theſe Queſtions; let them ſtrike near your Heart, and convince you of your Unholineſs and Unlikeneſs to God. Why ſhould you deceive yourſelf? If you have the Spirit of Chriſt in you, you will feel the Bent and Biaſs of your Soul carrying you to the higheſt Meaſures of Purity and Sanctification; a faithful Man " hath white Hands " and a clean Soul, fit to lodge God in; " all the Rooms whereof are ſet apart for his " Holineſs*." Is your Soul thus dedicated to God? And are your Words and Actions conformable thereto? Do you avoid all idle and frothy Converſation? Is your Speech with Grace ſeaſoned with Salt? Doth no corrupt Communication proceed out of your Mouth, but that which is Good to the uſe of edifying? Do you put off all fooliſh talking and jeſting which are not convenient? And is it your Delight to talk of God and his dear Son Jeſus Chriſt? Do you feel your heart warmed by holy Conference and heavenly Meditation? Be diligent likewiſe to adorn the Doctrine of God our Sa

viour

* Biſhop *Hall*'s Character of a faithful Man.

viour in all things. Be swift to hear, slow to speak and slow to wrath. Let your Moderation be known to all Men. Love all who love Christ without respect of Persons or Distinction of Parties. Be ready to forgive Injuries and bear Offences. Labour after that Charity which is not easily provoked. Walk in the Spirit, and ye shall not fulfil the Lusts of the Flesh. *Sanctify the Lord* GOD *in your Heart, having a good Conscience, that whereas they speak Evil of you as of Evil-doers, they may be ashamed who falsely accuse your good Conversation in Christ,* 1 Peter. iii. 13, 16. Alas! how doth the Cause of Christ suffer through the vain and trifling Behaviour of the Professors of his Gospel! How many talk of the Spirit of God, and yet live in the Spirit of the World, in the Pomp and Pride of Life, and in the Indulgence of the Flesh? Some People's Religion is made up of Mirth and Jesting; they are light and trifling upon all Occasions, and discover nothing so much as a talkative Tongue, and an airy ridiculous Turn of Mind. Such Persons may ask themselves, does this Discourse, this Behaviour become one who is to act according to the Inspiration of the Divine Spirit? The very Thoughts of the Presence of God within us would condemn many of our allowed Ways of speaking and acting, or else baffle all our Pretensions to Christianity. Who hath more Reason to be afraid of acting below his Dignity than he whose Soul is the Temple of the Holy Ghost? Certainly none ought more carefully to watch over their Conduct,

than

than they who are to live and act according to the Dictates and Motions of the Spirit of God. The Sense therefore of this divine Inhabitant in us should be a Motive to universal Holiness and undissembled Piety. We are also to be reminded, that by our idle Words and vain foolish Actions we *grieve* the Spirit, Eph. iv. 30. and cause him to withdraw from us, and leave us in the Darkness and Misery of our Nature. God seldom or ever forsakes his People, unless they first forsake him, as *David* saith to his Son *Solomon, if thou forsake him, he will cast thee off for ever,* 1 Chron. xxviii. 9. Souls first forsake God by some inward or outward Sin, and then he forsakes them; and so they fall into Doubts and Darkness, and are often at the Point of Despair. What a dreadful Thing is it to be deserted by the Spirit of God! They who have felt the Misery of such Desertions, know that no Pains are like those Pains, no Sorrows like those Sorrows. As when God speaks Peace, who can trouble? So when God troubles, none can speak Peace. Watch therefore, and strive against Sin, and avoid every thing that may displease God, or cause his Holy Spirit to depart from you.

To conclude; have you the Spirit of God in you? Then wait in Expectation of future Glory. The Holy Spirit is the Seal *whereby ye are sealed unto the Day of Redemption,* Eph. iv. 30. What God *seals* he appropriates for his own, and it cannot be alienated from him. Hath God then *sealed you with that Holy Spirit of Promise?* Then he hath made you his own, you are his

in

in an eternal and inviolable Covenant; and although the Mountains depart, and the Hills be removed, yet *my Kindness shall not depart from thee, neither shall the Covenant of my Peace be removed, saith the Lord, that hath Mercy on thee,* Isa. liv. 10. The Spirit of God is also called *the Earnest of our Inheritance,* Eph. i. 14. God hath given his Children many great and precious Promises, but left that should not suffice, left they should distrust his Goodness or question his Faithfulness, he gives them an Earnest of the purchased Possession. An Earnest is Part of the Estate, and a Security of the Conveyance of it. Hath God therefore *given us the Earnest of the Spirit in our Hearts?* As certainly as we have the Spirit of God dwelling in us here, we shall dwell with God in Heaven hereafter, If we have the *Earnest,* we cannot miss of the Inheritance. *Lastly,* the Spirit is a Witness, 1 John v. 6. *it is the Spirit that beareth Witness.* And what doth he bear witness to? The Apostle Paul tells us, *the Spirit beareth witness with our Spirit, that we are the Children of God,* Rom. viii. 16. The Spirit is infallible, and his Testiomny is to be depended upon. His Evidence is clear and convincing, so that they to whom he witnesseth, cannot possibly doubt of their being Children of God. Their Faith and Hope are built upon the Testimony of the divine Spirit. And how is it possible they should doubt their being Children of God, when God by the inward Witness of his Spirit tells them they are? Hence they draw near to God in *full Assurance of Faith,* as

the

the Apostle speaks, Heb x. 22. they are sure
that God is their Father, that Christ is their
Saviour; they are sure their Sins are forgiven,
and that they are at Peace with God; they are
as sure of going to Heaven as if they were there
already. This is a Part of Experimental Religion which *Despisers will not believe though a
Man* who hath experienced the Truth thereof
declare it unto them, Acts xiii. 41. "World-
"lings (saith Bishop Davenant) will not be-
" lieve that such a full Assurance of Faith is
" impressed upon the Hearts of Believers; but
" the Pious who continue stedfast in the Gos-
" pel experience it."

II. The Illumination of the Spirit is necessary to a right and saving Knowledge of the
holy Scriptures: I say, a *saving* Knowledge of
the holy Scriptures, because Men may have a
notional Acquaintance with them, a speculative
Knowledge of them, and yet not be in a State
of Salvation. This Knowledge is not sufficient
to bring them to Heaven. A competent Skill
in Grammar, History and Criticism will give
Men an insight into the Letter of Scripture,
but to see the true Light, and feel the saving
Power thereof an internal Operation of the Spirit is required; and without this no Man can
understand the Scripture to any saving Purpose.
The natural Man (saith the Apostle) *receiveth not
the Things of the Spirit of God.*, 1 Cor. ii. 14. A
Person can no more discern Spiritual and Divine
Things without the teaching and Illumination
of

of the Divine Spirit, than a Man without Eyes can behold the Sun. In the Fall of Man all his Faculties were vitiated and debafed; amongft the reft his Underftanding was darkened and his Judgment corrupted: Hence he is rendered incapable of beholding fpiritual Objects, and forming a right Judgment concerning them. He remains in grofs Ignorance of the Things of God and Religion, till the Holy Spirit darts an heavenly Beam into his Soul, and fills him with a divine Light: For it is the Spirit which fearcheth all Things, yea, the *deep Things* of God, and revealeth them unto us, ver. 10. in fuch a Manner and Meafure as is neceffary to our eternal Salvation. We cannot know thefe divine Depths any farther than the Holy Ghoft reveals them unto us.

In the fecond Part of the Homily of the Information of certain Places of Scripture, the People are thus inftructed, " If ye will be pro-
" fitable Hearers and Readers of the holy Scrip-
" tures, ye muft firft deny yourfelves, and keep
" under your *carnal fenfes* taken by the *outward*
" Words, and fearch the *inward meaning*: Rea-
" fon muft give Place to God's Holy Spirit;
" you muft fubmit your worldly Wifdom and
" Judgment unto his divine Wifdom and Judg-
" ment." How would that Expreffion, " Keep
" under your *carnal fenfes*, taken by the *outward*
" *Words*," be laughed at, if it was not found in one of our own Homilies! And how difagreeable to fome People is the Doctrine of an *outward* and *inward meaning* in Scripture; Yet this Homily makes exprefs mention of both thefe, and ex-

horts

horts the People to fearch into the *inward Meaning* of Scripture, and to fubmit their Reafon to God's Holy Spirit.

The Homily entitled, *A fruitful Exhortation to the Reading and Knowledge of Holy Scripture*, hath this Paffage : " The Words of Ho-
" ly Scripture be called Words of everlafting
" Life, for they be God's Inftrument ordained
" for the fame Purpofe.   They have Power to
" turn through God's Promife, and they be
" effectual through God's Affiftance ; and be-
" ing received in a faithful Heart, they have
" ever an heavenly fpiritual Working in them."
To which add the Conclufion of the Homily
for *Whitfunday* ; " He that is the Lord of Hea-
" ven and Earth of his great Mercy fo work in
" all Men's Hearts, by the mighty Power of
" the Holy Ghoft, that the comfortable Gof-
" pel of his Son Chrift may be truly preached,
" truly received, and truly followed in all pla-
" ces". The comfortable Gofpel of Chrift cannot be truly preached without the mighty Power of the Holy Ghoft. Preachers who have not
the Holy Ghoft are no Minifters of Chrift.
They who have the Holy Spirit attending
their Miniftry, fpeak not with the enticing
Words which Man's Wifdom teacheth, but
which the Holy Ghoft teacheth.   When they
are thus influenced and infpir'd, their Word
is in Power, and in the Holy Ghoft, and 'in
much Affurance.   The Holy Spirit warms
their Heart, and they feel what they fay : Their
" Expreffions are affectionate and cordial, as
" proceeding from the Heart, and an experi-
" mental

" mental Acquaintance with thofe Truths
" which they deliver. 'Tis a hard Matter to
" affect others, with what we are not firft af-
" fected ourfelves. 'Tis faid of John the Bap-
" tift, that *he was a burning and a fhining*
" *Light*. This is to fpeak in the Evidence
" and Demonftration of the SPIRIT and
" Power.*"

The Homily of reading the Holy Scripture
fays, " in reading of God's Word he not al-
" ways moft profiteth that is moft ready in turn-
" ing of the Book, or in faying of it without
" Book, but he that is moft turned into it, that
" is moft infpired with the Holy Ghoft,
" moft in his Heart and Life altered and chang-
" ed into that Thing which he readeth." 'Tis
not he that is moft clear in his Ideas, moft accu-
rate in his Conceptions, or moft refined in his
Speculations, nor he whofe Head is moft phi-
lofophically or geometrically turned, that is the
moft profitable Reader of Holy Scripture; but
he who is moft infpired with the Holy Ghoft,
and whofe Heart and Life are moft changed into
that which he readeth. Without the Infpiration of the Holy Ghoft all our human Wifdom and Science will no more enable us favingly to underftand the Scriptures than to create
a new World. " Man's human and worldly
" Wifdom or Science (as faith the fame Homi-
" ly) is not needful to the underftanding of
" Scripture, but the Revelation of the Holy

O   " Ghoft

---

* Bifhop *Wilkins's Gift of Preaching.*

" Ghoft who infpireth the true Meaning un-
" to them that with Humility and Diligence
" fearch therefore." Now, do you think our
Reformers were Enthufiafts? Why then are
you ready to call thofe Enthufiafts who fpeak of
the Infpiration of the Holy Ghoft? How do
you expect to underftand the Scriptures? You
are here taught, that 'tis not all your Skill in
Arts and Sciences will help you to a right Underftanding thereof; but 'tis the Revelation of
the Holy Ghoft, and his Infpiration, that muft
advance you to this high Attainment. And
note by Infpiration here we do not mean any
Power to write a new Scripture, but only to underftand the antient Writings of the Old and
New Teftament aright to all Intents and Purpofes of Salvation. This is what our Church
prays for in the Collect for the fecond Sunday
in Advent; " Bleffed Lord, who haft caufed all
" Holy Scriptures to be written for our Learn-
" ing, grant that we may in fuch wife hear
" them, read, mark, learn, and inwardly digeft
" them, that by Patience and Comfort of thy
" holy Word we may embrace and ever hold
" faft the bleffed hope of everlafting Life, which
" thou haft given us in our Saviour Jefus
" Chrift." And have we not all Reafon to
join in fuch a Prayer?

The Scriptures are very clear and exprefs in
this Particular. Thus faith the holy Pfalmift,
*Open thou mine Eyes, that I may behold wonderous
Things out of thy Law.* cxix. 18. The infpired
Author, from the Senfe of the Weaknefs of his
own Underftanding, and the Sublimity of divine

vine Myfteries, breaks out into this devout Petition.   He prays God to open his Eyes, that he might behold the Wonders of the divine Book; implying, that without this heavenly Illumination he could not underftand it.   The Cafe is the fame with us, unlefs the Spirit of Grace enlightens our dark Minds we cannot favingly difcern the Myfteries of the Kingdom of God.   The fame divine Writer fpeaks to the fame Purpofe, ver. 12. *Bleffed art thou O Lord, teach me thy Statutes*; where we fee the holy Man of God firft bleffes the Lord for paft and prefent Manifeftations of his Grace, and then prays for further Revelations and Difcoveries, *teach me thy Statutes*; *i. e.* give me the inward *Teaching* of thy Spirit, whereby I may have a clear View of the Doctrines, Precepts, and Privileges contained in thy holy Word.   And this Petition is repeated ver. 26, 33, 64, 68, 124, 135, which fhews how earneft the Pfalmift was in this his Requeft.   And when we have a Senfe of the Need of this divine Teaching, we fhall be ceafelefs and importunate in our Supplications to God, that he would afford us the Guidance of his infallible Spirit to conduct us in all our facred Refearches.

We are informed in *Luke* xxiv. 45. that our Saviour *opened the Underftanding* of his Difciples *that they might underftand the Scriptures*; which fhews us that they could not have underftood them, unlefs the bleffed Jefus had thus opened their Underftanding.   Now then it may be afked, can we underftand the Scriptures without having our Underftanding oper~d in the

fame

fame Manner? Have we not as much need of this fpiritual Illumination as the Apoftles had? Or do we think we can underftand the Scriptures without it, though they could not? If Men are thus conceited of their own Wifdom and Abilities, may not God juftly leave them to the Guidance of their natural Intellects, to walk on in the Darknefs of their own Hearts to Blacknefs of Darknefs for ever? How earneftly therefore fhould we call upon God to do the fame Thing in our Hearts, which he did in the Hearts of his Difciples? For otherwife we fhall never underftand the Scriptures to any faving Purpofe. The Time when our Lord Jefus thus opened their Underftanding, is remarkable: For *firft*, they had before this been fent out to preach;* they muft then therefore have had fome Knowledge of Chrift and his Offices; yet now after his Refurrection the bleffed Jefus *opens their Underftanding, i. e.* gives them a frefh Difplay of his Grace and Mediatorfhip. The moft aged Minifters, the moft advanced Believers receive an Augmentation of fpiritual Light and Wifdom. All our Knowledge is finite, and fo is capable of perpetual Addition and Increafe. *Secondly*, this Opening of their Underftanding was before the plenary Effufion of the Holy Ghoft on the Day of *Pentecoft*, Acts ii. and therefore cannot mean any extraordinary Donation of the Spirit peculiar to the Apoftles only, but muft fignify fuch a Communication thereof as all experienced Chriftians are endowed with. Accordingly,

---

* Luke ix. 1. 2.

ingly, when it is faid the Lord *opened Lydia's* Heart, Acts xvi. 14. the very fame Greek Word is there ufed, which the divine Evangelift here makes ufe of. When *Lydia's* Heart was opened, fhe attended to the Things which were fpoken by *Paul*, and God opened her Heart for this very End and Purpofe. Had not the Lord opened her Heart, fhe would have remained in Blindnefs and Ignorance for ever. And till the fame gracious Lord, opens our Hearts, as he did faithful *Lydia's*, we fhall never favingly attend to Things eternal and divine.

The Apoftle *Paul* prays for the *Ephefians*, that the *Eyes of their Underftanding might be enlightened*, Eph. i. 18. and Chap. v. ver. 8. faith he, *Ye were fometime Darknefs but now are ye Light in the Lord*. Darknefs and Light are ab-ftract Terms and fo denote to us the extreme Mifery of a natural and the extreme Felicity of a regenerate State. They alfo acquaint us with the diametrical Oppofition of thefe two States. Chrift is called the *Light of the Gen-tiles*, Ifa. xlii. 6. xlix. 6. Luke ii. 32. Acts xiii. 47. He calls himfelf *the Light of the World*, John viii. 12. ix. 5. He was fent to *open the blind Eyes*, Ifa xlii. 7. *To give Light to them that fit in Darknefs*, Luke i. 79. and *recovering of Sight to the Blind*, Luke iv. 18. So the Apof-tle *Paul* was fent to the *Gentiles to open their Eyes, and to turn them from Darknefs to Light*, Acts xxvi. 18. And 2 Cor. iv. 6. faith he, *God who commanded Light to fhine out of Darknefs, hath fhined in our Hearts*. All which I alledge (and much more might be alledged) to fhew

the

the total Darkneſs of Men in their natural Condition and the abſolute Neceſſity of the enlightening Grace of God.

Experience is the Mother of all knowledge, natural and ſpiritual, and this Doctrine is con-firmed by the Experience of all Saints. The Scriptures are full of Inſtances of a divine Light and Power attending the Word. When St. *Paul* was converted, the Light that ſhined round about him was but an Emblem of the in-ternal Irradiation of his Mind by the Holy Ghoſt. When our Saviour called *Simon* and *Andrew*, *James* and *John*, they heard, beſides the outward Call of his Voice, the inward Call of his Spirit; otherwiſe they would not have immediately *left their Nets, the Ship, and their Father, and followed him* Matt. iv. 18. 22. So likewiſe when the bleſſed Jeſus called *Matthew*, he was *ſitting at the Receipt of Cuſtom*, Matt. ix. 9. getting Riches, engaged in Buſineſs, and ſharing largely in this World's Goods; and we cannot ſuppoſe he would have ſo readily for-ſaken All to follow Chriſt, if the Holy Spirit had not inclined him thereto. " When the " inward Call of the Spirit accompanies the " outward Call of the Word, the Soul readily " complies, and preſently yields Obedience to " the Voice of God. Chriſt ofttimes ſpeaks " by his Word to our Ear, and we hear not, " we ſtir not; but when he ſpeaks by his Spirit " to our Hearts, Satan ſhall not hold us down, " the World ſhall not keep us back, but we " ſhall ariſe and follow our Lord and Maſter.*"

And

---

* Biſhop Hall.

And when Chrift called Zaccheus, a divine Power and Energy went along with his Words, as we may gather from the Effect they had upon him; for he *made hafte, and came down, and received him joyfully*, Luke xix, 6. And fo innumerable Inftances might be heaped together to evince this Doctrine and to fhew that the Holy Ghoft adds a vital Power and Influence to the Word, and makes it effectual to the Iilumination and Converfion of Souls. Yea, I might add, every frefh Convert is an Inftance of the Truth of it; and if you are converted, you will need no further Arguments to prove it.

The Application of this is eafy. Hence we learn not to lean to our own Underftandings, nor to think by our own natural Abilities, without the Affiftance of divine Grace, to attain a faving Knowledge of God's Word.

" Abfurd (faith a learned Bifhop of our
'· Church) is the Doctrine of the *Socinians,*
" and fome others, that unregenerate Men by
" a mere natural Perception, without any
'· divine fuperinfufed Light, (they * Sine Lumine
" are the Words of *Epifcopas,** Supernatura-
" and they are wicked Words) lis Potentiæ
" may underftand the whole Law, fuperinfufo.
" even all Things requifite unto *Epifcop. Difput. 3.*
" Faith and Godlinefs; foolifhly
" confounding, and impioufly deriding (as too
" many do in this prefent Day) the fpiritual
" and divine Senfe of holy Scriptures with the
" Grammatical Conftruction‡." Many read

O 4

the

---

‡ Bifhop Reynolds's Sinfulnefs of Sin.

the Scriptures, yet never understand them because they trust to their own Understanding, instead of depending upon the Teaching and Influence of the Holy Spirit. A Person can no
more understand the Scriptures savingly without the Illumination of the Holy Ghost, than
a Man can understand Greek or Hebrew or any
other Language which he hath never learned.
The Scriptures are all an unknown Language
to an unenlightened Heart. Learned Men often think they understand the sacred Writings,
because they know the literal Meaning of the
Words: Dictionaries and Lexicons are the Tutors and Governors, and the Letter of the Text
is the highest of their Attainments. And thus
far natural Men may aspire: They may com-
pass the Grammatical Construction of the
Words; when yet they have no inward Experience of Evangelical Doctrine in their Hearts.
Men may be well versed in Science and Philosophy; and well instructed in the Languages,
but unless they are taught, not by Critics and
Commentators, but by the Spirit of God, they
know nothing yet as they ought to know, 1 Cor. viii.
2. A moderate Skill in the Languages is service-
able in determining the true Sense of Words,
yet if Men stop here, how far short do they fall
of the one Thing needful? They are acquainted
with the *Letter that killeth,* but ignorant of *the
Spirit which giveth Life,* 2 Cor. iii. 6. The
Veil is yet *untaken away in reading the Old Tes-
tament* and the New, ver. 14. A great deal of
Learning in the Head with no Grace in the
Heart, does frequently fill Men with Pride,

blind

blind their Minds, and harden their Hearts, and sink them into eternal Darkness and Destruction.

Never therefore take the sacred Volume in your Hand without lifting up your Heart to God: Beg of God to give you the Light of his Spirit to lead you into the Light of Divine Truth. The reason why Persons read the Scriptures to little or no Purpose is, because they do not call upon the Lord for a Blessing upon their Reading; they take up the Scriptures with as much Carelessness and Indifference as any other Book, neither considering the Weakness and Shallowness of their own Judgment, nor yet the mysterious Nature of scriptural Truths: Hence the Word of God is to them a dead Letter, a Book sealed, and it strikes with no Power or Demonstration upon their Hearts. And besides I think it is no Wonder Men fall into dangerous Errors and Heresies, if they trust to their own natural Parts, and make the illuminating Grace of the Spirit neither the Object of their Faith, nor the Subject of their Prayers. Does God do them any Injustice in leaving them to their own Wisdom and Understanding, seeing they place so much Confidence therein as to acknowledge no Necessity of a supernatural and divine Illumination? Reading the Scriptures without the Light of the Spirit is but an unprofitable Exercise; it is in Effect reading without Eyes. We cannot understand the inspired Writings but by the same Spirit which indited them. The Holy Ghost, which dictated them at first to the Apostles, must interpret

terpret and explain them to us, or elfe we fhall
never acquire a faving Knowledge of them.
" Wicked Men (faith Mr. *Herbert*) however
" learned, do not know the Scriptures, becaufe
" they feel them not, and becaufe they are not
" underftood but with the fame Spirit that writ
" them" This may feem ftrange Doctrine to a
carnal Mind, and to a Perfon unacquainted with
the Power of Godlinefs; but a Soul that knows
by Experience what it is to be in Doubt when
Salvation is at ftake, will be glad to hear of the
Direction of the Spirit, and will readily depend upon it, and heartily acquiefce in it. And
indeed when we are under a due Senfe of the
Weaknefs of our own Judgment, and caft our
Eyes abroad on the World and obferve what
innumerable Errors there are, and how many
abler and wifer Heads than our own are and
have been deceived, how do our Souls tremble?
What Hope could we have? Or where fhould
we flee for Relief but to the Teaching and
Unction of the Eternal Spirit? This is what we
are to rely upon; this is what we are to truft
to: and thofe who are under a right Apprehenfion of Things will find themfelves conftrained to pray to God for the Illumination
and Manuduction of his Holy Spirit. And
Prayer is the Life of Study: thofe who ftudy
the Scriptures with inceffant Prayer, will not
fail to be led into the True Meaning of them.
They ftudy beft who pray the moft. And
God will certainly vouchfafe his Help to all
fincere and devout Supplicants. " The Eyes of
                              " our

" our Underftanding fhall be irradiated with a
" celeftial Beam, and we fhall feel an Inter-
" nal Operation of the Spirit on our Hearts
" communicating Light and Wifdom*." And
how glorious is it when Souls experience this
heavenly Illumination! Then, as the Apoftle
fpeaks, they are brought out of Darknefs into
marvellous Light : *Marvellous Light* indeed:
Wonderful Light ! ‡ They are filled with Wonder and Aftonifhment at every Thing they fee
in the fpiritual World: They wonder to fee
how blind they were before, they wonder to fee
how enlightened they are now *:* They read the
Scriptures as if they had never read them before, and all therein appears new, and comes
with a quick, vital, comfortable Influence upon
their Hearts. Then they become fettled in all
Doctrines, not by an external Speculation, but
by an internal Senfation of the Goodnefs of
them; they fee the fitnefs and Propriety, they
tafte the Sweetnefs and Felicity of every Evangelical Truth: They walk with Pleafure in the
Ways of God; and his Precepts, which before
were burdenfome and grievous, now become
perfect Freedom, Life, Liberty and ftrong Confolation to their Hearts.

III. The comfortable Influences of the Holy
Ghoft are really felt by thofe Souls to whom
they are communicated. There is much wrang-
ling and difputing about this Propofition;
fome fay one thing and fome fay another; and

yet

---

* See Dr. Edwards on the Excellency and Perfection of
the Scriptures.   ‡ 1 Pet., ii. 9,

yet one might juftly wonder (was it not for the Blindnefs and Corruption of human Nature) there fhould be fo much Contention about fo plain a Matter; for this Propofition feems to me no fooner ftated but demonftrated; for what fort of Comforts muft thofe be which cannot be Felt? They will be in Effect none at all; if therefore you deny the poffibility of Feeling the Comforts of the Spirit, you do in Effect deny their Reality. Befides, I might obferve, the Denial hereof is not only Unfcriptural, but alfo Unphilofophical. The Soul is the Seat of Life and Perception in Man, and by Confequence muft itfelf be endued with Senfibility and Perceptibility. If therefore God is pleafed to make any Impreffions of Pleafure or Comfort upon the Soul, the Soul will have a real Senfe and Perception thereof. But how Irrational as well as Irreligious is it to affert, that the Soul is the Spring and Source of all Senfation and Perception, but yet incapable of Feeling divine Joys and fpiritual Confolations? 'Tis true indeed, fpiritual Senfation or Feeling is as different from bodily, as the Soul is from the Body, neverthelefs the one is as real as the other. This I doubt not I fhall make good from the Homilies and Liturgies. The third Part of the Homily on Faith is directly to our Purpofe, " if you " Feel and perceive fuch a Faith in you, rejoice " in it, and be diligent to maintain it, and keep " it ftill in you; let it be daily increafing, and " more and more by well working, &c." Our Reformers we hope were good Men, and felt that Faith of which they here fpeak. If you

do

do not Feel this Faith in you, you fhould not immediately ridicule and condemn the Doctrine of Feeling Faith, but pray to God to fhew you this Truth both by an Information of the Judgment, and an Experience of the Heart. An hiftorical Faith may make you a Member of a Church Vifible, but nothing lefs than a Feeling Faith in the Heart will conftitute you a Member of Chrift's Body Myftical. And let thofe who have this Faith follow the Exhortation here given, viz. to increafe in it, and to exert it more and more by well working.

The Homily for Rogation Week hath thefe Words, " if after Contrition we feel our Con-
" fciences at Peace with God through Remif-
" fion of our Sins;" here is mention made of Feeling-our Confciences at Peace with God, which fome Men count Enthufiafm; but indeed how fhall we know we are at Peace with God, unlefs we Feel it? Peace and all other Evangelical Bleffings are made known to us only by this inward Feeling, and we can no farther know our Intereft in them than as we have a Feeling Poffeffion of them. Therefore in another Place we meet with thefe Words, " God
" give us Grace (good People) to know thefe
" Things and to Feel them in our Hearts."
And obferve what follows, " This Knowledge
" and Feeling is not in ourfelves, by ourfelves it
" is not poffible to come by it." What Words can be plainer? And if this will not convince People of Spiritual Feeling, what will?

'The Homily on Repentance thus encourageth the true Penitent, " neither let the Remem-
" brance

" brance of thy former Life difcourage thee,
" yea, the more wicked it hath been the more
" fervent or earneft let thy Repentance or Re-
" turning be, and forthwith thou fhalt feel the
" Ears of the Lord wide open to thy Prayers."
What Foolifhnefs do fome People think it to
talk of Feeling the Ears of the Lord wide open
to our Prayers! And yet we fee the Church
holds this and the People of God experience
it, and what an unfpeakable Happinefs is it for
thofe who do feel it! This Expreffion of Feeling
the Ears of the Lord wide open to our Prayers,
is to be underftood Metonymically, viz. with
regard to the Effect, and fo it denotes our receiving thofe Comforts and enjoying that Peace
and Pleafure which God confers in Confequence
of his hearing our Prayers, and in Anfwer to
them.   And then is fulfilled that Promife in
Ifaiah, *Before they call, I will anfwer, and while
they are yet fpeaking, I will hear.* " Sometimes
" (faith Bifhop Wilkins) a Man fhall Feel his
" Heart more warm, his Defires more vigorous,
" and his Expreffions more copious and ready,
" And in this Cafe he fhould not fuffer himfelf
" to be ftraitned or confined with any old Form;
" but may expatiate more freely, according as
" he finds his inward Enlargements*." Thefe
inward Comforts and Enlargements are not always infallible Proofs, that God will grant the
particular Thing we then requeft. The contrary might be fhewed in feveral Inftances.
The truth is, thefe Confolations are Tokens of
God's Love in general, and Earnefts in particular,

---

cular, that he will either grant what we then afk or fomething better.

In the Ordering of Deacons the Queftion is afked, " Do you truft that you are inwardly " moved by the Holy Ghoft to take upon " you this Office and Miniftration, &c." Now unlefs a Perfon feels this inward Motion, how can he tell whether he hath it or not? And if he cannot, he anfwers this Queftion at a venture, and fo perhaps may tell a direct Falfhood; and then hear what Bifhop *Burnet* fays, " If any " Man fays *I truft fo*, that yet knows nothing " of any fuch *Motion*, and can give no Account " of it, he lies to the Holy Ghoft; and makes " his firft approach to the Altar with a Lie in " his Mouth; and that not to Man, but to God." And pleafe to hear how this learn-ed Divine afterwards explains this Queftion. " The true Meaning of it muft be refolved " thus; the Motives that ought to determine a " Man to dedicate himfelf to the Miniftering " in the Church, are a *Zeal* for promoting the " Glory of God, for raifing the Honour of the " Chriftian Religion, for the making it to be " better underftood, and more fubmitted to. " He that loves it, and feels the Excellency of " it in himfelf, that has a Due Senfe of God's " Goodnefs in it to Mankind, and that is en- " tirely poffeffed with that, will feel a Zeal " within himfelf for communicating that to " others."* We fee here the Bifhop holds with fpiritual Feeling, and mentions thofe Motives

and

----

* Bifhop Burnet's Paftoral Sermon.

and Difpofitions which every one ought to feel
in himfelf, who anfwers the Queftion in the
Affirmative.

In the Collect for the *Sunday* after Afcenfion
Day the Church prays, " fend to us thine Holy
" Ghoft to comfort us," and in the next Collect, " evermore to rejoice in his holy Com-
" forts." How can we rejoice in his Comforts
unlefs we feel them? Accordingly in the Vifita-
tion of the Sick, it is faid, " The Almighty
" Lord make thee know and feel, that there is
" none other Name given to Man in whom
" and through whom thou mayeft receive
" Health and Salvation, but only the Name of
" our Lord Jefus Chrift." Here the Minifter
prays that the Sick Perfon may not only know
by a Conviction of the Underftanding, but alfo
Feel by an inward Senfibility of the Heart, that
Jefus is the only Saviour. I once in Difcourfe
with a Man, produced this Paffage; he artfully
replied, that know and feel were fynonymous
Terms, and fo concluded, that Feeling was no
more than knowing. But tho' Feeling is one
fort of Knowledge, does it follow that all Knowledge is Feeling, or that knowing and Feeling
are the fame Thing? The Truth is, this was
the only plaufible Evafion this Artift could
poffibly make. But what will this Artifice avail
him in the following Citation? " The godly
" Confideration of Predeftination, and our
" Election in Chrift is full of fweet, pleafant
" and unfpeakable Comfort to godly Perfons,
" and fuch as feel in themfelves the Work-
" ing of the Spirit of Chrift, mortifying the
" Works

" Works of the Flesh."‡ How will this Person or any other do to synonymize away the Word Feel here, seeing there is no other. Word to resolve or incorporate it into! And since here is mention of sweet, pleasant and unspeakable Comfort; if this is not to be truly and really felt, it is time to ask what is, or what may be Felt? This therefore is a full Eviction that the Church holds the Doctrine of spiritual Feeling, and if you absolutely deny, that the Comforts of the Holy Spirit are to be felt, you reject the Homilies, Articles and Liturgies of the Church of *England* all at once. I would ask then, are they Members or Ministers of the Church of *England*, who say that the Comforts of the Holy Ghost cannot be felt?

But what saith the Scripture? St. *Paul* writing to the *Romans*, prays, that the God *of Hope* would *fill them with all Joy and Peace in believing*, ch. xv. ver. 13. But could they be thus filled, and not *feel* it? And because these divine Consolations are Earnests of future Glory, and so increase the Believer's Hope, the Apostle adds, *that ye may abound in Hope thro' the Power of the Holy Ghost . An abundance of Hope* accompanies and follows these gracious Manifestations. It is further observable, the Apostle here mentions *Joy* and *Peace* as distinct Things; for oftentimes Persons have great Measures of *Joy*, who yet have no solid *Peace* when those Joys are gone off; and on the other hand, many truly Christian Souls walk in a constant abiding *Peace*, who yet are not transported with Raptures and Extasies.

P   The

---

‡ *Art.* 17.

The same inspired Writer reckons *Joy* and *Peace* among the Fruits of the Spirit, Gal. v. 22. and in Phil. iv. 7. he mentions a *Peace of God which paſſeth all Underſtanding*. He reminds the *Theſſalonians*, that *they receive the Word in much Affliction, with Joy of the Holy Ghoſt*; 1 Theſſ. i. 6. Although they had much outward *Affliction* and Perſecution, yet they had much inward Joy from the Holy Spirit; and they Felt their Joy as truly and really as they did their Affliction. When our Hearts are full of Sorrow and Vexation, do we not really feel it? Have we not as deep a Senſe and Perception thereof, as of any bodily Pain whatſoever? Will it not therefore follow, by the Rule of Contraries, if our Souls are full of ſpiritual Joy and Comfort, that we muſt feel that alſo? Is not one of theſe as reaſonable as the other? And may you not upon the ſame Principle that you reject one, reject both? But if you allow the one, you muſt allow the other alſo.

Our Saviour ſaith to his Diſciples; *Your Heart ſhall rejoice and your Joy no Man taketh from you*, John xvi. 22. All bodily Goods and external Goods, Men may take from us; but the Joys of the Spirit neither Men nor Devils may deprive us of. Our Lord mentions a *Fulneſs of Joy*, John xv. 11. xvi. 24. xvii. 13. So St. Paul ſpeaks of being filled with *Joy* and *Comfort*, 2 Tim. i. 4. 2 Cor. vii. 4. And it would be endleſs to bring all the Texts that ſpeak of ſpiritual Joy and Solace. You may think perhaps this Fulneſs of Joy was peculiar to the Apoſtles and Primitive Chriſtians: I

would

would have you therefore take notice, the Apoftle fpeaks of Believers as *rejoicing with Joy unfpeakable and full of Glory*, 1 Pet. i. 8. And faith the Evangelift John, Thefe Things write we unto you, that *your Joy may be full*, 1 John i. 4. which may convince us, that this Fulnefs of Joy is the Priviledge of all Chriftians in general. As carnal and fenfual Pleafures and Gratifications are really felt by carnal Men, fo are fpiritual Delights by thofe that are fpiritual; only with this Difference, as the Soul is fuperior to the Body, fo thefe Enjoyments are more exquifite and refined than thofe.

The Pfalmift *David* fpeaks, *I will run the Way of thy Commandments, when thou fhalt enlarge my Heart. Pfal.* cxix. 32. The holy Man was ftraitened and contracted in his own Soul (as the People of God often are:) This hindered him in the Way of his Duty and Obedience to the divine Commandments: Hence he prays for fpiritual *Enlargement*, that he may walk, yea *run*, in the Ways of God with Pleafure and Delight. When Souls are thus *enlarged*, with what Courage and Succefs do they run their Chriftian Race! Their ardent Love to God is a powerful Motive to all holy, humble evangelical Obedience: Their flaming Affection for him carries them through all Difficulties, Dangers and Tribulations, in his Service. The Apoftle *Paul* experienced this *enlargement of Heart*, 2 Cor. vi. 11. *Our Heart is enlarged.* Who can tell what the Apoftle *Felt* in his Soul when he wrote thefe Words? What a heavenly Tranfport was he in! The Love of God was fhed abroad in his Heart,

  and

and this produced in him such a seraphic Love for his Brethren, *Be ye also enlarged*, ver. 13. He was desirous (as all Christians are, for Grace is communicative) that they might be Partakers of this Joy in common with himself. This therefore shews, that the *Corinthians* through Grace might taste this divine *Enlargement* of Soul, and so many Christians in all ages. Let us not then think that this Blessing was confined to the Apostles and first Christians, but seek that we ourselves may be possessed of it. And I admonish all those who laugh at inward *Enlargements*, and ridicule those as Enthusiasts and Schismaticks who make mention of them and experience them, to consider these Texts, lest haply by their Opposition they discover their malice and Ignorance, and shew themselves quite unexperienced in this spiritual Dilation of the Heart.

The Author of the Epistle to the Hebrews saith, *Strong Meat belongeth to them that are of full Age, even those who by Reason of Use have their Senses exercised to discern both Good and Evil*, Heb. v. 14. He makes mention of Senses, for the Senses of the Mind are as real as those of the Body, and spiritual Feeling is as true as corporal. The Apostle prays for the Philippians that their *Love may abound yet more and more in Knowledge, and in all Judgment :* i. e. Sense or Feeling, as the original Word* denotes; and so it is translated in the Margin of the Bible. In Acts xvii. 27. the Apostle exhorts the Athenian Philosophers (who to be sure thought spiritual feeling as arrant Cant and

En-

---

* *Philip.* 1. 9.

Enthufiafm as our modern Chriftian Philofophers do) *to feek the* LORD, *if haply they might
feel after him, and find him.* And Eph. iv. 19.
he fpeaks of thofe who were paft Feeling, to
which miferable Condition thofe heatheniz'd
Chriftians labour to reduce Men, when they
deny all inward Feeling, and tell them they
may have the Spirit of God, and not Feel
it. But till they can erafe thefe Texts out of
the Bible they will never be able to prove
their point. While thefe exprefs Teftimonies
of Scripture remain on our Side, we fhall have
all the Reafon imaginable to affirm, that the
Influences of the Holy Spirit are to be felt.

I might further appeal to Experience: when
you are full of Pride, Envy, Malice, or Hatred,
do you not Feel it? When you are prone to
Covetoufnefs, Senfuality, or Worldly-mindednefs, do you not Feel it? And do you really and
fenfibly Feel thefe corruptions, when they arife
in your heart? Now then fuppofe you are
full of Love, Joy, Peace, Long-fuffering,
Gentlenefs, Goodnefs, Faith, Meeknefs, and
Temperance; what think you? Do you not
think you fhall feel thefe Fruits of the Spirit?
Or, do you think you may have them in you
without Feeling them? May the Corruptions of
a brutal, and the malevolent Affections of a
diabolical Nature be Felt? And may not the
Graces of the Spirit, and the benign Influences of the Holy Ghoft be felt by thofe Souls
who are fo happy as to be poffefs'd of them?
Can the Devil work fo powerfully as to be felt
in the hearts of his Children? And cannot the

Operations of the Eternal Spirit be felt in the hearts of the Faithful? If therefore you allow the Poſſibility of Feeling the Devil's Operations on the one hand, why ſhould you deny the Poſſibility of Feeling the Holy Spirit's Operations on the other? But the caſe generally is, Men ſpeak evil of the Things they know not; and revile and condemn what they never experienced. If Perſons really enjoy'd theſe divine Communications, they would no longer doubt whether they are to be felt or not: The Poſſeſſion of theſe ſpiritual Pleaſures would convince us of their Truth and Reality, and ſilence all our Cavils and Scruples concerning them. Now therefore what remains but to exhort all Profeſſors of Chriſtianity to follow after theſe ſenſible Influences and Communications of the Holy Ghoſt?

Let who will deny the Doctrine of inwardly feeling the Holy Spirit, the Church People cannot confiſtently with their own prinples. This I have clearly demonſtrated. And their own Articles, Homilies and Liturgies, lay them under the ſtrongeſt Obligations to aſſert and maintain this Doctrine. Neither would I have Perſons eſpouſe and vindicate it only as a ſcientifick Truth, but ſeek to enjoy the experience of it in their hearts. What ſignifies all our Religion, unleſs it makes us happy? Some People have juſt Religion enough to make them miſerable; they miſtake the ſhadow for the ſubſtance, and reſt in the letter without the Spirit: yet 'tis not Religion, but the want of it, that makes men miſerable. True Religion and

true

true Happiness are inseparable; and so far as we possess the one we shall enjoy the other. Some nominal Christians talk of the Doctrines of the Gospel, the Graces of God's Spirit, and the Privileges of God's Children, and yet feel none of these Things in their hearts; and therefore all their Religion is but lifeless Profession and vain Imagination. Unconverted Moralists and formal Christians may please themselves with Modes of Worship, and ceremonial and legal Performances; but a soul that is truly awakened can never rest satisfied without tasting the comforts of Religion, and enjoying the Pleasures of Christianity. The Happiness of Religion, consists in feeling the comforts of the Spirit of God. Seek therefore after God, and never think yourselves happy till you find him in your hearts and feel his comfortable Presence.

Some People are filled with a great deal of Joy and Mirth, and experience sudden Flashes of Comfort, which they take to be from the Spirit of God; but how frequently do they deceive themselves herein? These warm Emotions of the Mind often proceed from the State and Disposition of the Body; they spring from the Motion and temperature of the Blood and Animal œconomy. How often do we see vigorous, healthy Christians transported with false Joy? It is common for young converts to mistake natural Zeal and Affection for the Influxes of the Divine Spirit : They are very apt to ascribe that to the Operation of the Holy Ghost, which is owing to the Mechanism of the Body. This I just mention by Way of

P. 4

caution

Caution. I would not difcourage the weakeft Believer. I know fome Chriftians are very fcrupulous in this cafe; they are afraid to take comfort when God gives it them; and are too ready to attribute that to the Temperament of their Bodies, which really comes from God, and is owing to the Influences of his Holy Spirit. I would not offend one of the leaft of thefe: Let fuch weak Souls know, that they who are moft cautious are in leaft Danger. 'Tis in this Cafe as in Regard to the Sin againft the Holy Ghoft, they who are in moft Fear and Concern about it are generally fartheft from committing it. Their Vigilance is through Grace their Prefervative: So here, Perfons Scrupuloufnefs is frequently a Means of keeping them from being deceived. The Hafty, the Carelefs, and the Unguarded, are in moft danger of being carried away with falfe Joys and imaginary Tranfports. But then the weak Chriftian is often afking, "How fhall I know whether "my Comforts come from God or not?" I anfwer; were thefe Comforts derived to your Soul by Prayer, by the Word of God, by receiving the Sacrament, or any other appointed Means? If they were, you have Reafon to think they came from God. Again, do you find that thefe Comforts and fpiritual fenfations carry you not to Softnefs, Indolence, or Lukewarmnefs; not to Pride, Senfuality, or Contempt of the Weak; but to Humility, to the Love of Jefus, and to the tendereft Sympathy and Compaffion for his weakeft Difciples? If

the

the inward Confolations you enjoy promote thefe Ends, doubt not, but be affured they came from God, and are the Effects of his Spirit, and Evidences of his Love to you. Laftly, Soul, have you had fome inward Comfort? And do you doubt whether it was from God or not? Do you think you caufed it yourfelf? Well, try if you can make yourfelf fo again; fee if thofe Comforts are at your Command, and if you can have them again juft when you pleafe: If you could make yourfelf fo comfortable once, why cannot you make yourfelf fo again? If you cannot, this plainly fhews thefe inward fenfations of Comfort were not from yourfelf, and therefore you may be fatisfied God was the author and giver of them. This I fpeak for the Benefit of thofe feeble Chriftians who are in their Minority. Thofe who are more acquainted with God, and walk in clofer communion with God, know the Confolations of his Spirit, by the Light, Power, and Evidence they bring along with them. The pleafures of God's Spirit are infinitely fuperior to all other Pleafures; and they who have tafted them once, know them again. Perfons that never tafted them have no Knowledge of their incomparable fweetnefs and tranfcendency. As the fweetnefs of Honey is known by tafting it, fo the Delights of the Spirit are known by enjoying them. " What an Heaven do I Feel in myfelf, when " (after many Traverfes of Meditation) I find " in my heart a feeling poffeffion of my God!"

faith

faith *Bishop Hall**. Yet do not depend upon these inward feelings, but upon the Merits of Christ for Salvation. If you trust to these inward feelings for Salvation, then you will have hope so long as these continue; but when they are gone, your hope will wither, and your Faith fail. Our hope of Heaven is all founded not upon any thing in ourselves, but only upon the meritorious Death, and All-sufficient Righteousness of the Lord Jesus Christ. When you are under the sensible Manifestations of the Divine Favour, rejoice and give God Glory: But know this, that when the Light of his Countenance is hid, his Love is the same: His Love is eternal and immutable. His Saints will soon get to Heaven, and then they will see his Face without a Cloud, and enjoy his beatifick Presence without Interuption, and without End.

---

* *Dec.* ii. *Ep.* 1.

End of the First Part.

The MARROW of the CHURCH.

PART II.

Of CHRIST's Righteousness IMPUTED.

CHAP. I.

I-ENTER upon this head with much the more Freedom and Pleasure, becaufe it is One Main Branch of the Grand Doctrine of Juftification, which is a Doctrine as Wholefome as it is True, and as Comfortable as it is Neceffary; and this Article with me is never irkfome or unfeafonable; but it is a Subject I could dwell upon for ever.

Righteoufnefs is a perfect Conformity to the Righteous Law of God: a Perfon is Righteous when all the Thoughts and Inclinations of his heart, and all the Words and Actions of his Life are every Way agreeable to the Divine Will and Commandment. A righteous Man's Will coincides with the Will of God, his Underftanding is filled with the Knowledge of the Lord, and all his Faculties are exerted in obeying his God: all his Affections centre in God; God is the Object of his Delight and Happinefs, and in his heart there is no deviation from

God;

God; no, not one. In this State of Perfection and Righteousnes was *Adam* at his First Creation: he was created in Knowledge, Righteousnes, and true Holines.* He was a perfect Pattern of his Maker, and a Living Image of that God who formed him: his Nature answered to the Divine Nature just as the Impression upon Wax answers to the Seal that made it. Thus holy and righteous was Man in his First Estate; and he continued to be possessed of this Righteousnes as long as he was Obedient to his Creator; but as soon as ever he disobeyed the Divine Command, he lost All his holines and righteousnes at once; he emptied himself of every spark of Goodnes, and was full of all Manner of Wickednes; he forfeited all his Primitive Purity, and became a sinful, impure, and unrighteous Creature. Hence it is that all Mankind are destitute of Original Righteousnes, and there is none of the Children of Men Righteous, *no, not one: There is none that doeth Good, no, not one.* Rom. iii. 10, 12. How then shall Man be Righteous before God? Or by what Means shall he recover that Righteousnes which he hath lost? This indeed is a Question which Natural Reason could never answer; and although Men have tried various Ways to obtain a perfect Righteousnes, yet All their Labours have proved Abortive, and their Attempts succesles; and none of those who followed after Righteousnes

---

* Col. iii. 10. Eph. iv. 24.

obtained

obtained it, excepting thofe only who followed after the Righteoufnefs that is of Faith. Rom. ix. 30, 31, 32.   The Gentile Philofophers fought after Righteoufnefs by following the Dictates of Natural Reafon, and obferving the common Rules of Morality.   The Jewifh Pha-rifees expected to attain a Juftifying Righteouf-nefs by practifing the moral Commands and ceremonial Inftitutions of the Mofaic Law. Formal Chriftians think to gain Righteoufnefs by obeying the Morals of the Gofpel, as they ufually exprefs themfelves.   But neither Jewifh nor Pagan Morality will juftify us before God. All Self-Jufticiaries, whether Heathens, Jews, or Chriftians, ftand upon the fame Foundation, viz. their own Righteoufnefs, which is a fandy Foundation, upon which whofoever builds his hope of Salvation, his Building will certainly fall, and Great will be the Fall of it.   All felf-Righteoufnefs, by whatfoever Name it is call-ed, whether you ftile it Natural Religion, or Chriftianity, is equally Defpicable in the Sight of God, and equally Unavailable to our Jufti-fication.   The only Righteoufnefs that will re-commend us to God, and gain us Accefs into the Kingdom of Heaven, is the Righteoufnefs of Chrift Imputed to us by God, and ap-prehended by Faith.   We have no Righteouf-nefs of our own, but the Righteoufnefs of Chrift it is wherewith we are invefted, and wherein we appear Righteous before the Moft High GOD.   This Righteoufnefs is not of Nature, but of Grace; and therefore it is not faid to be Innate, but Imputed; becaufe our

hea-

heavenly Father moft freely and gracioufly imputes or accounts it ours to all Intents and
Purpofes of Juftification and Salvation.

The Word Impute is ufed no lefs than in
Ten different Places * in the Fourth Chapter
of the Epiftle to the Romans; and it properly
fignifies to efteem a Perfon who hath not done
a Thing as though he had done it; thus the
Apoftle Paul defires Philemon, if Onefimus
had wronged him, or owed him any Thing, to
place it to his Account ‡, or efteem the Injury or
Debt his, though he had never contracted it.
On the contrary, *not to impute*, is to efteem him
who hath done a Thing as though he had not
done it: Thus the Apoftle prays that the Sin
of thofe who forfook him *may not be laid to
their Charge* † though they had committed it.
And this Interpretation of the Word very well
fuits our prefent Purpofe, and clearly illuftrates
the Cafe before us; for our Sins which we have
actually committed are *not imputed* to us. We
who have done Evil are looked upon by God
in Chrift as if we had not done it, becaufe
God doth *not impute our Trefpaffes unto us*, Rom.
iv. 8. 2 Cor. v. 19. On the other Hand, that
Righteoufnefs, which not We, but Chrift himfelf performed, is neverthelefs *imputed* unto us,
as if We Ourfelves had performed it; Rom.
iv. 24. 2 Cor. v. 21. Accordingly, our Jufti-

---

* Ver. 3, 4, 5, 6, 8, 9, 10, 22, 23, 24.
‡ Philem. Verfe 18.
† 2 Tim. iv. 16.

fication

fication confifts (as I have before fhewed *) both in the *Non-Imputation* of our Sins to us, and alfo in the *Imputation* of Chrift's Righteoufnefs to us.

We are juftified both by the Active and Paffive Obedience of Jefus Chrift. A Soul that hath True, Living, Juftifying Faith, looks both to the Blood, and alfo to the Righteoufnefs of Chrift. She beholds the Sufferings of Chrift's Death, and the Obedience of his Life, and fo receives the Remiffion of Sins, and Free Juftification.

There are Many who feem to allow the Atonement and Satisfaction Chrift made by his Death, who yet deny the Imputation of his Active Righteoufnefs unto us ; and yet one of thefe is as clearly contain'd in Scripture as the other, and they both are declared in the Homiles, Articles and Liturgies of the Church of *England.*

The Homily of the Salvation of Mankind avers, that Chrift paid " the Price of our " Redemption by the Offering of his Body and " Shedding of his Blood, with *fulfilling of the* " *Law perfectly* and throughly." Not only the Oblation of Chrift's Body and Blood, but alfo his fulfilling of the Law for us, is Requifite to our Eternal Salvation. There is no Salvation without *fulfilling the Law perfectly* ; we do not *fulfill the Law perfectly* ourfelves, but Chrift hath fulfilled it for us, and therefore

we

---

* See the Firft Part of my Medulla, Chap. II.

we are faved. We are look'd upon as *fulfillers of the Law*, becaufe Chrift hath fulfilled it for us. The Infinite Juftice of God requires not only a full Satisfaction for all our Breaches of the Law, but alfo a Perfect Obedience to the Law; wherefore it is foon after added, " the Juftice of God confifteth in paying our " Ranfom and *fulfilling of the Law:*" Chrift did both thefe, and fo fatisfied the Divine Juftice, and procur'd the favour of God for us.

This Wholefome Doctrine is elfewhere in the fame Homily delivered to us in thefe Words, " He (God) provided a Ranfom for us, that " was the moft Precious Body and Blood of " his own moft Dear and Beloved Son, Je- " fus Chrift; who befides this Ranfom *ful- " filled the Law for us perfectly.*" If Chrift had been only Man (as the *Socinians* affert) then his Obedience to the Divine Law would had been his Bounden Duty, and fo would have profited none but Himfelf : But fince he was God as well as Man, this added an Infinite Merit to his Active Obedience, and rendered it infinitely Available for the Reconciliation and Salvation of all who put their Truft in Him. The *Socinians* deny the Divinity of Chrift, and fo (confiftently enough with themfelves, how Inconfiftent foever with the Gofpel) deny the Imputation of his Legal Righteoufnefs unto us; and all they who hold this Latter Opinion of theirs, do unwarily fall into the Former.

The Homily on Chrift's Nativity informs us, that " the End of his Coming was to fave " and deliver his People, *to fulfil the Law for*

" *us*, &c. We have broke the whole Law, Christ hath *fulfilled* it; we have omitted all Righteousness, and committed all Unrighteousness; Christ hath *fulfilled all Righteousness*, Matth. iii. 15. and He fulfilled it for us and in our Stead, and this was the End and Intent of his Coming into the World. " So that (as the First Part of the Homily of Salvation concludes) " Christ is now become the Right-
" eousness of all them that do truly believe in
" Him *He for them paid their Ransom by his*
" *Death. He for them fulfilled the Law in his*
" *Life.*" What Words can be plainer? And I would also ask, in what Sense, or with what propriety of Speech could Christ be said to have *fulfilled the Law for us in his Life*, unless his Perfect Obedience or Conformity to the Divine Law was imputed to us? It is therefore admirably well said by our Excellent Church in her Eleventh Article " We are *accounted righ-*
" *teous* before God, only for the Merit of our
" Lord and Saviour Jesus Christ *by Faith.*"
—— Observe, we are *accounted* *, for this Righteousness is not ours by Nature, but we

---

* This exactly agrees with the Apostle's way of speaking, Rom. iv. 3. *Abraham* believed God, and it was *counted* unto him for Righteousness; and Ver. 5. Faith is *counted* for Righteousness; and Ver. 6. God *imputeth* Righteousness without Works; and Ver. 9. Faith was *reckon'd* to *Abraham* for Righteousness; and Ver. 24. to us also shall Christ's Righteousness be *imputed*, if we believe.——So that you see how our Church and the Scriptures coincide; and you cannot but observe at the same Time how grossly mistaken they are who pretend to say that there is no mention of *Imputed* Righteousness in Scripture.

Q_

have

have it of the Free Grace of God in Christ. This Righteousness is ours, not by Infusion, nor by Inhesion, but by Imputation. God does not account us righteous in ourselves, or, "for "our own Works or Deservings," as it follows afterwards, but "for the Merit of our Lord and Saviour Jesus Christ, by Faith." We have no Righteousness of our own, but the Righteousness of Christ is imputed to us, and God accounts us righteous in Him. We know of no Righteousness but the Righteousness of Faith. We trust in no other Righteousness for Salvation, but the Righteousness of the Mediator, which is imputed to us by God, and apprehended by Faith. The Judgment of God is according to Truth: God therefore does not account us Righteous in ourselves, (for this would not be True) but he accounts us Righteous in the Righteousness of our Lord and Saviour Jesus Christ, as faith the Scripture, *we are made the Righteousness of* God *in Him,* 2 Cor. v. 21.

Further, here is an Objection obviated, for whereas some are ready to ask, if we have Remission of Sins by the Death and sufferings of Christ, what need have we of the Imputation of his Active Obedience unto us? Or otherwise, if we are justified by his Active Obedience, what occasion have we for his Passive? Our judicious Reformers here teach us that Christ's Active and Passive Obedience both go together, and ought never to be separated. If you separate these, one from the other, you run yourself into endless Error

and

and Confusion; always therefore remember to take them both together, and never attempt to put asunder what God hath joined together. And may the Son of God write these two Evangelical Truths in all our Hearts, " *He* " *for us paid our Ransom by his Death: He* " *for us fulfilled the Law in his Life:* So " that now in Him, and by Him, every True " Christian Man may be called a Fulfiller of the " Law, forasmuch as that which their Infirmi- " ty lacked, Chrift's Justice hath supplied."

I think I should not do well in passing over a particular Passage in our Common Prayer, which by many is little taken notice of, tho' it clearly contains this Doctrine: You will find it in the Communion Service; the Words are these, " We do *not* presume to come to this " thy Table *trusting in our own Righteousness,* " but in thy manifold and great Mercies,"— Now, if we do *not trust in our own Righteous-ness,* we must trust in Chrift's; for there is no Medium; and you will not (I suppose) venture to affirm we may come before God without any Righteousness at all; yet we have no Righteousness of our own wherein to appear before the Moft High; where then should we have Righteousness, but in Chrift? This we possess by Faith, and so (as the Apoftle speaks) *we have* great *Boldness and free Access* to God *with Confidence by the Faith of Him.* Some think to compromise the Matter by joining our own Righteousness and Chrift's together; and so the Prayer of the *Papist* juft answers their purpose: " Lord Jefu, join, I pray Thee, *my*

Q 2   " Righ-

" Righteousness with all that Thou haft done
" and suffer'd out of thy great Love and Obe-
" dience." Now, should you like to make
use of such a Prayer as this? And yet it exactly suits your Case, if you join your own
Righteousness with Christ's in the Affair of
Salvation. Remember therefore, as often as
you receive the Lord's Supper in the Eftab-
lish'd Church, you renounce your own Righteousness, and truft in Christ's; otherwise,
you are an Hypocrite, an unworthy Commu-
nicant, a Mocker of God; and you *eat and
drink Judgment* to yourself.*

The Scriptures are full of this Doctrine; *for
therein is the Righteousness of GOD revealed
from Faith to Faith*, Rom. i. 17. It shines
both in the Old Teftament, and in the New.
We shall at prefent confine ourselves chiefly to
the latter. And no where in Scripture is the
Imputation of Christ's Righteousness more
clearly fet before us than in *Rom.* iii. 21, 22.
*But now the Righteousness of God without the
Law is manifefted, being witneffed by the Law
and the Prophets; even the Righteousness of
God, which is by Faith of* Jesus Christ *unto
all, and upon all them that believe* — Obferve
here firft, the Righteousness of Christ is
twice called the *Righteousness of* God, and that
for thefe two Reasons; firft, becaufe it is

God's

God's ftated Method of juftifying finners by imputing it to them: All who are juftified are juftified by Chrift's Righteoufnefs. This is the only Way of Juftification and Salvation; and without this Righteoufnefs no Soul ever was, no Soul ever will be juftified before God. Secondly, Chrift is God, John i. 1. GOD *over All bleffed for ever*, Rom. ix. 5. and therefore his Righteoufnefs is truly and properly the Righteoufnefs of God, fo called by way of Eminence, and in Contra-diftinction from, and in Oppofition to all Creature-righteoufnefs whatfoever. And this I take to be the Principal Reafon why Saint Paul fo much delights to call Chrift's Righteoufnefs the Righteoufnefs of God.* Secondly, this Righteoufnefs is faid to be without the Law, *the Righteoufnefs of God without the Law is manifefted*—We muft never attempt to mix our own Legal Righteoufnefs and Chrift's Righteoufnefs together, for this is in Effect mingling Light and Darknefs. We muft therefore always keep thefe feperate, as the Greek Word juftly informs us. And indeed the Righteoufnefs of Chrift is fo Perfect and Complete in itfelf, that it ftandeth in no Need of the Addition of our Legal Obedience to it, either before, at, or after our Juftification. *Thirdly*, this Righteoufnefs is *witneffed by the Law and the Prophets.*—Thus faith *Mofes*, he (Abraham) *believed in the* LORD; *and he counted it to him for Righteoufnefs*, Gen. xv. 6. And

---

* See Rom. i. 17.----x. 3. Phil. iii. 9.

the

the Prophets bear Ample Teftimony to this Truth; thus Ifaiah, *furely, fhall one fay, In the* LORD *have I righteoufnefs and ftrength,* xlv. 24. —And again, xlvi. 12, 13. *Hearken unto me, ye ftout-hearted, that are far from righteoufnefs, I bring near my righteoufnefs : It fhall not be far off, and my Salvation fhall not tarry*—And liii. 11. *by his Knowledge fhall my righteous fer-vant juftify many*—So alfo Jer. xxiii. 5, 6, I will *raife unto David a righteous branch*—and *this is the name whereby he fhall be called* THE LORD OUR RIGHTEOUSNESS. And Ch. xxxiii. 15, 16, *I will caufe the branch of righteoufnefs to grow up unto* David—*fhe fhall be called, The* LORD *our righteoufnefs.* So alfo the Pfal-mift defcribing a citizen of Chrift's Spiritual Kingdom faith, *he fhall receive the Bleffing from the* LORD, *and righteoufnefs from the* GOD *of his Salvation,* xxiv. 5. And the fame Divine Writer declares that he preached the Doctrine of CHRIST's *righteoufnefs in the Great Congrega-tion,* Pfal. xl. 9, 10. and Ethan the Ezrahite fpeaking of the People of God faith, *In thy Name fhall they rejoice all the Day: And in thy righteoufnefs fhall they be exalted,* Pf. lxxxix. 16. The Prophet *Daniel* bears as Clear a Teft-imony to this Doctrine as any of them; *Se-venty Weeks are determined upon thy People, and up-on thy Holy City, to finifh the Tranfgreffion and to make an End of Sins, and to make reconciliation for Iniquity, and to bring in Everlafting righ-teoufnefs,* Dan. ix. 24. *Fourthly,* This *righ-teoufnefs* is *by the Faith of* JESUS CHRIST *unto All and upon All them that believe:* So that All who

who have Faith have this Righteoufnefs. Wou'd
you know how to obtain a faving Righteoufnefs?
The only Way is to believe in Jefus Chrift.
This Righteoufnefs is freely given to all them
that believe: Therefore only believe, and you
fhall *receive the gift of righteoufnefs*, Rom.
v. 17. God is willing to give you this Righteoufnefs, and if you don't receive it, 'tis becaufe
of your Unbelief. God holds out this Righteoufnefs to you; and if you will not accept it,
it fhews that you are Obftinate and Self-righteous. Nothing hinders you from embracing this
Righteoufnefs, but your own Infidelity. Hath
therefore this been an Obftacle in your Way for
a long Time? Now by the Grace of God break
thro' it, hearken to the Devil and Unbelief no
longer, in the Strength of God burft all the
Bars of Mifery and Iron that lie in your Way,
and take hold on Chrift for Strength and
Righteoufnefs. But why does the Apoftle fay
not only *unto all*, but *upon all* them that believe? To account for this we are to take Notice that this Righteoufnefs is called *Fine Lin-
nen*, Rev. xix. 8, *White Raiment*, Rev. iii.
18, *the Beft Robe*, Luke xv. 22, the *Wedding
Garment*, Matth. xxii. 11. Accordingly the
Apoftle fays to the Romans, *put ye on the* Lord
Jefus Chrift ——— The Greek Word * fignifies
to *put on* as a Garment, and fo is figuratively
applied to the Soul, whofe *Filthy Garments* are

---

* *Rom.* xiii. 14. and *Gal.* iii. 27.

taken

taken away, and who is *clothed with Change of Raiment,* * viz. with the Righteousness of the Lord Jesus. This therefore shews us with what a Beauty and Propriety the Phrase *upon all,* is here used by the inspired Orator.

Rom. iv. 6, *Even as* David *also describeth the Blessedness of the Man to whom* God *imputeth Righteousness without Works.* If by Righteousness we allow our Adversaries here to understand Justification, it will follow that Justification is *without Works,* which is a Doctrine they dislike as much as the Imputation of Christ's Righteousness. But when the Apostle speaks of God's imputing Righteousness, he plainly points at the Active Righteousness of our Saviour, which is made over to us by an Act of Imputation, whereby God justifies Sinners. The formal Cause of our Justification is " the " Gracious Imputation of God the Father, ac- " counting his Son's Righteousness unto the " Sinner, and by that accounting making it his " to all Effects, as if he himself had performed " it." † And observe, this Righteousness is imputed *without Works,* just as in the foregoing Text *without the Law.* This Act of Imputation is an Act of God's Grace, whereby he confers Christ's Righteousness upon us, and places it to our account without any Works of ours to make us Worthy or Meet to receive it. This Righteousness is given to Sinners who

---

* *Zech.* iii. 4. † Archbishop Usher.

have

have done no Good Works, yea, on the contrary, all Manner of Evil Works; thus it was freely beftow'd on *Rabab*, on the *Jailor*, *Acts* xvi. on the Thief on the Crofs, yea, on thofe Vile Wretches who *crucified the Lord of Life and Glory* who wrought out this Righteoufnefs for us, *Acts* ii. 23, 41. iii. 25. iv. 4. If it fhou'd be afked, how can this Interpretation of the Text be accommodated to the Apoftle's Quotation, *Bleffed is the Man to whom the* Lord *will not impute Sin?* The Anfwer is, where the Lord doth not impute Sin, there he imputes Chrift's Righteoufnefs. The Non-Imputation of Sin and the Imputation of Righteoufnefs always go together: *David* very well knew this, and confequently while he defcribes the Bleffednefs of the Man to whom the Lord will *not impute Sin*, he does at the fame Time defcribe the Bleffednefs of the Man to whom God *imputeth* Chrift's *Righteoufnefs*. The *Jews* gloried much in having *Abraham* for their Father, the Apoftle therefore very fuitably fhews them that *Abraham* was juftified by having Chrift's Righteoufnefs imputed to him; and fince *Abraham*, the Father of us all, was accepted of God by Virtue of a Righteoufnefs Imputed, the Apoftle from thence juftly concludes that all the Faithful are reconciled to God in the fame Way and Manner: *Now it was not written for his Sake alone, that it was imputed to him, but for us alfo to whom it fhall be imputed, if we believe on him that rais'd up* Jefus *our* Lord *from the Dead*, Ver. 23, 24.

R   So

So again, Chap. v. Ver. 19, *For as by one Man's Difobedience Many were made Sinners; fo by the Obedience of one fhall Many be made righteous.* The Apoftle here draws a plain Parallel between the Sin of *Adam* and the Righteoufnefs of CHRIST, informing us, that as by the Imputation of *Adam's Difobedience* to us *Many,* i. e. all are *made Sinners,* fo by the Imputation of CHRIST's Active *Obedience* to us *Many,* i. e. all Chriftians are *made righteous.* As we are made or *conftituted Sinners* in *Adam,* fo we are *made righteous* in CHRIST; but we are *conftituted Sinners* in *Adam* by Imputation, therefore we are *made righteous* in CHRIST by Imputation alfo. This is the Plain Meaning of the Words of the Text without any Violence or Diftortion. And this I clearly faw fome years ago. I once oppos'd the Doctrine of the Saviour's Righteoufnefs Imputed, (as we all do while we are in a State of Self-Righteoufnefs) but when this Text was produc'd in Proof of that Salutary Doctrine, it ftruck with fuch Power and Conviction upon my Mind that I knew not how to withftand the Evidence. And I heartily pray God, if any of you who hear me this Day are Ignorant of, or Enemies to this Spiritual Truth, this Text may be a means of opening your Eyes and turning you from Darknefs to Light, and from the Power of Satan unto God. If any fhould here object that the Word here tranflated *Obedience* only fignifies Chrift's Death and Sufferings, i. e. his Paffive Obedience, becaufe it is faid *he became Obedient unto Death,*

and

and *he learned Obedience by the things which he suffer'd,* Phil. ii. 8. Heb. v. 8. It may be fufficient to reply, Firft, that fince the Obedience here fpoken of ftands oppofed to *Adam's* Act of Difobedience, it muft mean CHRIST's Active Obedience. Secondly, what is ftiled in the Greek, and tranflated Righteoufnefs in both Places, properly fignifies Chrift's Active Righteoufnefs. Thirdly, Chrift's Active and Paffive Obedience always go together, and are never to be feparated, as we have before fhew'd.

In the Tenth Chapter of this Epiftle the Apoftle complains of the People of *Ifrael* that *they being Ignorant of* God's *Righteoufnefs, and going about to eftablifh their own Righteoufnefs, have not fubmitted themfelves unto the Righteoufnefs of* God. The Righteoufnefs of our Bleffed Saviour is here twice called *the Righteoufnefs of* God, as in Rom. iii. 21, 22. The Jews were Ignorant of this Righteoufnefs, and fo highly conceited of the Worth and Excellency of their own Righteoufnefs, that their Proud Hearts would not fubmit (for indeed 'tis a great Act of Submiffion wholly to renounce our own Righteoufnefs and wholly to truft in Chrift's Righteoufnefs) *themfelves unto the Righteoufnefs of* God. And fo 'tis in our Day, Pride and Ignorance are the Caufe of Men's not *fubmitting* to the *Righteoufnefs of the* Son *of* God. Self-righteous People are Ignorant of the Infufficiency of their own Righteoufnefs, they are Ignorant of the All-fufficiency of Chrift's Righteoufnefs; they fee not the Sin, Folly and Danger

of

of trusting in themselves that they are righteous, and therefore they seek, they try this Way and the other to establish a Righteousness of their own, and despise and reject the Righteousness of God. This is the way of Self-righteous Unbelievers. But Christ is the End of the Law for Righteousness *to every one that believeth*, Ver. 5. All who believe in Christ, possess a perfect Righteousness in him, and the Righteousness of the Law is at an End. The Jews *followed after righteousness by the Works of the Law*, but then it was in Appearance only, and not in Reality; as it were * i. e. seemingly, and not really: They were not Hearty and Earnest in the Pursuit of it. The Case is just the same with our Modern Legal Justiciaries; they seek Righteousness by their own Good Works, but then it is apparently, not really: If they would once set themselves in Earnest to fulfil every Jot and Tittle of the Law, they would be soon convinc'd they could do Nothing, they would find themselves Miserable, Undone Sinners, and be obliged to fly to Jesus Christ for Refuge, Righteousness, Salvation and Redemption.

The Apostle delivers the same Doctrine in both his Epistles to the *Corinthians*. In his First Epistle, Chap. i. Ver. 30, he saith, *but of him are ye in* Christ Jesus, *who of* God *is made unto us Wisdom, and Righteousness, and*

---

* Rom. ix. 31, 32.

Sancti-

Sanctification, and Redemption. We are Nothing, but Chrift is our All. Chrift is One, Perfect and Undivided Saviour, but he is faid to be made to us all thefe Particulars in Relation to our Neceffities. Chrift is all we want, and whatfoever we ftand in need of we poffefs in Him. Chrift is our Wifdom: *in him are hid All the Treafures of Wifdom and Knowledge,* Col. iii. 3. and *of his Fulnefs all we receive,* John i. 16. Chrift is our Righteoufnefs; becaufe his Righteoufnefs is imputed to us. Chrift is *made unto us of* God *Sanctification* or *Holinefs.* In ourfelves is no Sanctification: All our Sanctification is in Chrift. Chrift is our Sanctification. We have no Holinefs at all in us : All our Holinefs is in Chrift our Head. When we fee ourfelves Unholy and Unfanctified, we look up to Chrift our Sanctification, and we know of no other Holinefs or Sanctification than what we poffefs by Faith in Him, hence *we receive Forgivenefs of Sins, and an Inheritance among all them that are Sanctified by Faith in Him,* Acts xxvi. 18. Laftly, Chrift is our Redemption : *He gave himfelf a Ranfom for All,* 1 Tim. ii. 6. *He hath given himfelf a Sacrifice for us,* Eph. vi. 2. Heb. ix. 26. By the Oblation of his Body and the Effufion of his Blood he hath purchafed *Redemption of the Body,* Rom. viii. 23. and *Eternal Redemption* both of Soul and Body, Heb. ix. 12.

So 2 Cor. v. 21.———*that we might be made the Righteoufnefs of* God *in Him.* Chrift

R 3

was

was made Sin, and we are made Righteousneſs. God *made him who knew no Sin to be Sin for us; that we might be made the Righteouſneſs of* God *in him.* As Chriſt was made Sin or a Sinner (for the Abſtract is here put for the Concrete) by the Imputation of our Sins to Him, ſo we are made Righteouſneſs or Righteous Perſons by the Imputation of his Righteouſneſs to us. And as Chriſt knew no Sin, i. e. perſonally and intrinſically, but yet was a Sinner imputatively; ſo we perſonally and intrinſically know no Righteouſneſs, i. e. have no Righteouſneſs of our own, but yet we are righteous imputatively, and are therefore ſaid to be *made the Righteouſneſs of* God *in him.* This is Clear : And I know no Text of Scripture wherein this Double Imputation of Sin and Righteouſneſs is more clearly exhibited, and oppoſed to each other. Our Sins are imputed to Chriſt, and Chriſt's Righteouſneſs is imputed to us.

Phil. iii. 7, 8, 9, *But what things were Gain to me, thoſe I counted Loſs for* Chriſt; *yea doubtleſs, and I count all things but Loſs for the Excellency of the Knowledge of* Chriſt Jeſus *my* Lord : *for whom I have ſuffer'd the Loſs of all Things, and do count them but Dung that I may win* Chriſt, *and be found in* Him, *not having mine own Righteouſneſs which is of the Law, but that which is thro' the Faith of* Chriſt, *the Righteouſneſs which is of* God *by Faith.* How Earneſt the Apoſtle here is! He, with all his Might, diſclaims his

own

own Righteoufnefs, and the one Sole Defire of his Heart is to be found in Chrift's Meritorious Righteoufnefs. The Apoftle calls his own Righteoufnefs, a *Righteoufnefs which is of the Law*, i. e. an Obedience to the Moral and Ceremonial Law of *Mofes*. Of this the Apoftle gives us a Particular Account, Ver. 5, 6, *Circumcifed the eighth Day, of the Stock of Ifrael, of the Tribe of Benjamin, an Hebrew of the Hebrews; as touching the Law, a Pharifee; concerning Zeal, perfecuting the Church; touching the Righteoufnefs which is of the Law, Blamelefs.* All thefe things the Jews gloried in, and the Apoftle himfelf once efteem'd them Gain; but after he faw the Grace and Righteoufnefs of Chrift, he counted them Drofs, Lofs and Dung, or Offals, fit for Nothing but to be thrown to Dogs; and therefore he threw them away *for the Excellency of the Knowledge of* Chrift Jefus his Lord, *for whom he fuffer'd the Lofs of all things*, not only his Worldly Honours, Interefts and Preferments, but his Self-wifdom, Self-righteoufnefs, Self-holinefs, &c. &c. So altho' you, my Beloved Brethren, have been born within the Pale of the Chriftian Church, and baptiz'd the Eighth Day; altho' concerning Zeal you may have perfecuted all that were not of your own Way of thinking, and have liv'd *concerning the Righteoufnefs of the Law* (according to our Modern Expofitions of it) *Blamelefs*; tho' you have repeated Forms of Prayer without Number, and Fafted twice a Week,

Week, and have had Many Good Thoughts, Good Difpofitions and the utmoft Sincerity; tho' you have been ever fo Careful to abftain from all Sin, and have done as much Righteoufnefs as ever you poffibly could, yet you muft *fuffer the Lofs of all thefe Things*; all this is but a Legal Righteoufnefs, and you muft count it Lofs, you muft abfolutely renounce it as to all Truft and Dependence, or elfe you can never be faved. Obferve further the Apoftle renounces his Righteoufnefs done after Converfion as well as before, he had faid in the Paft Tenfe I counted, Ver. 7. but then in the Eighth Verfe he fays I count, I do count, in the Prefent Tenfe. The Apoftle *Paul* had been a converted Man near thirty Years when he wrote this Epiftle; he had preached the Gofpel from Jerufalem to Illyricum, Rom. xv. 19, he had *labour'd more abundantly than they all*, 1 Cor. xv. 10. he had fuffer'd more than the Reft, 2 Cor. xi. 21, *ad Finem*, he had enjoy'd Vifions and Revelations, xii. 1, 2, &c. Yet all this he tramples under foot, he counts it but Lofs and Dung in comparifon of Chrift's Righteoufnefs. And thus you muft ferve all your own Righteoufnefs. Your Legal Righteoufnefs both before and after Juftification fignifies Nothing; it has no Caufal Influence into your Salvation. Never therefore mention your own Righteoufnefs; make mention of Chrift's Righteoufnefs, and his only. Chrift hath done All, Chrift

hath

hath fuffer'd All. Talk not what you fuffer, but of what Chrift hath fuffer'd for you. Never think of what you do, but rejoice in what Chrift hath done for you. Laftly, St. Paul calls it the *righteous which is through the Faith of Chrift, the righteonfnefs which is of God by Faith.* What a ftrefs the Apoftle here lays upon Faith! Faith in Chrift is All in All in the Chriftian Religion; and if you have no Faith you have no Religion. What do you want? Have Faith in Chrift, and you poffefs it. Do you want Wifdom? Have Faith in Chrift. Do you want Righteouf-nefs? Have Faith in Chrift. Do you want Holinefs? Have Faith in Chrift. Do you want Redemption? Have Faith in Chrift. By Faith we are juftified, by Faith we are fanc-tified, by Faith we are faved, Rom. v. 1. Acts xxvi. 18. Eph. ii. 8. All our Religion confifts in believing in Chrift. This is a Myftery to Carnal People: They cannot receive it; they fcoff at it, and ridicule us for this *Foolifhnefs of Preaching,* 1 Cor. i. 21. They cry out, " you " preach up an Implicit Faith; you make Faith " in Chrift the Whole of Chriftianity——'tis " but Believing in Chrift, and All is well." Now fee how thefe Modern Defpifers and Ri-diculers agree with the Old Heathen Perfecu-tors; for thus Origen tells us the Heathens ridicul'd the Primitive Chriftians, faying " Don't ftand examining, only believe, your " Faith will fave you.*" This is the Language of our Prefent Adverfaries; they laugh at the

Word

Word Faith, and ridicule believing as a Cant Term. Especially the Imputation of Christ's Righteousness is a Doctrine which Nature cannot bear, although 'tis as True as the Scriptures of God.

And as this Doctrine is founded upon Many Direct Texts of Scripture, so it is confirmed and illustrated by a Variety of Scriptural Arguments, which are these that follow.

First, Christ and his Church are One: Believers are one with Christ and Christ with them, as our Church expresses it. * There is a Real, Vital, Spiritual Union between the Lord Jesus and All the Faithful. Accordingly our Lord prays that *they All may be One, as Thou Father art in me, and I in Thee; that they also may be One in us*, John xvii. 21. What an Intimate and Mysterious Union is here intended! Our Lord compares it to the Union there is between the Father and Himself. This Union is sometimes represented to us by the Union of the *Members with the Body* or *the Body with the Head*, 1 Cor. xii. 12, 13. Eph. iv. 15, 16. Col. ii. 19. Sometimes it is compared to the Union of the Vine and Branches, John xv. 5. And sometimes it is resembled to the Conjugal Union of Husband and Wife, Eph. v. 23, 29. *&c.* For as the Head and Members make One compleat Body, or as the Vine and Branches make One Natural Tree, or as

---

* Communion Service.

the

the Husband and Wife constitute One Legal Person, so Christ and his Disciples are One. And a very Deep, Close and Mystical Union it must be which the Scripture represents to us under so many Figures and Similitudes; all which are used by the Holy Ghost to adapt it to our Finite Capacities. By Virtue of this our Ineffable Union and Conjunction with Christ, Christ and we are One Body. Hence when we believe in Christ we partake of his Righteousness which is by God imputed to us for our Justification. For Faith is (as One of our Divines* calls it) " the Bond of " Union between us and Christ, and by that " Means makes Way for the Imputation of " Christ's Righteousness to us."

Secondly, Christ was our Representative; he personated us all, and represented us before God, and upon this Account his Righteousness is imputed to us. One Reason why *Adam*'s Sin is imputed to all Mankind, is because *Adam* represented all his Natural Posterity, and therefore they all are look'd upon by God as having committed the Offence which he committed. So Christ being the Representative of all Christians, his Righteousness is imputed to us and placed to our Account as much as if we had perform'd it, *Rom.* v. 19, Christ and we made an Exchange; we exchang'd our Sins for his Righteousness. Christ stood in

* Bishop REYNOLDS.

the Sinner's Place; He took upon Him our Sins, and He puts upon us his Righteoufnefs. We are Sinners, but Chrift is our Saviour: We are dead, but Chrift is our Life: We are Nothing, but Chrift is our all: We are Empty, but Chrift is our Fulnefs; and of his *Fulnefs have all we received, and Grace for Grace*, Joh. i. 16. " Every Grace in Chrift
" is reckoned ours, and eftecm'd as fuch.
" For the Prepofition which is here tranflated
" *for*, is a Word of Imputation and of Com-
" mutation. It is ufed in the Sacred Wri-
" tings, and in other Good Authors, when
" one is reckoned in the Place of another,
" and one thing is fubftituted and changed
" for another. *Give unto them the Tribute-*
" *Money for me and thee*, Matth. xvii. 27, that
" is, in thine and my ftead. *For one Morfel*
" *of Meat he fold his Birthright*, Heb. xii. 16,
" that is, he chang'd his Birthright for it.
" From which Acceptation of the Word we
" learn how to underftand and apply it in the
" Text before us. When 'tis faid, that of
" Chrift's Fulnefs we receive even *Grace for*
" *Grace*, the Genuine Senfe is, that every
" Grace in Chrift is made over to us, and is
" reckon'd as ours. There is a change made
" between him and all True Believers. As
" he takes upon him their Sins, fo his Righ-
" teoufnefs is imputed to them. This is fitly
" exprefs'd by the Prepofition *for*; and to
" *receive Grace for Grace* is as if it had been
" faid, all that Grace and Righteoufnefs which
" is in Chrift Jefus our Lord is tranferr'd to
" us

" us by God and accounted as our own, when
" he juftifies us.*"

Thirdly, Chrift is our Fœderal Head, or
Head in Covenant. God covenanted with the
Firft *Adam* for himfelf and all his Race, fo
that they all were to ftand or fall in him. If
he had fulfilled the Conditions of the Covenant,
all his Children would have enjoy'd the Benefit of it. But he finned againft God, broke
the Conditions of the Covenant, ruin'd himfelf,
and entailed a Curfe and Condemnation upon
himfelf and all his Pofterity. They all finned
in him and fell with him in his firft Tranfgreffion. The Covenant of Works being broke,
a Way is opened for a Declaration of a Covenant of Grace. Now Chrift is our Covenant-Head; He enter'd into Covenant with
God for us; He fhed his Blood for us, which
is therefore called *the Blood of the Everlafting
Covenant*, Heb. xiii. 20. The Lord Jefus
perfectly fulfill'd all the Conditions of this Covenant; He made Full Satisfaction for our Sins,
and perform'd a Perfect Righteoufnefs for us.
He yielded an Unfinning Obedience to the Divine Law. This he did in our Stead; and
we ftand in Him as our Covenant-Head; and
being confider'd in this Relation to him we are
look'd upon by God as if we had fulfilled all
the Articles of the Covenant. His Obedience
is reputed ours, aud we are efteem'd Righteous

---

* See Dr. *Edwards* on Faith and Juftification.

and

and Obedient for his Sake. Compare *Gen.* ii. 16, 17, *Hoſ.* vi. 7. *Rom.* v. 14. 1 *Cor.* xv. 22, 45, 47, 48.

Fourthly, Jeſus was our Surety. *By ſo much was* Jeſus *a Surety of a better Teſtament or Covenant,* Heb. vii. 22. What a Surety does is reckoned to the Account of him in whoſe Stead he acts. If a Man becomes Surety for a Debt, he is as much obliged to pay it, (if the Perſon whoſe Surety he is proves Inſolvent) as if he had contracted it himſelf. And if a Surety pays a Debt, 'tis look'd upon by the Creditor as if the Original Debtor had paid it himſelf, and hereupon he diſcharges him. This juſt illuſtrates the Caſe. Sins are Debts, and Sinners are Debtors : God is the Creditor. We all are Sinners, and have contracted a Debt, the Leaſt Mite of which we are Unable to pay. Chriſt voluntarily became our Surety, and took upon him the whole Debt, and paid it all off by the Oblation of his Death and the Righteouſneſs of his Life. This is intimated to us by the Word which the Apoſtle ſo often uſes, *Rom.* iv. This Word is taken from the Accompts that ſtand between a Creditor and his Debtors. And ſince Chriſt was our Surety, God our Creditor places to our Account the Sufferings and Obedience of Chriſt, he makes them over to us and imputes them to us as much as if we had done and ſuffer'd what Chriſt did and ſuffer'd, and ſo we are diſcharg'd. When therefore the Devil, *the Accuſer of the Brethren,* ſpreads a long Bill or

Cata-

Catalogue of our Sins before us, we only look*
to Jesus our Surety, and we see the whole
Debt paid and the Bond cancell'd.

Fifthly, We have no Righteousness of our
own to justify us, we must therefore be justified by Christ's Righteousness, or not at all.
*In Many Things we offend all, and whosoever
shall keep the whole Law, and yet offend in one
Point, he is guilty of all*, Jam. ii. 10. iii. 2.
Who is there then among us can plead, Not
Guilty? What then is All our Righteousness
worth? It is no better than Filthy Rags, Isa.
lxiv. 6. It cannot stand the Test of God's
Justice, it will not bear examining, it falls infinitely short of the Demands of the Divine
Law, and can never justify us before God. All
our Good Works are defiled with Sin, and
Odious in the Sight of God. Jerusalem who
trusteth in her own Righteousness *is as a Men-
struous Woman*, Lam. i. 17. But those who
are Citizens of Jerusalem which is above cast
away their own Righteousness as a Menstruous
Cloth, Isa. xxx. 22. They take hold of the
Covenant, they take hold of Christ for
Strength and Peace, Isaiah xxvii. 5. lvi, 4.
For our own Righteousness affords us neither
Strength nor Peace. We must utterly despair
of Salvation if we had no better Righteousness
than

---

* Saving Faith is express'd by looking. If. xvii. 7. xlv. 22.
Heb. xii. 2, &c. As Moses lifted up the Serpent in the Wilderness, so was the Son of Man lifted up Job. iii. 14. As the
Jews were cur'd of the Bite of the Fiery Serpents by looking up
to the Brazen Serpent, Numb. xxi. 7, 8, 9. so are the Souls cur'd
of Sin and the Bite of that Old Serpent the Devil by looking to
Jesus Christ by Faith.

than our own to truſt in. Therefore the Ne-ceſſity we have of Chriſt's Righteouſneſs, and the Extremity we are in without it, may ſerve to convince us of the Goodneſs of God in ſo ſeaſonably providing it for us. And this Righteouſneſs every way ſuits our purpoſe, it fully anſwers all our Neceſſities, ſtands Com-menſurate with the Divine Commands, ſatisfies the Divine Juſtice, and is in every Reſpect Sufficient to purchaſe the Remiſſion of our Sins and merit our Juſtification before God. There-fore we believe in Chriſt, we rely upon his Righteouſneſs, (for Faith is expreſs'd by relying 2 Chron. xiii. 18. xvi. 8.) and ſo are juſt and Righteous in the Eyes of our LORD and Maker.

Some object that our Bleſſed Lord in his Sermon on the Mount preaches up Moral Du-ties, and makes no mention at all of Imputed Righteouſneſs, or of Juſtification by the Obe-dience of another, which to be ſure (ſay the Objectors) he would have done, if that had been an Article of ſo great Importance, and ſo very Neceſſary to Salvation. This Objection does Nothing more than ſhew the Ignorance of thoſe who make uſe of it. For whoſoever reads the fifth of St. *Matthew* with a Diſcerning Eye, will there find that our Saviour aſſerts the Doctrine of Imputed Righteouſneſs Two Ways: Firſt, implicitly, by giving the Moral Law its Full Scope and Tenour, and exhibiting it in its Largeſt Extent and Utmoſt Spirituality. Ac-cordingly he ſaith, *Bleſſed are the poor in Spi-rit, the Mourners, the Meek, the Merciful,*

the

the Pure in Heart, &c. &c. This implies that thofe who have not thofe Graces are accurfed; and who is there of us that hath them in us by Nature? Therefore we all naturally fall under the Curfe. Again, in Ver. 28. our Lord faith, *whofoever looketh on a Woman to luft after her, hath committed Adultery with her already in his Heart.* Is a Luft or Defire of the Heart Adultery? Who then is Innocent? Let him go free. If what our Lord here faith be True, (as it moft certainly is) will not this condemn every Man Living for an Adulterer, and every Woman Living for an Adulterefs? Obferve further, *whofoever fhall fay to his Brother, thou Fool, fhall be in Danger of Hell-fire,* Ver. 22: And the Difciple whom Jefus lov'd learns his Mafter's Language, and fays, *whofoever hateth his Brother is a Murderer,* 1 John iii. 15. Is Hatred of our Brother Murder? Does Calling our Brother Fool endanger us to Hell-fire? Who then can expect to efcape? Therefore to fum up the whole, are all deftitute of the Meeknefs, Purity and Poverty of Spirit here recommended? Have all committed Adultery in their Hearts? Are all Murderers? Then what a Damnable Condition fhould we all be in if we ftood upon our own Works for Juftification before God? Is not our own Morality, or rather Immorality enough to damn us? And do we not tremble at the Thoughts of depending upon it for Salvation? All this may infallibly convince us of the Abfolute Impoffibility of being juftified by our own Righteoufnefs, and of the Abfolute Ne-

S

ceffity

ceffity of being juftified by Faith in the Righteoufnefs of Chrift only. Secondly, explicitly, Ver. 20, *except your Righteoufnefs fhall exceed the Righteoufnefs of the Scribes and Pharifees, ye fhall in no wife enter into the Kingdom of Heaven.* Here the Righteoufnefs of the Scribes and Pharifees is condemned, and herein all the Righteoufnefs of all Natural Men and Unbelievers univerfally. And mention is made of a Righteoufnefs that exceeds it, and what can this be, but the Righteoufnefs of the Lord Jefus, applied by the Holy Spirit, and apprehended by Faith? So that here we have an Explicit Declaration of Chrift's Righteoufnefs, which God places to our Account, and for which he juftifies us.

Again, it is objected that our Lord fays to the Rich Youth, Matt. xix. 17, *if thou wilt enter into Life, keep the Commandments:* From hence it is concluded that keeping the Commandments is the Condition of entering into Life. It is True, indeed, if we do keep the Commandments, we fhall enter into Life ; fo faith the Law, *the Man that doeth them fhall live in them,* Gal. iii. 12. But then who is there keeps the Commandments? And what will become of thofe who do not keep them? *Curfed is every one that continueth not in all Things which are written in the Book of the Law, to do them,* Ver. 10. If, therefore, you will be faved by the Law, you muft do all Things the Law requires, yea, you muft continue to do them from the Firft Moment of your Life to the Laft, or elfe you are loft and curfed to all Eternity.

Eternity. What Flesh can be faved then by the Works of the Law? But it is ufually afked, Why did our Saviour prefcribe this to the Young Man, if he knew 'twas Impoffible for him to obey his Advice? Firft, our Lord faw he was too highly conceited of his own Works: this the Queftion plainly fhews, *what Good Thing fhall I do that I may have Eternal Life?* He was for doing fomething eminently Good and Great in order to merit Eternal Life. Our Lord therefore fends him to the Law to humble his Pride, and convince him that he could do no Good Thing, and that in his Flefh dwelt no Good Thing. Secondly, the Youth fays, *all thefe things have I kept from my Youth up,* Ver. 20. This fhews that he was totally Ignorant of the Corruption of his Heart, totally Ignorant of the Unrighteoufnefs of his Life, and totally Ignorant of the Purity and Perfection of the Divine Law. Otherwife, his Language would have been juft the Reverfe of this: and inftead of faying, all thefe have I kept, he would have faid, all thefe have I tranfgrefs'd from my Youth up. But he perfifting to juftify himfelf, our Saviour put him upon the Trial, *go fell that thou haft, and give to the Poor,* Ver. 21. At this the Self-righteous Creature went away forrowful, difcovering thereby his Inordinate Love of the World, and fhewing that he preferr'd Earthly Treafures before Heavenly. Thirdly and Laftly, *the Law is a Schoolmafter to bring us to* CHRIST, *that we might be juftified by Faith,* Gal. iii. 24. When a Man is convicted of his Guilt and Danger by the Law of Works, he is forced to flee from

the

the Wrath to come and lay hold of Chrift that he may be juftified by Faith. This is a Way wherein Souls are led from under the Law to Chrift. Our Saviour feems to have taken this Courfe with the Young Man, but his Difobedience prov'd his Ruin.

But I fhall not ftand to anfwer any more Objections; for they are all founded in the State of the Heart. Men know not the Want of this Righteoufnefs, and therefore they object againft it; they know not the Value of it, and therefore they flight it. The Infenfibility of their Indigence fupplies them with a Fund of Cavils and Objections, all which are anfwer'd at once as foon as they are convinced of Sin, Unbelief, Internal Iniquity, External Impiety, and Self-righteoufnefs. When Men find the Want of Chrift's Righteoufnefs, they will then know the Worth of it; they will have nothing to object againft it, but blefs God for providing it for them.

The Imputation of Chrift's Active Obedience and his Satisfaction for Sin are both founded upon the fame Principle, viz. that one may undertake or become Surety for another, and that what the one does and fuffers may be transferr'd to the other. Thofe therefore who allow that Chrift was our Surety muft grant not only that he made Satisfaction for our Sins, but alfo that his Active Obedience is imputed to us: And they that deny the Latter do in Effect renounce the Former. If Chrift might in Confequence of his Suretifhip fuffer for our

Sins,

Sins, why might he not alfo upon the fame Principle work out a Perfect Righteoufnefs for us? Is not one of thefe as Reafonable as the other? And if you admit one of thefe, have you not as good Reafon to admit both? But if you reject either, you have as good Ground (and that is juft none at all) to reject both. The Socinians deny the Atonement of Chrift's Death, and fo in Confiftence with their own Scheme renounce the Doctrine of his Righteoufnefs Imputed; and if you difclaim this latter, you muft cafhier both.

We are juftified by Chrift's Righteoufnefs or Active Obedience: This is the Matter of our juftification. God imputes this Righteoufnefs to us; Faith apprehends this Righteoufnefs, and fo we are juftified before God. We are juftified by Faith, not by the Act of Faith, as an Act which we (through Grace) exert, or as an exercife of our own Minds. To affert this would be in Effect to maintain Juftification by Works, and to fay we are juftified for fomething in us or done by us, which is directly oppofite to that of the Apoftle, Rom. iii. 24. *being juftified freely by his grace through the redemption that is in* Chrift Jefus. Now we fhould not be juftified freely and of Grace, but of Debt, if we were juftified by Faith as an Act, Work or exercife of ours, Rom. iv. 4. We are no more juftified by Faith as an Act of ours, than by Hope, Love, or any other Fruit of the Spirit. When therefore we fpeak of being juftified by Faith, we do not mean by

S 3

Faith

Faith as our Act, but by the Object of Faith i. e. Jesus Christ. And this is no Needless or Frivolous Distinction ; for you will observe many Preachers, who with a great Zeal and Air of Free Grace declare for Justification by Faith, by Faith alone, in the strongest Manner possible; yet for Want of duly making a Distinction between the Act of Faith and the Object, they do all the while unawares preach Justification by Works. Faith is nothing of itself; it must always be taken with its Object, or else it is nothing worth. The Blood and Righteousness of Christ are the Ground and Foundation of our Acceptance with GOD. And what is Faith without these? It is nothing but a wither'd Hand. Therefore all the Glory of our Justification is to be ascribed to Christ alone, and not to our Faith, nor any thing in us, nor any thing done by us.

Hence therefore we see how full and Perfect the Righteousness of Christ is : It is Sufficient to justify us without any Thing of our own. This Righteousness was accomplish'd by the Eternal and only-begotten Son of God, and therefore its Worth and Excellence must bear Proportion to its Divine Author. The Righteousness of Christ is in every Respect Answerable to the Strictest Demands of God's Law, and the Severest Exactions of his Justice. Is the Divine Commandment Exceeding Broad ? Yet the Obedience of Christ is as Broad and Extensive. It is so Pure that the Holiness of God can discern no Spot in it ; it is so Universal and

and Uniform that his Infinite Juſtice can find no Fault with it. Hath not God therefore magnified the Law? Hath he not made it Honourable? Is not the Obedience of Chriſt a greater Honour to the Divine Law than if Men and Angels, and all Finite Creatures whatſoever had obey'd it? All theſe could have yielded but the Obedience of Finite Creatures, but the Obedience of Chriſt is the Obedience of the Creator, and is Infinite. As by the Sacrifice of Chriſt's Death a greater Recompence was made to the Injur'd Juſtice of God, than if all Mankind had ſuffer'd eternally, ſo by his Abſolute Conformity to the Divine Commandments, the Law was more highly honour'd than if it had been fulfill'd by all Intelligent Beings, whether Human or Angelical. Chriſt hath ſuffer'd all, Chriſt hath done all for us, and we have Nothing to do but to believe that he hath done all for us. And this Faith is the Gift of God, *Eph*. ii, 8. *Only believe* ſaith our Saviour, *Luke* viii. 50. This is a Myſtery to the Children of this World, and Carnal Reaſoners eſteem it Fooliſhneſs. " If we walk worthy of Chriſt (ſays *Polycarp*) we ſhall alſo reign with him, i. e. if " we believe." So that according to this Apoſtolick Father, believing in Chriſt is walking worthy of him, and we have nothing to do but to beleive in Chriſt. And even this Belief, or this Faith, is not our own Work, but the *Work of* God and his *Gift, John* vi. 29. *Eph*. ii. 8. Therefore all is of Grace.

S 4

Indeed

Indeed if Chrift had left one Sin Unfatisfied for, we could never have made Satisfaction for that Single Offence, and fo muft have perifhed for ever. And if Chrift had left but one of the leaft Commandments Unfulfill'd, that Commandment we could never have fulfill'd, and fo we could never have been faved Suppofe we had finned only in one fingle Turn or Thought of the Heart, fuppofe that afterwards we had kept the whole Law in Thought, Word, and Deed, yet our Prefent or Future Obedience could never make amends for that One Offence, tho' it were but a Single Deviation of the Heart from God for the Space of a Moment. All our Prayers, Tears, Humiliation, Confeffions and Penances, can never wafh out the ftain of the Leaft Sin. The Fire of Hell itfelf cannot Purify us from the Pollution of Sin. Nothing but the Precious Blood of Chrift can purge our Souls from Sin. And his Blood cleanfeth us from all Sin. He hath atoned for all our Sins, the greateft as well as the leaft, therefore in Him and by Him we *are juftified from all*, Acts xiii. 39. The Satisfaction of his Death is Complete, and the Righteoufnefs of his Life is Complete; and this is the only Foundation of our Comfort and Salvation. What fay you then, my Brethren; Do you not fee the Compleatnefs and All-fufficiency of the Saviour's Righteoufnefs? And does not this fweetly allure and incline your Hearts to rely upon it? 'Come then, put your whole Truft in the Righteoufnefs of the Lord Jefus. Depend upon Chrift, and nothing elfe. Have
vou

you lived in Sin? Yet the Righteousness of Christ is Free for you? Have you lived in Uncleanness, in Swearing, in Lying, Perjury and Drunkenness? Yet the Righteousness of Christ is sufficient to cover all your Unrighteousness. Put on this Robe by Faith, and all your Sin, Shame and Nakedness is hid. In this Righteousness you stand Holy, unblameable and unreprovable before the Throne of God. Build upon this Foundation, and your Building shall stand. Venture upon Christ's Righteousness, and you shall never miscarry, you shall never be confounded. This Righteousness is the only Source of Comfort and Peace of Conscience. This Righteousness will be your Support when your Flesh and your Strength fail you. This Righteousness is the only Medicine to heal a broken Heart, 'tis the only Remedy against the Power of Sin, the Terrors of Satan and the Symptoms of Despair.

But further, if the Fulness and All-sufficiency of this Righteousness does not attract and invite you, does not the Necessity of your Condition force and constrain you to take hold of it? Sinners, what will you do without Christ's Righteousness? What will become of you? Dare you appear before God as you are? Will you presume to appear at the Tribunal of God in your own Filthy Rags? Will not the Presence of God frighten you into Hell? How will you stand in the Day of Judgment? All who have not Christ's Righteousness must go to Hell. And without this Righteousness you will have no Comfort at the

Hour

Hour of Death. Now perhaps you live in Carnal Eafe and Security; but how foon will Death overtake you? And then what will become of your vain Confidence, and Worldly Happinefs? Will the Multitude of your Riches fave you from going down to the Pit? Or will the Number of your Friends and Relations afford you any Relief? *Beware left he take thee away with his ftroke: then a Great Ranfom cannot deliver thee. Will he efteem thy Riches? no, not Gold; nor all the Forces of Strength,* Job xxxvi. 18, 19. *They that truft in their Wealth, and boaft themfelves in the Multitude of their Riches: ncne of them can by any means redeem his Brother, nor give to* God *a Ranfom for him: for the Redemption of their Soul is Precious, and it ceafeth for ever,* Pf. xlix. 6, 7, 8. When therefore you are at the Point of Death, and the Prefcriptions of Phyficians, the Endeavours of your neareft and Deareft Relatives, and all Human Affiftances fail you, what will you do if you have not Chrift's Righteoufnefs to take Comfort in? " A Death bed (fays Mr. *Jenks*) may bring " them to *Bellarmine's* Tutissimum est —— " and the Worft that I wifh them is that they " may find Mercy from the Lord in that Day. " ——But at prefent I cannot think they are " in any Good Way for it. And O! how " Juft were it with God at laft to bar up that " Refuge out of which they now fo ftudioufly " fhut themfelves.*

---

* See *Jenks's* Submiffion to the Righteoufnefs of God. Printed 1700, in Octavo, page 155.

But

But some there are who trust in themselves that they are Righteous, and despise others; they think themselves Righteous enough without the Righteousness of Christ. These are they of whom our Saviour speaks. *I am not come to call the Righteous, but Sinners to Repentance,* Matt. ix. 13. *These are of the Number of those Ninety and Nine Just Persons which need no Repentance,* Luke xv. 7. If you discourse with one of this Sort, he will immediately justify himself by giving you a Long Catalogue of his Good Works, he will make a Confession of his formal Righteousness and almost Christianity: " I believe all the Articles
" of the Christian Faith; I do as well as I can,
" and what do you require more? I have been
" a Christian all my Life Time, I have be-
" liev'd in Christ from my Youth up; I go
" to Church and say my Prayers, and receive
" the Sacrament; I have many Good Thoughts
" and Dispositions, and I would be better if I
" could; I am constant at saying my Morning
" and Evening Prayers, I take Care to pay
" every Body their own; If I sin, I repent; I
" know God requires no more of me than I
" am able to do; I do not live in any Wilful
" Sin, I practise my Duty (as far as I know)
" in every Particular; and therefore I hope I
" shall be saved at last—I am in the Way to
" Heaven, am I not?" And is this all your Religion? Is this all your Christianity? Then it is just Equivalent to none at all, only with this Difference, if you had not so much Self-righteousness to trust in, perhaps you might be

more

more eafily induc'd to truft in the Righteoufnefs
of Chrift. All the Works of Righteoufnefs
you have reckoned up you may perform, and
yet be in a Natural State All your Religion
is but the Religion of Gentile Philofophers: It
is the Religion of Jewifh Pharifees, and of almoft Chriftians. The Devil often appears in
a Saint's Drefs. Thofe who think themfelves
the moft Righteous are always the moft Unrighteous. *Verily I fay unto you, that the Publicans and the Harlots go into the Kingdom of*
GOD *before you*, Matth. xxi. 31. If you are
Righteous in your own Eyes, then the Devil is
as Good a Chriftian as you. Have you ever
been convinc'd of your own Unrighteoufnefs?
Are your Idols abolifhed? Are you ftript of all
Self-Dependance? Are all your Falfe Hopes
thrown down? Is Tranfgreffion finifhed? Is
the Everlafting Righteoufnefs of Jefus brought
into your Soul? If not, all your Religion
is but Hypocrify, and your Solemn Duties are
an Abomination. When the Comforter is come,
he will convince you *of Sin, and of Righteoufnefs, and of Judgment*, John xvi. 7, 8, 9.
Then you will bewail the Lofs of Original
Righteoufnefs, you will fee thro' your Mock
Religion; the Mafk of a Pharifaical Righteoufnefs will be taken off, and you will juftify
yourfelf no longer; you will fpeak a quite Different Language, and your Speech will be the
Language of your Heart. My late Lord of
St. *Afaph* feems to have had a Conviction of
this, and therefore he declares his Mind in the
following Words: " I do not remember, nei-
" ther

" ther do I believe that I ever prayed in all
" my Life-Time with that Reverence, or heard
" with that Attention, or receiv'd the Sacra-
" ment with that Faith, or did any other
" Work whatfoever with that Pure Heart and
" Single Eye as I ought to have done. Info-
" much that I look upon all my Righteoufnefs
" but as Filthy Rags, and 'tis in the Robes on-
" ly of the Righteoufnefs of the Son of God
" that I dare appear before the Majefty of Hea-
" ven.*" To the Poor the Gofpel is preached.
To the Poor the Righteoufnefs of Chrift is
given; the Tidings of the Redeemer's Righteoufnefs is " moft Bleffed and Welcome News
" to thofe that are fenfible of their own Po-
" verty, and take it of Grace. But whofo
" thinketh his own Penny Good Silver, and will
" be putting in and bidding for it, will ftand
" upon his own Terms, as *David* did with
" *Araunah*, and will pay for it, or he will not
" have it, let that Man beware left *he and*
" *his Money perifh together*, and left he get
" *neither Part nor Fellowfhip* in this Bufinefs.†
There are fome who fay " We muft do as
" well as we can, and Chrift will do the
" reft: We muft begin the Work, and Chrift
" will finifh it: We muft Work as Good a
" Righteoufnefs as we can, and then add
" Chrift's Righteoufnefs to it, and fo we
" fhall be juftified." This is a common way

---

* Bp. BEVERIDGE's Private Thoughts.
† Bp. SANDERSON on *Ifa.* lii. 3.

of

of talking among Legalifts and Self-Jufticiaries: And the Papifts talk exactly in the fame Manner. For the Romanifts argue thus; if a Man trufts to his own Righteoufnefs, it may deceive him; if a Man trufts wholly to Chrift's Righteoufnefs he may perhaps be miftaken in being too Prefumptuous. But he that trufts to his own Righteoufnefs and Chrift's conjointly, cannot fail in both, but is in the fafeft way to Heaven; juft as if a Man ftands with one Foot upon one Branch of a Tree, and the other upon another, he is much Safer than if he ventures his whole weight upon either. This is their Way of illuftrating their Argument: but the Fallacy of it is eafily fhewn. That Chrift is compared to a Branch all allow who believe the Scriptures; for he is called a *Righteous Branch*, Jer. xxiii. 5. He is effentially Righteous, as God; and he is actually Righteous, as Mediator; and he is alfo the Lord our Righteousness. Now our own Righteoufnefs is a Rotten Branch: If we lay any Strefs upon it, it will break and let us fall into Hell. But the Righteoufnefs of Chrift is an able Branch, an Omnipotent Branch, a Branch that never will fail, a Branch that never will break, tho' Winds and Storms beat upon it. Therefore upon this Branch we ftand faft for ever. The Lord Jefus lays an Abfolute Claim to all the Honour of our Salvation; he will not fuffer our Righteoufnefs to ftand in Competition with his: he will not give his Glory (no, not the Leaft Degree of it) to another. Chrift is not divi-

ded,

ded. His Satisfaction is finished and perfected : His Righteousness is Complete, and stands in no Need of the Addition of any of our Righteousness to it. Jesus will be a whole Saviour, or he will be no Saviour. Never think to accommodate Matters by joining your own Righteousness and Christ's together; *for what Fellowship hath Righteousness with Unrighteousness? and what Communion hath Light with Darkness?* 2 Cor. vi. 14. Can you ever hope to reconcile such Contraries? And yet you may as soon do this as be justified before God by your own Righteousness in Conjunction with Christ's. Your own Righteousness hath nothing to do in the Affair. All Human Righteousness is but of short Continuance: It lasts for a few Months or a few Years: It is as the Morning Cloud or Early Dew which soon passeth away, and it expires for ever at the Time of Death. The Righteousness of Christ is Everlasting; it lasts to the Hour of Death, it lasts to the Day of Judgment, it lasts to all Eternity. This Righteousness is set up from Everlasting to Everlasting, and is therefore by *Daniel* fitly called an *Everlasting Righteousness*, Chap. ix. Ver. 24. Therefore throw away all Righteousness but the Righteousness of Christ. As for Self-righteousness, we abhor it, we break it down, as Jehu *brake down the House of Baal, and made it a Draught House,* 2 Kings x. 27. We tear away all but the Righteousness of Christ. This makes Creatures who are Righteous in their own Eyes cry out of us as *Zipporah* did of *Moses,* she said,

surely

furely a Bloody Hufband art thou to me, becaufe of the Circumcifion, Exod. iv. 25, 26. fo they fay of us, furely Bloody Preachers are ye to us, becaufe of Self-righteoufnefs. Renounce all Dependance upon your Imaginary Good Works and Hypocritical Obedience. Take Chrift as a whole Saviour, or elfe you will never have him at all.

As for you who are interefted in this Righteoufnefs, you are the Happy Souls. *Bleffed is the Man to whom the* LORD *will not impute Sin*, and Bleffed are they to whom GOD *imputeth Righteoufnefs without Works*. Therefore take the Comfort, and give God the Glory. How Good hath God been to you? When you had no Righteoufnefs of your own to cover you, he cloathed you with the Righteoufnefs of his Son Jefus Chrift. How Good hath Chrift been to you? He took you when you were Naked Beggars, and put on you the Rich Robe of his Righteoufnefs. You are Black in yourfelves, yet Comely in the Comelinefs which Chrift hath put upon you. Live therefore upon Chrift's Righteoufnefs. When you fee no Righteoufnefs in yourfelves, look to the Righteoufnefs of Jefus Chrift. Why are ye fo full of Doubts and Fears? What makes you fo Weak and Wavering? It is becaufe ye live partly upon your own Righteoufnefs, and partly upon Chrift's. If ye lived entirely upon Chrift's Righteoufnefs, you would not be fo Unftable and Difquieted. Look to the Blood of Chrift, and then doubt if you can. Look to the Righteoufnefs of Chrift, and then defpair

ſpair if you can. Live wholly upon the Blood
and Righteouſneſs of Jeſus Chriſt. Live out
of All that is in you upon All that is in
Chriſt. Then will you be always Quiet and
Eaſy in your ſouls; you will feel your Hearts
more deeply rooted, more firmly Grounded and
more ſolidly Eſtabliſhed on the Dear Lamb of
God. And when you are thus ſettled, do not
deſpiſe the Weak, but condole and comfort
them. When you have an Aſſurance of Faith,
and mount up with wings as Eagles, do not
ſlight and contemn All who do not ſoar to the
ſame Altitude with yourſelves, do not keep
Weak Believers at a Diſtance, but freely give
them the right-hand of fellowſhip. Many
there are who can *rejoice with them that do rejoice*; but few alas! know how to *weep with
them that weep*, Rom. xii. 15. And yet one of
theſe is as much a Chriſtian's Priviledge as the
other. A Sympathetick Spirit is a Great Sign
of a True Chriſtian, *Joh.* xiii. 35. Thoſe who
have been through much Tribulation themſelves
know how to pity others; and if Perſons are
not Tender-hearted and do not care to compaſ-
ſionate the afflicted, 'tis becauſe they have not
experienc'd much Tribulation themſelves: So
ſaith the Apoſtle Paul, *God comforteth us in
all our Tribulation, that we may be able to comfort them which are in any Trouble, by the Comfort wherewith we ourſelves are comforted of
God*, 2 *Cor.* i. 4. And the Apoſtle ſets us an
Excellent Example in this Caſe, 1 *Cor.* ix. 19,
20, &c. *Though I be Free from All Men, yet*

T

have

*have I made myself servant unto All, that I might gain the more. And unto the Jews I became as a Jew, that I might gain the Jews; to them that are under the Law, as under the Law, that I might gain them that are under the Law; to them that are without Law as without Law, (being not without Law to God, but in a Law, * to Christ) that I might gain them that are without Law. To the Weak became I as Weak, that I might gain the Weak: I am made All Things to All Men, that I might by All Means save some. And this I do for the Gospel's sake.*——If ye have a Love for the Gospel, go ye and do likewise. They *that are strong ought to bear the Infirmities of the Weak, and not to please themselves,* Rom. xv. 1. Think of the Condescension of Christ to you, and then you will not grudge condescending a little to your Weak Brethren. How much hath Christ done for You? How much hath Christ suffer'd for You? And will you do nothing, will you suffer nothing for his Weak Disciples? *We ought to lay down our Lives for the Brethren,* 1 Joh. iii. 16. *Bear ye one another's Burdens, and so fulfill the Law of*

---

* The Greek Word properly signifies this; and not under a Law, (as our Translators grossly render it) for that is apt to carry in it an Idea of Servile Subjection. *Under a Law,* as in Rom. vi. 14, 15. 1 Cor. ix. 20. Gal. iii. 23. iv. 4, 5, 21. v. 18.

Christ.

Chrift. Laftly, think of Chrift's righteoufnefs, and then you will do Good Works.
Think of nothing, fpeak of nothing, love nothing but Chrift. Be ravifhed with his Delights at all Times. Come nearer to the
Blood and Righteoufnefs of Chrift. *The
Righteoufnefs of God is revealed from Faith to
Faith,* that is, from one Degree of Faith, to
another: Therefore increafe in Faith, live nearer to Chrift; and the nearer you live to the
Saviour the farther you will be from Sin; *for
the Grace of God that bringeth Salvation hath
appeared to All Men, Teaching us that denying
Ungodlinefs and Worldly Lufts, we fhould live
foberly, righteoufly and godly in this prefent
World; looking for that Bleffed Hope, and the
Glorious Appearing of the Great* GOD *and our*
SAVIOUR JESUS CHRIST, *who gave himfelf for
us, that he might redeem us from All Iniquity,
and purify unto himfelf a Peculiar People, zealous
of Good Works,* Tit. ii. 11, 12, 13, 14.

But how fhall I conclude my Difcourfe
without fpeaking a Word to you who do not
yet know your Intereft in the Redeemer's
righteoufnefs? And what fhall I fay unto you?
For I would not willingly fay a Word to difcourage you, but do All I can to encourage
you to believe in Chrift's righteoufnefs. We
are Ambaffadors for Chrift, as tho' God did
befeech you by us: we pray you in Chrift's
Stead be ye reconciled to God. And I befeech
you Brethren, fuffer the Word of Exhortation.
The righteoufnefs of Chrift is Free: 'Tis

Free

Free for the *Chief of Sinners*, 1 Tim. i. 15,
'tis Free for All who believe: Therefore only
believe and 'tis yours. Don't ftand excufing
yourfelves by faying " *we cannot believe* "
Faith is the Gift of God, and no Man hath
it of himfelf naturally. St. Polycarp in his
Epiftle to the Philippians exhorts them to take
heed to the Epiftle St. Paul wrote them, that,
faith he, " ye may be edified in the Faith
" which is given you." For Faith is freely
given us of God. Therefore afk, and ye fhall
receive. If you do not believe, the Fault is
your own; therefore pray don't charge it upon
God. God will give you Faith, if you afk it:
But if you will not afk, you are juftly condemned. What fignifies making Excufes?
What fignifies inventing Quirks and Evafions,
and making this Pretence and the other to cover the Infidelity of your Hearts? It is no Trifling Matter; it is a cafe of Neceffity; and
you muft believe, or be caft into Hell for ever.
The righteoufnefs which your own Hands
have wrought is a Bed fhorter than that a
Man can ftretch himfelf upon it, and the covering narrower than that he can wrap himfelf
in it, Ifai. xxviii. 20. But the Righteoufnefs of
the Son of God is a foft and Eafy Bed, and long
enough for you to ftretch yourfelves upon; his
active obedience is a covering broad and wide
enough for you to wrap yourfelves in. Wrap
yourfelves in this White Raiment, that *ye may
be cloathed, and that the Shame of your Naked-*
nefs

nefs do not appear. God commands you to believe, 1 *John* iii. 23. *This is his Commandment, that we fhould believe on the Name of his Son Jefus Chrift* — This Command you are abfolutely obliged to obey, or elfe you muft perifh eternally. What fignifies obeying all other Commands? If you do not obey this, you may as well obey none. Do not fay we have no Power to obey this Command; for God who commands us to believe, does alfo give us Power to believe; if therefore we do not believe, we are Inexcufable. *He that believeth not is condemned already,* John iii. 18. . 'Tis the Eafieft Thing in the World to believe when a Soul is enabled; and a young Chriftian is often apt to wonder that he did not believe fooner. To believe is to renounce all that is in us, and to live upon all that is in Chrift. A True Believer renounces his own Merits, and lives upon the Merits of Chrift: He renounces his own Righteoufnefs, and lives upon the Righteoufnefs of Chrift: He renounces his own Sanctification, and lives upon Chrift for Sanctification: He renounces his own Obedience, and lives upon the Obedience of Chrift. Only renounce all that is your's, and all that Chrift hath is free for you. Are you Difobedient? Then truft in the Obedience of Chrift. Are you Unrighteous? Then truft in Chrift's Righteoufnefs. Are you Unholy? Then truft in the Holinefs of Chrift. Remember the Lord Jefus did not die for the Godly, but for the *Ungodly,* Rom. v. 6. Chrift fhed his Blood for you, he lived for

you

you, he died for you, he fulfilled all Righteoufnefs for you: Do but believe, and you will find it True. Believe, tho' you fee not. Our Saviour faith, *bleffed are they that have not feen and yet have believed.* Therefore believe that Chrift loves you, believe that he gave himfelf for you, that he fulfilled the Law for you, and that he hath purchafed Salvation for you; altho' you by your Natural Reafon fee nothing at all of this. Believe, tho' you fee no reafon in yourfelf for fo doing: Only depend upon the FREE GRACE of God, and you will be Happy. Sinners, don't ftay a Moment; come to Chrift immediately; caft yourfelves upon him juft as you are. Only venture upon Chrift, and fee if he will caft you out: indeed he never will. Did ever any one truft in Chrift, and was confounded? Truft in him, hope in him, believe in him, and you will never be difappointed. If ye ftay away from Chrift longer, ye will be never the better: But the longer you ftay away, the worfe you will be. Do not look into yourfelves for a Fitnefs. All your Fitnefs is in Chrift. What you want is Chrift. Believe in him, and he is yours. In Him dwells all Fulnefs. Believe in Chrift, and all that Chrift hath is yours: his Blood is yours, his Wifdom is yours, his Righteoufnefs, his Sanctification is yours; yea CHRIST JESUS HIMSELF is yours, he is yours in this World, and in the World to come; he is yours in Time, and in Eternity. Even fo, Amen, Lord Jefus, Amen and Amen.

CHAP.

C H A P. II.

Of REGENERATION.

IT is the Office of every Minister of the Gospel to declare all the Counsel of God, and
not to build one Evangelical Doctrine upon the
Ruins of another, nor so to preach Justification
by Faith, as to exclude the Regeneration of the
SPIRIT. 'Tis Good sometimes to be Suspici-
ous of our own Judgment, and not too hastily
to run into any Thing. *Est Modus in rebus* ——
Extremes are Dangerous. The best Way is to
keep a due Medium, and not so to insist upon
Christ without us as to exclude the Doctrine
of Christ within us, nor so to affirm what
Christ hath done for us, as to deny what
Christ does or works in us. That God
works in us is Evident beyond all Contradiction
from *Phil.* i. 6. God hath begun a GOOD
WORK *in you* —— from *Phil.* ii. 13. God
worketh in you —— from *Heb.* xiii. 21. God
working in you —— from 1 *Thes.* ii. 13. The
Word of God worketh effectually in you that
believe.——2 *Thes.* i. 11. We pray that God
would fulfill all the Good Pleasure of his Goodness,

uefs, and the Work of Faith with Power, and 1 Cor. xii. 6. God *worketh all in all.*

Our Saviour fets Regeneration and Juftification both upon the fame Level, Joh. iii. 3. *Except a Man be born again he cannot fee the Kingdom of* God, and Mark xvi. 16. *he that believeth not fhall be damn'd*——fo that you fee as well the Unregenerate, as the Unbeliever is excluded the Kingdom of Heaven. This therefore is a clear Demonftration that Regeneration is as Neceffary to Salvation, as Juftification by Faith, and that we can no more be faved without being born of the Spirit, than without believing in Chrift. As by our Juftification we live legally, i. e. are acquitted from all Guilt, delivered from the Curfe of the Law, and are entitled to Eternal Life; fo by our Regeneration we live Spiritually, i. e. are made alive in Soul and Spirit: *Heb.* x. 38. *Eph.* ii. 1. And thefe Two always go together. The Scriptures are Full of this Doctrine, and fo are the Homilies of the Church of *England.* We defcend immediately to the Proof of it.

The Homily on Chrift's Nativity fays, " according to his Great Mercy he faved us by " the Fountain of the New Birth, and by the " Renewing of the Holy Ghoft, which he pour- " ed upon us abundantly, through Jefus " Chrift our Saviour:" *Tit.* iii. 5, and 6, is here referr'd to; and thefe Words teach us that the New Birth is Neceffary to our being faved, and that this Renewing or Regeneration is the Work of the Holy Ghoft; which is faid to be poured upon us abundantly through Jefus

Chrift

Chrift our Saviour, becaufe Chrift procured for us fo Excellent and Unfpeakable a Bleffing.

The Homily on Whitfunday fpeaks thus,
" if otherwife he (viz. *Nicodemus*) had known
" the great Power of the Holy Ghoft in this be-
" half, that it is he which inwardly worketh the
" Regeneration and New Birth of Mankind,
" he never would have marvelled at Chrift's
" Words." Here the Work of Regeneration is
attributed to the great Power of the Holy Ghoft,
who is God, Eternal, Infinite and Equal with
the Father in every Attribute; and therefore his
Act muft be Omnipotent. Accordingly the
Homily for Rogation Week hath thefe Words,
" to juftify a Sinner, to new create him from a
" Wicked Perfon to a Righteous Man, is a great-
" er Act (faith St. *Auguftine*) than to make fuch
" a new Heaven and Earth as is already made."
And is it an higher and greater Act to new create a Sinner, than to make a new Heaven and a
new Earth ? Can any Power lefs than the Divine effect this Work? Do Men believe thefe
Homilies ? If they do, why are they ftartled
when they hear our Regeneration afcribed to a
Supernatural and Divine Energy ? Do not they
keep clofe to the Church of *England*, who attribute it to an Almighty Power ? And do not
they depart from her, who afcribe it to any
lefs Efficiency ? Again, are Men Senfible of
their Spiritual Death and utter Indifpofition to
God and Goodnefs ? And can they think that
any Power but that which raifed *Lazarus* from
the Dead (*John* xi. 43, 44.) fufficient to

U quicken

quicken them to Spiritual Life ? Yea, doth not the Scripture attribute this Marvellous Work to the felf-fame Omnipotency that raifed Chrift from the Dead ? Compare *Eph.* i. 20. with Ch. ii. Ver. 1 and *Col.* ii. 12, 13. Agreeable hereto the Homily for Whitfunday admonifheth us to befeech God " fo to work in our Hearts " by his Holy Spirit, that we being Regenerate " and newly born again in all Goodnefs, Righ- " teoufnefs, Sobriety and Truth, may in the end " be made Partakers of Everlafting Life in his " heavenly Kingdom." And the Homily for Ro- gation Week fpeaking of glorified Saints in Hea- ven, fays, " If they were afked again who " fhould be thanked for their Regeneration, for " their Juftification, and for their Salvation ? " Whether their Deferts or God's Goodnefs on- " ly? Altho' in this Point every one confefs " fufficiently the Truth of. this Matter in his " own Perfon : yet let them all anfwer by the " mouth of *David* at this Time, who cannot " choofe but fay, Not to us, O Lord, not to " us, but to thy Name give all the Thanks, for " thy loving Mercy, and for thy Truth's fake." From all this taken together we learn that Re- generation is the Work of the Holy Spirit; that if we have it, we are to thank him for fo Un- fpeakable a Bleffing, and that the Fruits thereof are Goodnefs, Righteoufnefs, Sobriety and Truth.

In the Book of Common Prayer there is fre- quent Mention of this Divine and Heavenly Doctrine. In the Collect for Chriftmas-Day we pray " Grant that we being Regenerate and
" made

" made thy Children by Adoption and Grace,
" may daily be renewed by thy Holy Spirit." In
the Firſt Clauſe we aſk for Regeneration ſtrictly
ſo called, i. e. the Act of God's Spirit in turning the Soul from Darkneſs to Light : in the
Laſt, where mention is made of being daily renewed, we pray for Sanctification ; and ſo the
Apoſtle prays for the *Theſſalonians*, that God
*would ſanctify them wholly, that their whole
Spirit and Soul and Body might be preſerved
Blameleſs*, 1 Theſ. v. 23. 2 Cor. iv. 16.

In the Collect for Aſh-Wedneſday we beg of
God to " create and make in us new and con-
" trite Hearts." This new Heart is the ſame
which St. *Paul* calls the *New Creature*, 2 *Cor.*
v. 17. and a *true Heart*, *Heb.* x. 22. This
the Regenerating Grace of God creates in us ;
and hereupon follows Contrition, Lamentation
and Unfeigned Sorrow for Sin, according to
that of the Prophet, *after that 1 was turned, I
repented ; and after that I was inſtructed I ſmote
upon my thigh.* Jer. xxxi. 19.

At the beginning of the Office of Baptiſm it
is ſaid, " None can enter into the Kingdom of
" God, except he be Regenerate and born anew
" of Water and of the Holy Ghoſt :" accordingly the Church prays afterward, " Give thy Ho-
" ly Spirit to this Infant, that he may be born
" again, and be made an Heir of everlaſting
" Salvation." In theſe Two Places we are
taught that Regeneration is neceſſary to our entering into the Kingdom of God, or becoming
Heirs of everlaſting Salvation. And 'tis Ob-

U 2

ſervable

fervable the Holy Ghoft is nominated as the Proper Author and Efficient of our Regeneration.

From what hath been faid we may deduce the Three following Propofitions:

I. That Regeneration is neceffary to our obtaining Eternal Life and Happinefs.

II. That this Second Birth is not the Effect of Man's own Will or Power, but of the SPIRIT of GOD, and

III. That the Fruits of Regeneration are Faith, Love, &c.

Each of thefe I fhall endeavour to prove from the Holy Scriptures. As to the Firft our Saviour exprefsly declares to *Nicodemus*, that *except a Man be born of Water and of the Holy Spirit, he cannot enter into the Kingdom of* GOD, John iii. 5. Obferve Firft, *Nicodemus* being a Pharifee, ver. 1. was undoubtedly an Honeft, Sober, Moral Man, as the beft of that Sect were, *Luke* xviii. 11, 12, yet our Saviour lets him know that all his Morality would never carry him to Heaven, that he would never enter therein unlefs he was born again. This our Divine Prophet ufhers in with a double Affeveration, Verily, verily, to exprefs his earneft Concern for *Nicodemus*, and to inculcate his Words more deeply upon *Nicodemus*'s Heart. This teaches us that our higheft Attainments in Morality will never bring us to

Heaven.

Heaven unlefs we are born again. Secondly, *Nicodemus* was a *Ruler of the Jews, a Mafter in Ifrael,* ver. 1, 10. yet totally Ignorant of the New Birth, as appears from the Queftions he propounded, ver. 4, 9. How dreadful a Cafe is it when they who fhould preach this Doctrine to others know nothing of it them-felves! Will not that Accufation St. *Paul* brings againft the *Jews* fall very heavy upon the Heads of all fuch Teachers, *Thou which teacheft another, teacheft thou not thyfelf?* And how will they bear that other Reproof of the fame Apoftle in his Epiftle to the *Hebrews, when for the Time ye ought to be Teachers, ye have need that one teach you again which be the Firft Principles of the Oracles of* GOD ? But to come to the Text, when our Lord fays, *except a Man be born of Water and the Spirit,* fome fuppofe that thefe Words contain an Hendyadis, and fo fignify no more than being born of the Spirit, who for his fanctifying and refrefhing Influences refembles *Water, John* iv. 14. vii. 38, 39, &c. &c. Others by Water underftand Baptifm according to *Mark* xvi. 16. *He that believeth and is baptifed fhall be faved.* But take which of thefe Interpretations you pleafe, (or both if you think proper, for they are both very Confiftent with each other) the Confe-quence will ftill be the fame, viz. that without being born again Men cannot enter into the Kingdom of Heaven. Obferve, our Lord doth not fay fhall not, as if Unregenerate Men were only excluded Heaven by the Decree and

Purpofe

U 3

Purpofe of God, but cannot, to afcertain us of the Abfolute Impoffibility of the Thing: fo St. *Paul*, 1 Cor. xv. 50. *Flefh and Blood cannot inherit the Kingdom of* GOD. There is an utter Contrariety in the Heart of an Unregenerate Man to Heaven, and the Felicities of that Bleffed State. If a natural Man was admitted into Heaven, he would find no Pleafure nor Satisfaction there; all the Joys of that Bleffed Place would be to him Taftelefs and Infipid, and afford him no more Happinefs than Concerts of Mufic to a Deaf Man, or a variety of Colours to a Man born Blind: yea, fuch an one would rather flee to Hell for Company like himfelf, than ftay in Heaven to be tormented and tantaliz'd with Pleafures whereof he could have no Relifh nor Enjoyment. Laftly, Chrift here argues the Neceffity of Regeneration from the Spiritual Uncleannefs or Pollution of Man's Firft Birth, *that which is born of the Flefh, is Flefh; and that which is born of the Spirit, is Spirit*, i. e. is Spiritual, ver. 6, where he not only infifts upon the Indifpenfible Neceffity of a Spiritual or Second Birth, but alfo ftates a Parallel between that and our Natural Birth, which is at the fame Time both very Elegant and very Inftructive; for as we have our Natural Being from our Natural Parents, we have our Spiritual being from the Spirit: As that bears the Image of Adam, this bears the Image of Chrift, 2 *Cor.* iii. 18, as by that we become Men, by this we become New Men, or Chriftians.

St. *Paul*

St. *Paul* fays to the *Corinthians,* 2 Cor. v. 17, *If any Man be in* CHRIST, *he is a New Creature,* that is, if a Man be in the Faith of Chrift, if he be vitally and myftically united to Chrift, if he be one Spirit with him, 1 *Cor.* vi. 17, then he is a New Creature. A Man may be in the Philofophy of *Ariftotle* or *Pythagoras,* he may be in the Morality of *Cicero* or *Antoninus,* and ftill remain Unrenewed in Heart, Unconverted and Unfanctified : A Corrupt Unregenerate Spirit frequently lurks under all this External Glofs and Pageantry. It is the Believer in Chrift, and he only that is a New Creature ; in fuch a Soul there is *a New Creation, Old Things are paft away, behold, all Things are become New ;* the corrupt Inclinations and Defires of the Old Adam are abolifh'd, and the Graces and Principles of the New Man inferted. In Regeneration the Spirit of God produces Light out of Darknefs, he makes the barren Heart fruitful, and out of Confufion and Difcord brings Order, Harmony and Tranquility. In a Soul thus wrought upon all Things are become New, a Man then receives a new fet of Hopes and Fears ; his Judgment is enlightened, his Will rectified, and his Heart *transformed :** his Eyes are open'd, and his Views are no longer terminated within the Horizon of this World ; he fees into Eternity ; his Hope is full of Immortality, Spiritual Appetites are excited in his Soul, his

---

* *Rom.* xii. 2.

U 4

Affections

Affections are raifed to God and Heaven, his Soul thirfteth for God, for the LIVING GOD; his conftant cry is, when fhall I come and appear before God?

To this add Gal. vi. 15, *In* CHRIST JESUS *neither Circumcifion nor Uncircumcifion availeth any Thing, but a New Creature.* By Circumcifion here we underftand the Moral and Ceremonial Duties of the *Mofaic* Law; by Uncircumcifion are meant the Moral Principles and Practices of the Gentile World: All thefe the Apoftle tells us will avail nothing to our Salvation; the only Thing that avails in this Affair is a New Creature, or a New Creation as fome render it. Need any Thing more be faid to fhew the Abfolute Neceffity of a New or Second Birth, in order to our entering into the Kingdom of Glory? Obferve, it is here faid a New Creature, and Gal. v. 6, *Faith which worketh by Love,* and 1 Cor. vii. 19, *the keeping of the Commandments of* GOD. Many People make a great ftir about keeping the Commandments; but what Commandments do they mean? If they mean the Commandments of the Law, who is there that keepeth them? Do they themfelves keep them? When I fpeak of keeping the Commandments, I mean thofe Two, 1 John iii. 23, *And this is his Commandment, that we fhould believe on the Name of his Son* JESUS CHRIST, *and love one another, as he gave us commandment.* As the whole Law is fumm'd up in Two Commandments, Matt. xxii. 40, fo here the whole Gofpel is fumm'd up in thefe Two Commandments, of *believing in*
CHRIST,

CHRIST, and *loving one another as he loved us*, John xiii. 34. Thefe Two are the Commandments that Chrift gave his Difciples, and every Chriftian is obliged to obferve them. It is therefore rightly faid by *Ignatius* the Martyr, " Faith and Love is all our Religion "

I might further evince the Neceffity of the New Birth from thofe Exhortations in Scripture, we meet with to this Purpofe, *Rom.* xii. 2. *Eph.* iv. 23, &c. from the abfolute Holinefs of God, *Exod.* xv. 11. *Jofh.* xxiv. 19. I *Sam.* ii. 2, vi. 20. *Job* iv. 17. xv. 15. *Rev.* iv. 8, &c. from the Original and Actual Sinfulnefs of Mankind, *Job* xiv. 4. *Pf.* li. 5, and from the utter Impoffibility there is that any Thing Unholy or Unclean fhould dwell with God, *Matt.* v. 8. *Hab.* i. 13. *Heb.* xii. 14. But what I have faid is fufficient, efpecially confidering however Men may differ in explaining the Nature of Regeneration, yet they generally agree in holding it Neceffary for our obtaining future Blifs and Profperity.

Is Regeneration fo neceffary? Is there no being faved without it? Then how highly doth it become us to fearch whether we are Regenerate or not? Our Saviour defcribes the State of Mankind in General when he fays, *Let the Dead bury their Dead*, Luke ix. 60. and fo does St. *John* when he fays, *the whole World lieth in Wickednefs*, I John v. 19. How many a Living Body contains a Dead Soul? How many are Alive in the Flefh, but Dead in Spirit? Perhaps you think yourfelf a Chriftian

becaufe

becaufe you are one outwardly; you think yourfelf Regenerate, becaufe you are outwardly Moral; but how many Unregenerate Moralifts are there in Hell? Don't miftake the Cafe, you may have all External Morality without having any Inward Chriftianity: what fignifies being outwardly Moral, unlefs you are inwardly Spiritual? If you have not an Experience of Inward Regeneration upon your Heart, however Sober, Juft and Laudable your External Converfation may be, yet you have no True Religion in you. Was you ever thoroughly awakened to a Senfe of your Mifery? Have you feen and felt the exceeding Sinfulnefs of Sin? Did you ever groan under the Burden of a Depraved Nature? Have you feen yourfelf Loft? Have you experienced your utter Inability to fave yourfelf? Hath God called you out of Darknefs into his Marvellous Light? Hath he tranflated you out of the Kingdom of Darknefs into the Kingdom of his dear Son? Are you converted, and become as a Little Child? Hath the Holy Ghoft taken Poffeffion of your Heart? Are you paffed from Death unto Life? Are thefe Things fo in your Soul? If they are not, all your Moral Virtues are but *Splendida Peccata*, and your Formal Religion will only ferve as an *Ignis Fatuus* to dazzle your Eyes, and lead you more fedately to Deftruction. Hear what Bifhop *Sanderfon* fays,——" Men " may reform themfelves in the general courfe " of their Lives in fundry Particulars, refraining " from fome Grofs Diforders, and avoiding the
.*"* Occafions

" Occasions of them wherein they have form-
" erly lived and delighted, and practising ma-
" ny Outward Duties of Piety and Charity,
" conformable to the Letter of the Laws of
" both Tables, and misliking and opposing
" against the common Errors or Corruptions
" of the Times and Places wherein they live;
" and all this to their own and others think-
" ing with as great a Zeal unto Godliness and
" as thorough Indignation against Sin as any
" others: All this they may do, and yet be
" rotten at the Heart, wholly Carnal and Un-
" renewed, quite empty of sound Faith, Repen-
" tance and Obedience, and every good Grace;
" full of Damnable Pride and Hypocrisy, and in
" the Present State of Damnation."* Observe
what this judicious Divine says, and hence
learn not to mistake Morality for Christianity:
how many secret Vices lurk under the mask
of a false Morality? This outward decency
of Behaviour is often a covert for Pride, Lust,
Covetousness, Worldly Mindedness, Envy,
Wrath, Malice, Revenge, and all Manner of
Spiritual Wickedness. Therefore see that your
Heart is changed,† see that your Soul is created anew: ‡ till this is done never look upon
yourself as Regenerate. But if the Self-righteous scarcely be saved, where will the Ungodly and Practical Sinner appear? How will you

---

* Sermon on 1 *Kings* xxi. 29.   † 2 *Cor.* iii. 18.
‡ *Eph.* ii. 10.

dare

dare to ſtand before God in Judgment? Yet there is Remiſſion of Sins for the worſt of you in the Blood of Chriſt. Now is the Accepted Time, now is the Day of Salvation. While you have Time believe in Chriſt. Saving Grace is free for you: God gives it unto you. But do not miſtake a few Legal Convictions of Natural Conſcience for Converſion. Do not think yourſelf a Chriſtian becauſe you endure a great deal of Terror. How many go to Hell with *Eſau*'s Tears, *Ahab*'s Humiliation, *Judas*'s Confeſſion, *Felix*'s Trembling, and *Agrippa*'s almoſt Chriſtianity? Some People have a Hell here, and a Hell hereafter. This is the Caſe of Final Apoſtates, and of thoſe who commit the Sin againſt the HOLY GHOST. Yet let not weak Souls be diſcouraged; for there is no being converted without being convicted.* Let thoſe therefore who are *convicted of Sin, hope and quietly wait for the Salvation of the* LORD, Lam. iii. 26. Jeſus Chriſt is a good Phyſician, he wounds deeply, that he may heal effectually. The ſharper your Convictions are, the ſweeter ſhall your Conſolations be. Are you in Pangs and Agonies of Soul? Chriſt will deliver you. Hath he brought to the Birth? and will he not give ſtrength to bring forth? *Stand ſtill, and ſee the Salvation* † *of God.* Are you now Afflicted, toſſed in Tempeſts, and not Comforted? You ſhall be the more ſettled hereafter. A Young Chriſtian

---

* *Joh.* xvi. 8. *Matth.* xviii. 3. † *Exod.* xiv. 13.

is

is like a Young Tree: The more a Young
Tree is shaken, blown about by Winds, and
loosened at the Root, the deeper Root it takes,
and the faster it is fixt in the Ground at last;
just so the more a Child of God is shaken with
Fears, Trials, and Anguish of Heart, the stron-
ger he will become in Faith at last, and have
the fuller Persuasion, the clearer Evidence, and
more constant, comfortable Assurance of God's
Love unto him. This is Agreeable to Scripture* and the Experience of Saints.

II. The Second Proposition is that the Second Birth is not the Effect of Man's own
Will or Power, but of the Spirit of God. As
in the Natural World all Things are of God,
so likewise are all in the Spiritual: As in the
Visible Creation God created the Sun, the Heavens, the Earth, the Sea and all that is therein; so in the New Creation God creates Faith,
Hope, Love, and all other Fruits of the Spirit. All Things in a New-born Soul are of
God. As Man could not create himself at
first, so neither can he regenerate or create
his Soul anew. This is clearly Demonstrable
from the Doctrine of Original Sin as before laid
down; for if all the Powers and Faculties of
the Human Nature are debased, then is the
Will depraved also; how then can a Man regenerate himself by his own Free Will? Hence

---

* *Pfal.* xxxviii. lxxvii. lxxxviii. *Lam.* iii.

you

you fee the Neceffity of the latter Part of the
Propofition, viz. that the Second Birth is the
Effect of the Spirit of God. This we fhall
endeavour to eftablifh by fome Texts of Scripture.

The Evangelift St. *John* fpeaking of the Regenerate fays, *which were Born not of Blood, nor
of the Will of the Flefh, nor of the Will of
Man, but of* God, John i. 13: In which
Words he acquaints us that New-born Souls do
not become fuch by Virtue of their Blood,
that is, their Natural Defcent and Lineage;
nor of the Will of the Flefh, that is, their Native Free-will and Mental Abilities ; nor of the
Will of Man,' that is, the Inftruction, Information and Inftitution of others ; but of God,
that is, by the fole Influence and Operation of
the Divine Spirit. So that here all other Caufes
are excluded from our Regeneration, but the
Will of God. To this we may add the Teftimony of St. *James*, Jam. i. 18, *Of his own
Will begat he us by the Word of Truth.* Here
you fee God of his own Will begat us; yet he
ufed the Word of Truth as a Means of our
Spiritual Regeneration. And this we fee is
commonly the Cafe: Souls are generally converted and regenerated under the Word: So St.
*Peter, being born again, not of Corruptible
Seed, but of Incorruptible, by the Word of*
God, *which liveth and abideth for ever,* 1 Pet.
i. 23. And St. Paul, 1 Cor. iv. 15, *In* Christ
Jesus *I have begotten you through the Gofpel.*

Our

Our Saviour delivers the same Doctrine, John xv. 5. *without me ye can do Nothing.* The double Negation in the Original gives the Words a peculiar Weight and Emphasis, and infallibly assures us that we can do Nothing to any Saving Purpose without the Divine Aid and Influence. Our Lord doth not say (as one justly observes) " ye cannot so *easily,* so *exactly,* " so *perfectly,* &c. but absolutely *ye* CANNOT: " He does not say ye CANNOT *do* every Thing, " or any *great* or *difficult* Thing; but simply " WITHOUT ME, i. e. separate from me, by " any Power of your own, and without my *in-* " *clining, quickening, affisting Grace ye* CAN DO " NOTHING, i. e. NOTHING AT ALL, whether " little or great, easy or difficult, in any Measure " or in any Degree." What clearer Proof can we have of the Weakness of Man's Will, and the utter Impossibility of his Regenerating himself ?

St. *Paul* gives us his Judgment in this Point 2 Cor. iii. 5. *Not that we are Sufficient of our-* *selves to think any thing as of ourselves : but our* *Sufficiency is of* GOD. Was the Apostle Insufficient to think a Good Thought ? And are not we much more ? How then can we by our own Strength regenerate ourselves ? Again, the Apostle speaks in the present Tense, we are; when he wrote this he was undoubtedly a Regenerate Man: this therefore shews us that without God we are as Insufficient to think a Good Thought after Regeneration as we were before; how wisely then doth the Apostle con-

clude

clude *our Sufficiency is of* GOD? And have not all we the highest Reason to make the same Conclusion? Indeed I readily allow the Apostle is here speaking of his Ministry and the Success thereof; but is not the same Power that renders our Ministry successful for the Regeneration of others, necessary for the Conversion and Salvation of our own Souls?

This Doctrine is further confirmed from the Prayer of *Ephraim*, *Turn thou me, and I shall be turned*, Jer. xxxi. 18. But what Occasion had he to pray to God to turn him, if he could turn himself? This shews that our Conversion is of God; and so does the Prayer of the Church, Cant. i. 4. *Draw me, we will run after thee*: before the Lord draws us we cannot stir a step; but afterwards we walk, yea run in his Ways: then we move freely and swiftly to him who is the centre of our Attraction, and the source of our Felicity. With all this agrees the Prayer of Zion, Lam. v. 21. *Turn thou us unto thee, O* LORD, *and we shall be turned*: so in the Liturgy of the Church of England, *Turn thou us O good* LORD, *and so shall we be turned* * We cannot turn ourselves;

unless

---

* Some People laugh and jeer at the Terms Converted and Conversion, especially when they hear Conversion insisted upon as necessary for Professors of Christianity. But are not the Church-People profess'd Christians? and yet in the Commination they pray, " *Turn Thou us, O good* LORD, *and so shall we be turned*: Now what is Turn but another Name for Convert? We see then that Conversion is necessary even for Christians. Indeed Profess'd Christians are by Nature no better than Profess'd Heathens. And let Scoffers take care left that

come

unlefs God by his Spirit turns us we fhall never be turned at all. "No Man is effectually
"turned unto God, unlefs the Spirit fpeaks
"unto him, and acts immediately upon him :
"for the Firft Converfion of the Soul unto
"God is from the immediate Influence of the
"Holy Ghoft upon it. This is the fole and
"proper Act of the Spirit, and no outward
"Means and Inftruments are able to do it of
"themfelves."* Some Men have too great and
arduous conceits of the Human Will to allow
this ; they think this Doctrine of Supernatural
and Efficacious Grace robs Man of the Freedom
of his Will, and fo deftroys his Nature. To
this I would reply a few Things : Firft, if it
was true that the freedom of Man's Will was
obftructed in the Work of Converfion, would
he fuftain any real Lofs or Detriment thereby ?
Did not God create Man and put him into this
World without afking the confent of his Will?
And does any Man think God hath done him
any Injuftice, or conceit this World a lefs happy
Place on that Account? Even fo if God is
pleafed to convert a Man without ftanding to
confult or afk Leave of his Will, is that any
Reafon why the Man fhould think the Spiritual
World lefs happy, or his Condition lefs Eligi-

---

come upon them which is fpoken of by our Saviour, *Matth*.
xii. 15. This People's Heart is waxed grofs, and their Ears
are dull of hearing, and their Eyes they have clofed ; left at
any Time they fhould fee with their Eyes, and hear with
their Ears, and fhould underftand with their Hearts, and
fhould be converted, and I fhould heal them.

* *Edwards's* Preacher, Part III.

X   ble?

ble? Yea rather hath he not Reaſon to bleſs God for not leaving him to the Obſtinacy and Perverſeneſs of his Natural Will? We ſee then that the Happineſs of Man will be never the leſs, tho' his Will ſhould be ſuperſeded or overpower'd in Converſion. Secondly, I would aſk, is Peccability ſo deſirable a Thing that we would not be without it? Or ſhould we not rather chooſe to be deliver'd from it? Why then do Men ſo warmly and indefatigably contend for ſo dangerous a Weapon? Do they not remember, do they not conſider, have they not heard, hath it not been told them, that Free-Will in its Pure and Uncorrupted State was a Means of ruining our Firſt Parents and all their Poſterity? Can we expect any Thing better from it, now it is depraved and inclined to Evil only? This Conſideration ought to abate and moderate Men's Zeal in contending for Free-Will in Fallen Man. Thirdly, if by Freedom be meant a Will and Power to ſerve God freely, (and nothing elſe deſerves the Name of Liberty) then we would exhort and perſuade Men by all Means to ſeek after ſuch a Freedom as this: and how ſhall they attain this but by believing in Chriſt? *If the Son ſhall make you free, ye ſhall be free indeed,* but *whoſoever committeth Sin is the Servant of Sin,* John viii. 34, 36. Whence we learn that none are free but thoſe whom the Son of God makes ſo, and that all who are not thus made free are the Servants of Sin; what Trifling and Colluſion is it therefore for Men to talk of Freedom while they are in a ſtate of Nature? They may pro-

miſe

mife themfelves Liberty, but the Word of God informs us *they themfelves are the Servants of Corruption*, 2 Pet. ii. 19. Fourthly, we do not fuppofe that God in converting Men deals with them as Stocks or Stones, he does not take away or deftroy the Will, but only gives it a right Turn; fo faith the Pfalmift, *thy People fhall be Willing in the Day of thy Power*, Pf. cx. 3. The Day of God's Power is the Time when the Spirit comes Purpofely and defignedly to convert Souls; then he makes his People willing, not by taking away any Power the Will had before, but by affording it a Power which it had not. And is this any Violence or Infult upon the Will? Suppofe a Man is fick, and unable to ftand or go, would a Power communicated to fuch a Man to ftand or walk be any Encroachment upon his Will? In like manner our Wills are difordered and unable to will what is Good till God enables them: Now will you fay that an Ability given to make a right Choice is any Invafion or Infringement upon our Volition or Liberty? Is not fuch a Power thus communicated a Cure for our Weaknefs, a Reftoration of our Soul's Health, and an Addition to our Spiritual Eftate? *Hofea* defcribes this Liberty thus, *I drew them with Cords of a Man, with Bands of Love, and I was to them as they that take off the Yoke on their Jaws*, Hof. xi. 4. We fee here God draws *with Cords of a Man, with Bands of Love*, that is, with Motives and Inducements fuitable to the Nature of an Intelligent Spirit, fuch as Man is; and he is moft powerfully

X 2

moved

moved by the Influences of Love, 1 *John* iv. 19. Hence this Divine Attraction or Drawing is said to be with Bands of Love. And when God thus draws Souls, he takes the Yoke off their Jaws, which well denotes that Evil Bias and Tendency whereby the Soul is sway'd to Sin; which when God takes off, the Soul feels itself at Liberty, juft as the Body does when a Yoke of Iron is taken off the Neck, And the Removal of this Spiritual Yoke is no more detriment to Liberty truly fo called, than the Removal of an Iron Yoke from the Body. Take the Suffrage of the Church concerning this Matter in the Tenth Article, " The Condition " of Man after the Fall of *Adam*, is fuch, that " he cannot turn and prepare himfelf by his " own natural ftrength and good Works to " Faith and calling upon God : Wherefore we " have no Power to do good Works, pleafant " and acceptable to God, without the Grace " of God by Chrift preventing us, that we " may have a good Will, and working with " us, when we have that good Will." To which the following Words were added in the Days of *Edward* the VIth, " The Grace of " Chrift or the Holy Ghoft by him given " doth take away the Stony Heart, and giveth " an Heart of Flefh : And altho' thofe that " have no Will to Good Things, he maketh " them to will, and thofe that would Evil " Things, he maketh them not to will, yet " neverthelefs he forceth not the Will."

To return. The Prophet *Ezekiel* fpeaks of this New Birth, Ch. xxxvi. Ver. 26. *A New Heart*

Heart will I also give you, and a New Spirit will I put within you, and I will take away the Stony Heart out of your Flesh, and I will give you an Heart of Flesh: so also Ch. xi. Ver. 19. By the stony Heart is intended the Heart of a Natural Man, which for its Obduracy, Impenetrability and Insensibility of Divine Things, is fitly compared to a Stone. *John* the Baptist calls the Gentiles (and all Natural Men for the same Reason) *Stones*, Matt. iii. 19. And our Saviour uses the same Figure of Speech, *Mark* iv. 5, where he mentions the *stony Ground.* All which may convince us of the suitableness and propriety of this Similitude. This stony Heart God promises to take away, and give instead thereof a new Heart, i. e. a soft, tender and pliant disposition of Soul, quite contrary to our former Obstinacy and Untractableness; a Heart capable of Divine Impressions, submissive to the Divine Will, and Obsequious to the Divine Commands. And observe by what a variety of Names it is called, a New Heart, a New Spirit, an Heart of Flesh, as well to denote the earnestness and sincerity of the Promiser, as the greatness and efficacy of that Power required to execute the Promise, and the compleatness and perfection wherewith it shall be fulfill'd in those Souls who rely upon it. Indeed 'tis well God hath promised to do this great Work, for we cannot do it ourselves; and we could have no Hope of having it done at all, unless the Almighty had engaged to do it. " Look into your " Heart (saith Bishop *Reynolds*) and you shall

X 3

" find

" find a very Hell of Uncleannefs, full of deep
" and unfearchable Deceit and Wickednefs,
" full of Hardnefs: no Sins, no Judgments,
" no Mercies, no Allurements, no Hopes,
" no Fears, no Promifes, no Inftructions,
" able to ftartle, to awaken, to melt or fhape it
" to a better Image, without the immediate
" Omnipotency of that God which melts the
" Mountains, and turns Stones into Sons of
" *Abraham.*"*

Tit. iii. 5. *Not by Works of Righteoufnefs which we have done, but according to his Mercy he faved us, by the Wafhing of Regeneration, and renewing of the Holy Ghoft.* Our own Works of Righteoufnefs are here excluded, and the Mercy of God affigned as the alone Caufe of our Salvation; and the Means hereof are, Firft, Regeneration, which expreffes our Firft being turned to God; and Secondly, the Renewing of our Minds: And both thefe are attributed to the HOLY GHOST as the Efficient thereof. In *Eph.* ii. 1, and *Col.* ii. 12, 13, we are informed that Men are *Dead in Sins,* and fo confequently can no more raife themfelves to Spiritual Life, than a Dead Body can raife itfelf to Natural. Hence this work is afcribed to the Infinite Power of God, the fame Power that raifed Chrift from the Dead, that created the World, and fpoke Light out of Darknefs, 2 *Cor.* iv. 6. And Chrift who is God equal in Power with the Fa-

---

* Sinfulnefs of Sin, p. 140.

ther,

ther undertakes this Work, faying, *the Dead
ſhall hear the Voice of the* SON *of* GOD : *and
they that hear ſhall live*, John v. 25:

But ſome are ready to aſk, if we have no
Power to renew ourſelves and turn unto God,
why are we commanded and exhorted thereto
in Holy Scripture? Doth not this imply that we
have a Power to turn? The Anſwer is twofold;
Firſt, the Exhortations to Regeneration which
we meet with in the New Teſtament, are generally expreſſed paſſively, to teach us that this
is not our own Work, but the Work of God
upon our Souls; thus St. *Paul* doth not ſay to
the Romans, *transform yourſelves*, but *be ye
transformed*, Rom. xii. 2. He doth not ſay
to the Epheſians, *renew yourſelves*, but *be ye
renewed*, Eph. iv. 23. And he doth not ſay,
we renew our Inward Man, 2 Cor. iv. 16,
but the *Inward Man is renewed Day by Day.*
All which ſhews us that we are Paſſive in our
Regeneration. Secondly, hath God commanded,
Waſh ye, make you clean, ceaſe to do evil, Iſa. i.
16? Hath he not alſo promiſed, *I will ſprin-
kle clean Water upon you, and you ſhall be clean*,
Ezek. xxxvi. 25? Hath he commanded, *circumciſe the Foreſkin of your Heart*, Deut. x:
16? Hath he not alſo promiſed, *the* LORD
thy GOD *will circumciſe thine Heart*, Deut.
xxx. 6? So that we ſee what God commands
his People, He himſelf hath promiſed to do
for them and in them : he hath engaged to
work that Regeneration in them which he requires of them : And let them only depend
X 4

upon

upon his Promife, they will find him as good as his Word.

How many great and glorious Privileges accrue to the Children of God upon their Spiritual Regeneration! They are the *Seed of Abraham*, Gal. iii. 29. the *Friends* of CHRIST, John xv. 15 *the Sons of* GOD, John i. 12. Gal. iv. 6. 1 John iii. 1. They do not trace their Pedigree from Kings or Princes, or Temporal Lords, but from GOD, from the KING of Kings, and the LORD of Lords; they are the Sons of God; and if Children, then Heirs, as the Apoftle argues; all Children have their Birth-Right; much more the Children of God: they are *heirs of* GOD, Rom. viii. 17. *heirs of Promife*, Heb. vi. 17. *heirs of Salvation*, Heb. i. 14. Heaven is their *Inheritance*, 1 Pet. i. 4. and they have as much a Right to it as an Heir hath to his Eftate. They have an Unalienable Title to it, becaufe Chrift hath purchafed it for them; and they fhall as furely poffefs it, as Chrift hath died, and now lives in Heaven. When our Lord comes to Judgment, he will invite them to *inherit* (which you fee is a proper Word to be ufed to Heirs who have an Indefeafible Right to a Thing) *the Kingdom prepared for them from the Foundation of the World*, Matt. xxv. 34. and thefe Words we are not to look upon barely as an Invitation, but alfo a Congratulation of their Happinefs. The Regenerate are *Kings, and Priefts unto* GOD, Rev. i. 6. they are *Free of the heavenly Jerufalem*, Gal. iv. 26, 31. Heb. xii. 22, &c. &c.

III. I come

III. I come now in the Third and Laſt Place to ſhew that Faith and Love, &c. are the Fruits of Regeneration. Tho' we are all by Nature Degenerate Plants of a ſtrange Vine, yet Souls that are grafted into Chriſt the True Vine, bring forth good Fruit as naturally as a good Tree doth. The Regenerate are *Partakers of the Divine Nature,* 2 Pet. i. 4. and of *his Holineſs,* Heb. xii. 10. they have the Image of God ſtamped upon their Souls, and *are changed into the ſame Image,* 2 Cor. iii. 18. hence they are *holy in all Manner of Converſation,* 1 Pet. i. 25.——That I may not needleſly puzzle and perplex the Reader, I ſhall only take notice of ſome of thoſe Fruits of Regeneration, which the Scriptures make expreſs mention of; thus, 1 John v. 1.. *Whoſoever believeth that* JESUS *is the* CHRIST *is born of* God; ſo that believing in Chriſt is the Effect of our being born of God, for all True Believers are Regenerate, and all the Regenerate are True Believers: tho' 'tis not People's ſaying they have Faith, but having Chriſt in their Hearts* that denominates them True Believers and Regenerate Perſons. Many, yea moſt who profeſs the Chriſtian Religion, look upon themſelves to be Believers and New-born Souls; if you was to judge by People's profeſſion, you would think there were few Unbelievers in the World; but if you examine into the

---

* *Rom.* x. 10.

Experience

Experience of their Hearts you will find it otherwife, and fee Reafon to conclude that the Number of Real Evangelical Believers is but fmall. Faith is an Affiance of the Soul upon Chrift, a living out of ourfelves upon Chrift Jefus alone for Life and Salvation. This Faith is the peculiar Priviledge of thofe that are born of God, and is accompanied with Love which makes the Evangelift add, *and every one that loveth him that begat, loveth him alfo that is begotten of him*, i. e. he that loveth God will love him that is begotten and born of him, 1 John iii. 14, 16. *Love is of* GOD faith St. John, and GOD *is Love*, 1 John iv. 7, 8, Love is the Univerfal Badge and Chaiacteriftick of Chrift's Difciples; all the Children of God love his Image wherefoever they difcern it, they love freely and difinfereftedly, without Refpect of Perfons or Diftinction of Parties. All Believers in Chrift love one another; all that are born of God are cemented together in the Unity of the Spirit and the Bond of Peace; but where Hatred and Malice reign, fuch Souls are not born of God, but of the Devil.

1 John iii. 9. *Whofoever is born of* GOD *doth not commit Sin*, i. e. doth not commit it wilfully and habitually, as Natural Men do, for the Reader may obferve that he that is born of God is oppofed to the Natural Man mentioned in Ver. 8. where it is faid, *he that committeth Sin is of the Devil*. Regenerate Men may fall into Sin after Regeneration: I fuppofe that St. *Paul* was regenerated, *Acts* ix. yet how did he fall into Inordinate Anger with *Barnabas*, *Acts* xv. 39 ? And

39 ? And how haftily did he fpeak againft the High Prieft, *Acts* xxiii. 3.? which he himfelf acknowledges to be a Crime, Ver. 5.   It is the defire of every Soul that is born again, to be free from Sin; yet if we allow none to be Regenerate but thofe who are perfectly Pure from Sin, where fhall we find a Regenerate Man? Who can fay I have made my Heart clean, I am Pure from Sin? A Chriftian is Perfect, not in himfelf, but in Chrift his Head.   Whofoever looks into himfelf for Perfection, he will never find it.   All our Perfection is in Chrift, and *every Man* who believes is *Perfect in* CHRIST JESUS, as faith the Apoftle, *Col.* i. 28.

Another Effect of the New Birth is Victory over the World, *For whatfoever is born of* GOD *overcometh the World,* 1 John v. 4. and this Victory is gain'd by Faith, as the following Words fhew, *this is the Victory that overcometh the World, even our Faith.*   Faith enables Souls to conquer, Firft, the Pleafures and Allurements of this World; it gives them a View of Heavenly Glories, and then the Trifles and Baubles of this World vanifh and difappear; it gives them a Tafte of Spiritual Joys, and then the Pleafures of Flefh and Senfe become Flat and Infipid.   Men do not love to drink Water when they have once tafted Wine. What a flur did our Bleffed Lord caft on all Human Glory and Grandeur when he refufed to be made a King?   And how glorioufly did his Servant *Mofes* defpife the World, and trample on the Magnificence of a Court, when he refufed to be called the Son of *Pharaoh*'s

Daugther,

Daughter, and chofe rather to endure Afflictions with the People of God, than to enjoy
the Pleafures of Sin for a feafon? And what an
admirable Example of Faith was *Abraham*,
who followed God into an Unknown Land,
when he might have lived at Home at Eafe,
and inherited his Father's Eftate? Secondly, by
Faith Chriftians overcome the Croffes, Afflictions, and Perfecutions of the World; thus the
Pfalmift in defcribing a Godly Man faith, *he
fhall not be afraid of Evil Tidings*, and the
Reafon hereof is immediately render'd, *his
Heart is Fixed, trufting in the* LORD, Pf. cxii.
Ver. 7. How victorioufly doth St. *Paul* tri-
umph over Tribulation, Perfecution, Diftrefs,
Famine, Nakednefs, Peril, Sword, &c.?——
What a world of Trials and Afflictions did the
Believers mention'd *Heb.* ix. undergo? And
how did the Primitive Chriftians endure Racks,
Stakes, Fire, Sword, Danger and Death, in
every fhape? Laftly, the Regeneráte live above
the Cares of the World; they take no Thought
for Life, or Food, or Raiment; they are not like
Martha, troubled about many Things, but with
Mary, they choofe that good Part which fhall
not be taken from them; they are careful for
nothing, but in every Thing by Prayer and
Supplication, with Thankfgiving, make known
their Requefts to God; they caft all their
Care upon him that careth for them; their
Will is refigned to his Will; they live upon
his Promifes, they truft in his Providences, and
are fatisfied with all his Difpenfations. They
blefs God in Profperity, they glory in Tribulation,

tion, they blefs God for all Things. And while Worldlings murmur and repine at Loffes, Troubles and Difappointments, they are glad they have any thing to give to God, they are glad they have any thing to lofe for God, and always cry out from the Ground of their Hearts, *the* LORD *gave, and the* LORD *hath taken away; bleffed be the Name of the* LORD.

Another, and the laft Effect I fhall at prefent enumerate, is a Love and Defire of God's Word, thus faith St. *Peter* the Apoftle of our Lord 1 Epiftle ii. 2, *As New-born Babes defire the Sincere Milk of the Word.* Chrift's Difciples are called New-born Babes becaufe of their Impotence and Helplefsnefs, and becaufe they are born into a World of New Trials and Troubles wherewith Natural Men are entirely unacquainted. The Word is called Milk, becaufe as Milk nourifhes Babes born after the Flefh, fo the Word of God nourifhes Souls born after the Spirit; it is called Sincere Milk becaufe of its Purity, and to diftinguifh it from the Doctrines and Traditions of Men, which are Corrupt, Fictitious and Counterfeit. This Sincere Milk New-born Babes defire as naturally, and covet as greedily as Infants do their Mother's Milk; and the End hereof is that they may grow thereby. Natural Infants do not grow unlefs they are conftantly fupply'd with the Breaft, no more do Spiritual Babes unlefs they are fed with the Food of God's Word. As little Children cannot live without their Mother's Milk, fo neither can the Children of God live, but they grow fick and languifh, if they have not

the

the fincere Milk of the Word frequently adminiftered unto them.   The Apoftle adds, (as the
Learned Dr. *Edwards* * takes Notice) " That
" they will not fail to defire this fincere Milk
" of the Word, which yields folid and proper
" Nourifhment for their Souls, *if they have*
" *tafted that the* LORD *is Gracious*, that is,
" they having had an Experimental Know-
" ledge of the Tender Love of Chrift to Sin-
" ners, namely to themfelves, they having felt
" the particular Goodnefs and Grace of God
" in changing and renewing their Hearts, they
" cannot but paffionately long for and breathe
" after this Spiritual Food and Nourifhment."
⁂ If Faith and Love and Victory over the World
are the Effects of Regeneration, then thofe who
do not bring forth thefe Fruits are not Regenerate.   *Every Good Tree bringeth forth Good*
Fruit, faith our Saviour : But if the Tree doth
not bring forth Good Fruit, how doth it appear
to be Good ?   And if Men do not exhibit the
proper Evidences of Regeneration in their Lives,
how doth it appear to others that their Hearts
are Regenerate ?   And pleafe to obferve, our
Lord doth not fay the Tree which bringeth
forth Bad Fruit; but *every Tree that bringeth*
not forth Good Fruit is hewn down and caft into
the Fire, Mat. vii. 19. Not only Trees that
yield corrupt Fruit, but they that yield no Fruit

----

* See his Hearer.

alſo ſhall be caſt into Hell Fire: *Every Branch in me that beareth not Fruit he taketh away,* John xv. 2. As our Saviour ſaith to the *Jews, If ye were Abraham's Children, ye would do the Works of Abraham,* John viii. 39. So we may ſay, if ye were born of the Spirit, ye would abound in the Fruits of the Spirit; now the Fruits of the Spirit are *Love, Joy, Peace, Long-ſuffering, Gentleneſs, Goodneſs, Faith, Meekneſs, Temperance.* If you have not theſe Fruits, and eſpecially, and above all, Faith in Chriſt, in vain do you pretend to be Regenerate. Where the Heart is internally renovated, the Life will be externally reformed; where the Inward Work really is, the Outward Work will follow. There may be an Outward Reformation without an Inward Regeneration, but there cannot be an Inward Regeneration without an Outward Reformation. How is it with your Soul? Do you Love all who Love God? Have you put off the Old Man and put on the New? Is your Converſation in Heaven? Do you walk as a Child of Light? Have you Chriſt in you the Hope of Glory? A Man may go a great way in Religion, and yet be Unregenerate: Yea, the Unregenerate frequently go farther in Externals than the Regenerate; but their Souls are Dead for want of Chriſt, and a Living Faith in him, All who are born of the Spirit believe in Chriſt. Chriſt is the Life of the Soul, juſt as the Soul is the Life of the Body; and the Soul is as Dead without Chriſt, as the Body is without the Soul. Hence Chriſt is called our *Life,* Col. iii, 4. And

iii. 4.   And *he that hath the Son hath Life,* 1 John v. 12.   *He that believeth is born of* God,   1 John v. 1.   fo that if you believe in Chrift, you need never queftion your Regeneration.   Therefore rejoice in Chrift Jefus, make him your all;   extol him highly, and give him all Honour and Praife.———

Though Thoufands of Doubts and Fears circulate around you, let none of them fettle upon you;   but drive them all away, as *Abraham* drove away the Fowls from the Carcafes, *Gen.* xv. 11.   No more doubt of your Second Birth than of your Firft.   This Faith in Chrift is the Beginning of the Gofpel in the Heart;   'tis Heaven in Miniature, and will dilate itfelf into all the Fullnefs of the Glory of the Eternal State.

A

DISCOURSE

ON

MARK v. 36.———*Only believe.*

AS *Mark* the Evangelift, the bleffed Author of this Gofpel, was not one of the
Twelve Apoftles, many have thought that he
wrote his Gofpel under the Care and Infpection
of *Peter*, who revifed and corrected it for him;
and fo it was received as authentic in the Church
of GOD. But this Conjecture feems as need-
lefs and infignificant as it is groundlefs and pre-
carious. For fince we are certain, that he was
infpired by the SPIRIT of the LORD JESUS,
and fpake and wrote (as alfo did the other Prophets and Evangelifts) *as he was moved by the*
HOLY GHOST, this is a fufficient Recommen-
dation of this Gofpel to all fincere Chriftians,
and a Reafon good enough to induce us to look
upon it as Infallible and Divine, as well as any
other Part of the Holy Scriptures.

Y

Some

Some are of Opinion that the Penman of this Gospel was a Jew born, and that his Name was *Mardocai*, but after he was converted to the Faith of CHRIST, his Name was changed from a *Hebrew* to a *Roman*, and accordingly he was surnamed *Mark*, Acts xv. 37. So likewise the Apostle *Paul* before his Conversion was called *Saul*, but afterwards he had the *Roman* Name of *Paul* given unto him. When Persons Hearts are [changed, 'tis well; when they are *turned from Darkness to Light, and from the Power of Satan unto* GOD, then they may change their Names from Heathens to Christians, or from Infidels to Believers. But otherwise for People to turn from one Church to another, or to exchange one Denomination for another, and so think themselves Religious upon that Account, is the greatest Folly and Self-Deceit.

But to consider the Text. *There cometh one of the Rulers of the Synagogue, Jairus by Name, and when he saw him,* [JESUS] *he fell at his Feet, and besought him greatly, saying, my little Daughter lieth at the Point of Death, I pray thee come, and lay thy Hands on her, that she may be healed, and she shall live. And* JESUS *went with him.*——And as our LORD was going, *there came from the Ruler of the Synagogue's House certain which said, thy Daughter is dead; why troublest thou the Master any further? As soon as* JESUS *heard the Word that was spoken, he saith unto the Ruler of the Synagogue, be not afraid, only believe.* Our SAVIOUR saw *Jairus* begun to be frighted at the Tidings of his Daughter's Death, therefore he says to him, *only believe.*

And

And this is written for our Benefit and Inftruction.   Our SAVIOUR preaches the fame Doctrine to us that he did to the Ruler of the Synagogue. He bids us *only believe*, and fo we pafs
from Spiritual Death to Spiritual Life, as *Jairus*'s Daughter was reftored to Natural Life.

Only believe: What a Divine Aphorifm is
this ! And how much do thefe Words contain !
Herein (as is ufual in Scripture) much is exprefs'd in a fhort Compafs.   This is an Evangelical Proverb.   This is the Chriftian's Motto.
And altho' this Sentence is but very concife,
yet it is very comprehenfive : For thefe Two
Words contain the Sum and Subftance of the
Gofpel; they briefly fet before us the true Way
of Salvation, and let us know that we poffefs
all Spiritual bleffings by believing in Chrift.   I
propofe therefore to fhew,

I. What it is to *believe*.

II. To confider the exclufive Adverb *only*. And

III. I fhall make fuch an Application as the
   Lord enables me.

I. What is it to believe? When our Saviour
was juft afcending to his GOD and our GOD,
to his Father and our Father, he commanded
his Apoftles, *Go ye into all the World, and
preach the Gofpel to every Creature*, Mark xvi.
15. and Luke xxiv. 46, 47. *It behoved* CHRIST
*to fuffer, and to rife from the Dead, and that
Repentance and Remiffion of Sins fhould be preached*

in his Name, among all Nations. Christ Jesus *came into the World to fave Sinners,* 1 Tim. i. 15. This is the Gofpel, and he that *believes* it *in his Heart fhall be faved,* Rom: x. 10. Mark xvi. 16. Tho' Salvation is fo Free, yet how unwilling and backward are Sinners to accept it? How few receive this Gofpel into their Hearts? Infomuch that the Prophet complains, *who hath believed our Report? And to whom is the Arm of the* Lord *revealed?* And fo 'tis in our Day; tho' we tell Sinners that Chrift died for them, and this Report tends fo much to their Comfort and Happinefs, yet but few *receive our Teftimony,* John iii. 32. and in them is the Arm of the Lord revealed.

As the Holy Spirit takes of the Things of Chrift, and fhews them unto the Soul, fo he gives us Power to believe, and by believing we apply them to our own Hearts. Faith is the Application. By Faith we apply the Blood and Righteoufnefs of Chrift to ourfelves, and fo we are faved. And indeed what is all the Salvation of the Gofpel to us, unlefs by Faith we embrace it, and appropriate it for our own? We fee *the Word preached did not profit* the Jews, *becaufe it was not mixed with Faith in them that heard it,* Heb. iv. 2. Even fo neither will the Word of the Gofpel profit us, unlefs we by Faith receive it, and clofe in with Jefus under the Miniftration of it. There muft be a clofe Application of Chrift's Heart's Blood to our own Hearts, and of his Righteoufnefs to our own Souls by Faith, elfe all our Religion is vain. The Pfalmift *David* was well ac‐
quainted

quainted with this, and therefore he prays, *Purge me with Hyſſop, and I ſhall be clean*, Pſalm li. 7. Hyſſop was made uſe of in ſprinkling the Blood of Birds and Beaſts under the Old Teſtament,* and Faith is the Means or Inſtrument which GOD is pleaſed to make uſe of in ſprinkling our Hearts with the Blood of Jeſus. Accordingly thoſe who believe have their *Hearts ſprinkled from an Evil Conſcience, and their Bodies Waſh'd with pure Water*, Heb. x. 22. ix. 14.

All our Happineſs conſiſts in believing in Chriſt. By Faith we have an Application and Poſſeſſion of Chriſt. As it is with the Body, ſo is it with the Soul: the good Things of this Life do our Bodies no ſervice unleſs they are applied, ſo neither do the Bleſſings of the Goſpel make our Souls Happy without a Saving Application of them. As our Food does not nouriſh us, unleſs we eat it, ſo except we by Faith *eat the Fleſh and drink the Blood of the Son of Man, we have no Life in us*, John vi. 53. As a Medicine will never cure a Sick Man, unleſs he takes it, ſo neither will the Medicine of Chriſt's Blood cure the Plague of Sin in our Souls, unleſs we receive it by Faith. And laſtly, as our Cloaths will not ſcreen us from the Severity of the Wind and Weather, unleſs we put them on, ſo in like Manner the Robe of Chriſt's Righteouſneſs will not ſcreen us

---

* Lev. xiv. 6. Heb. ix. 19. Exod. xxiv. 8.

from

from the juſt Judgment of GOD, unleſs by Faith we put on this Raiment. Therefore ſaith the Apoſtle, *Put ye on the* LORD JESUS CHRIST, Rom. xiii. 14. The Chriſtian Religion is founded in an Application of Chriſt. The Chriſtian Faith is an Applicatory Faith. Accordingly the Scriptures deſcribe Faith by coming to Chriſt, receiving him, leaning upon him, relying upon him, rolling on him, reſting in him, &c. All which Terms I need not particularly inſiſt upon now, becauſe I have explained them elſewhere.* But theſe Terms denote applying Chriſt by Faith, in which Application conſiſts a Chriſtian's preſent Happineſs, and this is alſo the Fore-runner of Eternal Glory.

The *Greek* Writers frequently ſet forth Saving Faith by a Word which ſignifies in Engliſh to appropriate, or make a thing our own. For by Faith we make GOD our own GOD, therefore ſaith the Pſalmiſt, GOD, *even our own* GOD, *ſhall bleſs us*, Pſalm lxvii. 6. An Unbeliever may ſay there is a GOD, and may call him Lord or God; but 'tis the Language of Faith only to ſay, *my* LORD *and my* GOD, John xx. 28. An Heathen or Infidel can talk of an Abſolute God, or a God out of Chriſt, but 'tis the Chriſtian only who knows that GOD *was in* CHRIST *reconciling the*

---

* Marrow of the Church, Part I. p. 68, 69, &c. And Part II. p. 29.

World

World unto himself, 2 Cor. v. 19. A Believer speaks the Language of Appropriation and Possession. Thus Cant. ii. 16, *My Beloved is mine, and I am his*; and so again Chap. v. Ver. 16. *This is my Beloved, and this is my Friend.* *Job* also speaketh the same Language, *I know that my Redeemer liveth*, Job xix. 25. So saith *Paul* the Apostle, *who* [CHRIST] *loved me, and gave himself for me*, Gal. ii. 20. And 2 Tim. iv. 8. *Henceforth is laid up for me a Crown of Righteousness.* The Possessives *my* and *me* sweeten all. For what is God to me, unless he is my God? God out of Christ is a *Consuming Fire*, Heb. xii. 29. And it would be better for me if there was no God at all, than that he should not be my God, reconciled in and thro' Christ Jesus. It is the Privilege of a Faithful Soul to know that God is his, and Christ is his. And a Person is truly happy when he reads the Scriptures and sees all that Christ hath purchased for Sinners by his Blood, and doubts not, but believes, and by Faith applies all the Blessings, Promises and Privileges of the Childrrn of God to his own Soul. How is a Christian then transported with the amazing View of the Grace of God in Christ? And what solid Joy does then overflow his Heart? Faith in Christ interests us in all that Christ did and suffer'd The Heart of a Believer is fixed on Christ, and the Language of his Soul is, " Christ loved me and gave himself for me; " he lived for me, he died for me, he rose again " for me, and he is now interceding for me, " at the Right-hand of God. All that Christ

Y 4

" did

" did, he did for me ; all that he fuffer'd, he
" fuffer'd for me, and for my Eternal Salva-
" tion." Can you fpeak thus, and fpeak the
Truth? Are you affur'd that Chrift loves you?
Yea, why fhould you doubt it? *Only believe*
that Chrift loves you, and you will find it really
True that he does love you. If indeed ye have
believed with the Heart unto Righteoufnefs,
then make Confeffion with the Mouth unto
Salvation.

II. We are next to confider the Meaning of
the Exclufive Adverb *only*. And this, indeed,
mightily exalts the Grace of Chrift, and teaches
us that we receive all Spiritual Gifts and Evangelical Mercies by believing in him. Tho' in
ourfelves we have nothing but Sin and Mifery,
yet in Chrift we *poffefs all things*, 2 Cor. vi. 10.
Whatfoever therefore you want, come to our
Saviour, and he will give it you: *only believe*
in him, and you have a *fupply of all your Need
according to* God's *Riches in Glory by* CHRIST
JESUS, Phil. iv. 19.
Do you want Forgivenefs of your Sins?
Only believe, and your Sins are forgiven. *The
Son of Man hath Power on Earth to forgive Sins,*
Matt. ix. 6. *Whofoever believeth in him fhall
receive Remiffion of Sins,* Acts x. 43. *Thro'
this Man is preached unto you the Forgivenefs of
Sins, and by him all that believe are juftified from
all Things, from which ye could not be juftified by
the Law of Mofes,* Acts xiii. 38, 39. Our
Saviour kindly invites Sinners unto him, and
promifes

promises them, *tho' your Sins be as Scarlet, they shall be white as Snow; tho' they be red like Crimson, they shall be as Wool,* Isa. i: 18. And the Lord Jesus declares, *I, even I am he that blotteth out thy Transgressions for mine own sake,* Isa. xliii. 25. and Ch. xliv. 22, *I have blotted out as a thick Cloud thy Transgressions, and as a Cloud thy Sins;* tho' your Sins are as many as the Watry Particles that make a Cloud, yet if you *only believe* in Jesus, he will blot them every one out. As Clouds and Vapours are disperfed, and vanish when the Morning Sun arises; so when Jesus, the Sun of Righteousnefs, shines upon the Soul, all our Sins are obliterated, and our Transgreffions erased. Our Dear Lord gives another Gracious Promise to this Purpose, Heb. viii. 12, *I will be merciful to their Unrighteousnefs, and their Sins and their Iniquities will I remember no more.* When we believe in Christ, our Sins are all pardoned; the Lord remembers them no more; he as it were forgets them, so that they shall never rise up in Judgment againft us; they shall be as tho' they had never been; they shall be no more imputed to us, than if we had never committed them. O Blessed Saviour, *Who is a* God *like unto thee, that pardoneth Iniquity, and passeth by the Transgression of the Remnant of his Heritage? He retaineth not his Anger for ever, because he delighteth in Mercy. He will turn again, he will have Compaffion upon us: he will subdue our Iniquities: and thou wilt caft all their Sins into the Depths of the Sea,* Micah vii. 18, 19. As if a Man takes a Milftone and cafts it into

the

the Sea, the Stone finks to the Bottom, and
rifes up no more; fo God takes all our Sins,
and cafts them into the depths of the Sea of
Chrift's Blood; there they fink, they are
drown'd, they are feen no more, they are remember'd no more againft us for ever. Thus,
my dear Brethren, fhall your Sins be wafhed
away if ye believe in the Son of God. This is
a fhort Way, and a fure one; and the Grace
of Chrift makes it Eafy. All other Methods
that you take to obtain Forgivenefs of your
Sins will prove Vain and Fruitlefs; but Faith
in Chrift is an Effectual Method to purge away
the Guilt and deftroy the Power of Sin. This
is a Way that never failed any who trufted in
it. Only make the Proof of it, and you will
find the Efficacy and Excellency of it. Believe in Chrift, and all your Sins from firft to
laft, from the greateft to the leaft, fhall be pardoned and done away.

Again, if you are feeking after Righteoufnefs, the only Way to attain it is to believe in
Chrift. What is all your own Righteoufnefs?
It is all Filthy Rags, and a very Unclean
Thing: therefore away with it. When you
have ufed your beft Endeavours, when you
have done all you can, and that too with the
utmoft Sincerity, yet you can never be juftified
by your own Good Works and Obedience to
the Law. How then muft we be juftified?
Why, Chrift fulfilled every Precept of the Law
for you, and by his Obedience you are juftified. All Chrift's Righteoufnefs fhall be imputed to you if you believe. This is the
Righ-

Righteoufnefs of Faith, Phil. iii. 9. Come to Chrift, and this Righteoufnefs is your own. O how do Self-righteous Perfons grieve Chrift by trufting to their own Righteoufnefs! Indeed this is an abomination in the Sight of God. For Self-righteoufnefs is the greateft Evil under the Sun. They who are Righteous in their own Eyes, are greater Enemies to Chrift than Drunkards, Swearers and Whoremongers; which makes our Saviour tell the Pharifees, *the Publicans and Harlots* go *into the Kingdom of* God *before you*, Matt. xxi. 31. Indeed when we tell Sober, Moral People, that they are as bad by Nature as Profligates, Debauchees, and the groffeft Sinners, it feems to them a hard faying, and immediately they are offended. Then they begin to vindicate themfelves. But when they tell us how good they have been, we can't bear to hear it; when they tell us what Virtuous Lives they have lived, we reply that they are building upon the Sand; when they fpeak how Sincere and how Righteous they are, we trample all their Righteoufnefs under our Feet, and confefs that we know no Righteoufnefs that will avail to Salvation, but the Righteoufnefs of Chrift. So they go away forrowful, becaufe they have large Poffeffions of Self-righteoufnefs; and they have laid up Treafures of Good Works in ftore for many Years: all this they are loth to part with; fo they perifh in trufting to their own Good Works of Righteoufnefs. But Sinners who have lived in all Manner of Outward Sin and Wickednefs, are glad to hear of the Righteouf-

nefs

nefs of Chrift, becaufe hereby they fee a Door
of Salvation open'd to their Souls, whereas before they thought they were abandon'd to Defpair, and configned to Eternal Deftruction.
Then they flee to the Righteoufnefs of Chrift,
they put their Truft therein, and are faved.
" What fhall we fay then ? That the Gentiles
which followed not after Righteoufnefs have
attained no Righteoufnefs, even the Righteoufnefs which is of Faith; but Ifrael which followed after the Law of Righteoufnefs, hath
not attained to the Law of Righteoufnefs.
Wherefore ? Becaufe they fought it not by
Faith, but as it were by the Works of the Law,
Rom. ix. 30, 31, 32.

Further, do you complain how Unholy you
are ? Do you want to be perfectly Holy ? Then
believe in Chrift, and in him you poffefs a complete Holinefs. As we have no Righteoufnefs
in us by Nature, fo neither have we any Holinefs in us by Nature; but we are beholden to
Chrift for both thefe. He is made to us of
God both Righteoufnefs and Sanctification, 1
Cor. i. 30. As by Chrift's Righteoufnefs we
are made Righteous, fo by his Holinefs we are
made holy. This I have fhew'd in a Difcourfe
I lately publifh'd on *Heb.* xii. 14. I only here
obferve that Self-holy People may defpife this
Way of Gofpel Holinefs and Sanctification;
but Souls who can fee no Holinefs in themfelves
will rejoice to hear of Chrift their Holinefs.
This will be welcome News to them, and they
will greedily embrace it. This Doctrine of
Evangelical Holinefs is fuch a Myftery, that
Carnal

Carnal Reasoners are stumbled at it. Indeed it is above the Comprehension of Natural Reason: if we go to reason about it, we are presently at a Loss, and we bring ourselves into Bondage; but if we heartily believe it we are Happy.

Lastly, by believing in Christ we obtain Everlasting Life and Happiness. So saith our Saviour, " he that believeth on him that sent me hath Everlasting Life," *John* v. 24. " He that believeth and is baptized shall be saved," *Mark* xvi. 16. " Whosoever believeth in him shall not be confounded," 1 *Pet.* ii. 6. " For whosoever shall call upon the Name of the Lord shall be saved," *Rom.* x. 13. So that we are saved not by working but by believing. " For the Lord will finish the Work and cut it short in Righteousness: because a short Work will the Lord make upon the Earth," *Rom.* ix. 28. Those " who had borne the Heat and Burden of the Day received every Man a Penny, and those who enter'd into the Vineyard at the Eleventh Hour, received every Man a Penny," *Matt.* xx. 1 — 16. If ye believe in Christ at the Eleventh Hour, you shall be saved; witness the Thief upon the Cross. If the Penny, i. e. Salvation, was conferr'd on us for our Works, then those who had borne the Heat and Burden of the Day should have receiv'd most, but we see they receiv'd no more than a Penny. For the Reward is not of Debt, but of Grace; " therefore it is of Faith, that it might be by Grace, to the end the Promise might be sure to all the Seed, not to that only which is of the Law, but to that also which is of the Faith of

Abraham,

Abraham, who is the Father of us, all." *Rom.* iv. 16.

III. I come now in the Third Place to make fome Application : and O, may the Spirit of the Lord apply the Word to your Hearts! You fee then, Brethren, there is a Fulnefs in Chrift to fupply all your Wants. By believing in Jefus you have Free Forgivenefs of Sins, a Juftifying Righteoufnefs, Evangelical Holinfs, and Eternal Salvation. Therefore *only believe*. But fome are ready to afk, " muft we not do Good " Works ?" But I would afk again, what Good Works can you do ? " But then muft we " not attend all the Ordinances ?" Our Saviour fays, *only believe*. " But muft we not " keep the Commandments of God ?" I anfwer, this is his " Commandment that we believe on the Name of his Son Jefus Chrift," 1 *John* iii. 23. " Is Salvation then only by be-" lieving ?" *Only believe*. " An Eafy Way of " Salvation Indeed !" Is it fo ? Then why don't you comply with it ? How comes it to be fo hard to you ? " If this was the Way, it " would not be Hard to me ; for I do believe." But what do you believe ? It may be you believe the Scriptures to be True, and you believe that Jefus is the Son of God. " Thou doft well, the Devils alfo believe and tremble," *James* ii. 19. Do you believe that Chrift hath forgiven you all your Sins and Trefpaffes ? *Col.* ii. 13. If not, your Faith is Vain ; and all your Pretenfions to Chriftianity are Groundlefs: you talk of Faith and believing, and know

nothing

nothing of the Matter. Indeed unless you believe Chrift hath forgiven your Sins, you do not believe to any Saving Purpofe. Believe in Jefus, and then you will know what Faith is, and you will have Forgivenefs of Sins, and enjoy all the Benefits of the Gofpel. As for you who do believe, happy are ye; only continue believing in Chrift, and you will be continually happy. Unbelief is the Caufe of all our Mifery. When Souls have an Unfhaken Faith in our Saviour, they are truly Bleffed, but when they begin to waver and difbelieve, they then become Miferable; have you not found it fo by Experience? Therefore take our Saviour's Counfel, *Continue ye in my Love*, John xv. 9.

Have your Eye upon Chrift, mind nothing but him alone; believe in him at all times. Are you befet with many Temptations? Do not ftrive to deliver yourfelf out of one; *only believe*, and Chrift will deliver you out of all. How often have you by attempting to make Things better, made them worfe, and so increafed your Burden inftead of leffening it? But when you have left all in the Lord's Hand you have always found that he hath order'd all for Good. There hath no Temptation befallen you, but what befel Chrift before yon: " He was in all Points tempted like as we are, yet without Sin. Let us therefore come boldly unto the Throne of Grace, that we may obtain Mercy and find Grace to help in Time of Need. For in that he himfelf hath fuffer'd being tempted, he is able to fuccour them that are tempted," *Heb.* ii. 18. iv. 15, 16.

Again,

Again, are you in Darkneſs or Diſtreſs of Soul? *Truſt in the* LORD *and ſtay upon your* GOD, Iſa. l. 10. Do not hurry here or there; do not go to do this Thing or another; for then you will only add to your Sorrow and aggravate your Miſery. *Only believe.* " Stand ſtill to ſee the Salvation of the Lord: Your ſtrength is to ſit ſtill. In returning and reſt ſhall ye be ſaved, in Quietneſs and in Confidence ſhall be your ſtrength," *Exod.* xiv. 13. *Iſa.* xxx. 7. 15.

To conclude: *Only believe:* This is all you have to do in order to Eternal Happineſs. Believe in Chriſt in every circumſtance and condition. Are you in Sickneſs? *only believe*; and Chriſt will reſtore your Health. Are you in Pain? *only believe*; and Chriſt will give you Eaſe. Are you in Heavineſs? *only believe*; and Chriſt will turn your Heavineſs into Joy, and cloath you with Gladneſs. In ſhort, believe in Jeſus in all Trials, Troubles, Dangers and Afflictions. Believe in him in Life and in Death: believe in him to the End of Time, and you ſhall ſee his Face to all Eternity: which may the Lord Jeſus, the King of Kings and Lord of Lords, be pleas'd to grant, for his Infinite Mercies Sake. Amen.

NOTES

N O T E S

ON THE

S E R M O N,

"*ONLY BELIEVE.*"

Page 274. *For People to turn from one Church to another, or to exchange one denomination for another, and so think themselves religious on that account, is the greatest folly and self-deceit.*——— I would obferve, on the other hand, that to be determined, at all events, to ftick to that Religion to which we were brought up, without knowing why or wherefore, betrays the groffeft ignorance and prejudice. In this moft important of all concerns, —— examine for yourfelves, —— prove all things——take no Man's word, but fearch the Scriptures for yourfelves. How many cautions to this purpofe do we find in the word of God? Our Lord fays, " Call no Man Mafter; beware of falfe Prophets." St. John tells us to " try the Spirits, whether they be of God, for many falfe Prophets are gone out into the world." There is fuch a thing as Truth,——there is fuch a thing as coming to the knowledge of the truth; and the effect of that knowledge will be liberty, or freedom of Soul. Ye fhall know the truth, and the truth fhall make ye free. Is there fuch a knowledge? How can this knowledge be attained? I anfwer, 'tis the gift of God. He hath given us an underftanding, St. John fays, to know him that is true. If any Man lack wifdom, let him afk of God, for every good and perfect gift is from him.

Z

Page 276. He gives us power to believe.---It is not only the work of the Spirit to reveal Chrift, by taking of the things of Jefus and fhewing them to us, but it is likewife the work of the fame Spirit to enable us to receive him; for no Man can receive thefe fayings fave thofe to whom it is given. If the Spirit reveals Chrift, and enables the Soul to receive him, is not Faith then, as St. Paul fays, an evidence.

Page 279. A Believer fpeaks the language of appropriation, or poffeffion.----It is the comfortable fatisfaction I feel in my own Soul that Chrift loved me, and gave himfelf for me, that alone can draw my affections off from Self and the World, and fix them upon that glorious and bleffed object, the Lord Jefus Chrift, in the knowledge and enjoyment of whom my heaven and happinefs entirely confifts.

Page 280. The exclufive adverb, Only. ---What ftrange miftaken notions do Men form of the Doctrine of Juftification by Faith alone, without works! Oh, fay they, what a licentious Doctrine! No matter what Men do, nor how they live, if they only believe they fhall be fure to go to Heaven. It is a bleffed faying which dropped from the lips of Truth, " He that believeth fhall be faved." But to fay that the Doctrine of Juftification by Faith alone, is a licentious Doctrine, is as vile a falfhood as ever was uttered by the Father of lies. What purifies the Heart? Faith. What faves from the guilt and power of Sin? Faith. What gives us the victory over the World? Faith. What makes us love God? Faith. What makes us hate Sin? Faith, and nothing but Faith. Without Faith it is impoffible to pleafe God. Only by believing we receive all Spiritual gifts and Evangelical mercies; but having received thefe, we are made free from Sin, and become Servants to God; we have our fruit unto holinefs, and the end everlafting Life. Woe be to them that call evil good, and good evil. Take heed how you fpeak evil of thofe things which you underftand not. If you are enabled to believe to the faving of your Souls, and have the witnefs within you, that you are a Child of God, (for he that believeth hath the witnefs in himfelf, the Spirit bearing witnefs with his fpirit that he is a Child of God) then you will find and feel that it is only by believing you can be either holy or happy.

A DISCOURSE

A

D I S C O U R S E

O N

G A L. iii. 24, 25.

The Law was our Schoolmafter to bring us unto Christ, *that we might be juftified by Faith. But after that Faith is come, we are no longer under a Schoolmafter.*

WHAT comfortable News is this! Efpecially to Souls who have been long exercifed with the fevere Rigour and Difcipline of the Law. Did *Ifrael* rejoice at their Deliverance out of the Land of *Egypt*, out of the Houfe of Bondage? How much more do poor Sinners rejoice, when they are delivered from Spiritual Captivity? Is not Spiritual Liberty infinitely Preferable to Temporal? If the Son of God makes you Free, ye fhall be Free indeed. All who are under the Law are in Bondage. "But now we are delivered from the Law," *Rom.* vii. 6. And this Deliverance from the Law is our Peculiar Freedom and Happinefs. O Sinners, do not your Hearts rejoice

joice

joice in hearing of this Glorious Liberty? Indeed my Soul delights in thinking and speaking of it.

How naturally are Men wedded to the Law! Tho' the Law condemns them, yet they are so Blind as to seek Life by it. All are born under the Covenant of Works, and they think to go to Heaven by keeping it, till the Lord Jesus shews them a more Excellent Way. Yea, we are all possess'd of so Legal a Spirit, and so deeply is the Old Covenant rooted in our Nature, that even in Christians we may frequently discern some Relicts of it. Those who have once tasted the Grace of Christ, do again gender to Bondage, and look back to the Law; " because they have cast off their First Faith, and left their First Love," 1 *Tim.* v. 12. *Rev.* ii. 4. This we may observe in ourselves; this we may observe in others; but of this we cannot have a more signal Proof than in the Instance of the Churches of *Galatia*, to whom this Epistle is directed.

The Apostle *Paul* preached the Gospel from *Jerusalem* to *Illyricum*, *Rom.* xv. 19. And if he was not the First Minister that preached the Kingdom of God in the Region of *Galatia*, yet " he went all over the Country of *Galatia* and *Phrygia* in order, strengthening all the Disciples," *Acts* xviii. 23. But by what the Apostle says in the Fourth Chapter of this Epistle, it seems as if he himself was the First Preacher of Christ among the *Galatians.*— " Through Infirmity of the Flesh (saith he) I preached the Gospel unto you at the first. And

as

as People generally like their Preachers beſt at firſt, ſo it was with the *Galatians*; they had a very high Eſteem and Veneration for the Apoſtle, " They received him as an Angel of God, even as Chriſt Jeſus." They lov'd him ſo heartily, " that if it had been poſſible, they would have plucked out their own Eyes, and have given them unto him." The Apoſtle declares, " the Goſpel which was preached of me is not after Man; for I neither receiv'd it of Man, neither was I taught it, but by the Revelation of Jeſus Chriſt." This Goſpel they embraced, they " did run well," they " begun in the Spirit; and Jeſus Chriſt had been evidently ſet forth crucified among them."

Now where God works, the Devil will work: Where the Lord Jeſus ſows the Good Seed, there the Devil will be ſure to ſow Tares. So it hath been, and ſo it will be in all Ages of the Church. Satan therefore ſeeing the ſucceſs of the Goſpel in *Galatia*, and envying the Happineſs of the Souls who received the Truth as it is in Jeſus, ſoon rais'd up ſome of his Emiſſaries to trouble the Diſciples, and to pervert the Goſpel of Chriſt. Judaizing Teachers came in like a Flood; they preached in *Galatia* the ſame Doctrine as at *Antioch*, " Except ye be circumciſed, and keep the Law of Moſes, ye cannot be ſaved," *Acts* xv. 1, 5. Theſe Preachers had more Reaſon than Faith; They had more Philoſophy in their Heads than Chriſtianity in their Hearts; and ſo they added *Moſes* to Chriſt, corrupted the Doctrine of Juſtification, jumbled Law and Goſpel together, and
Z 3
con

confounded the Covenant of Works with the Covenant of Grace. Hence Great Confusion follow'd in the Churches. The Souls of the simple were subverted. Their Affection for the Apostle and his Doctrine was lessen'd; they were ready to look upon him as their Enemy, *Gal.* iv. 16. They were again " entangled with the Yoke of Bondage," *Chap.* v. 1. and removed to " another Gospel," *Ch.* i. 6. Hence the Apostle, out of the Fulness of his Heart, sends them this Epistle, to rectify their Disorder, to correct their Errors, and to Establish them in the Faith. He writes with great Zeal and Earnestness against the Opposers, " tho' we or an Angel from Heaven preach any other Gospel unto you, than that ye have receiv'd, let him be accursed," *Ch.* i. *Ver.* 8. and *Ch.* v. *Ver.* 12. " I would they were even cut off that trouble you," He shews his Tender Care and Concern for the Souls who had been tainted with this False Doctrine, *Chap.* iv. *Ver.* 19, " My little Children, of whom I travail in Birth again until Christ be formed in you." The Design of the Apostle through this whole Epistle is to shew Two Things; first, that we are justified by Faith; and secondly, that we are no longer under the Law. Both these are comprized in the Text; but I shall now speak principally of the latter, because this seems to be the Main Drift and Scope of the Apostle in the Words before us. " Wherefore the Law was our Schoolmaster, to bring us unto Christ, that we might be justified by Faith. But after that Faith is come, we are no longer under a School-master."

master." In further difcourfing from thefe Words I propofe, thro' Divine Affiftance, to fhew

    I. Wherein the Law refembles a School-mafter.

    II. For what End it was our Schoolmafter, viz. to bring us unto Chrift. And

    III. That we are no longer under the Law.

I. And Firft, wherein does the Law refemble a Schoolmafter? This it doth in feveral Particulars; but efpecially in thefe that follow. Firft, in Refpect of its Purity and Perfection. A Schoolmafter is perfectly vers'd in all thofe Languages, Arts or Sciences, which he attempts to teach; otherwife he is not fit for his Office. How can a Man undertake to teach Greek or Hebrew, unlefs he very well underftands it himfelf? Or will any Perfon ever be able to teach Geometry, Aftronomy or Mathematics, unlefs he is himfelf Mafter of thofe Sciences? Now the Law is a Perfect Schoolmafter, very well inftructed in all the Will of God, and thoroughly vers'd in all his Commandments. " The Law is Holy; and the Commandment Holy, and Juft, and Good" — 'The Law " is Spiritual," *Rom.* vii. 12, 14. The Law is a Perfect Copy of the Divine Will, and a Tranfcript of the Divine Holinefs. We honour the Law of God, and efteem it very highly for it's Author's fake. The Law tells

us

us truly what we ought to do, and it directs us in the Right Way to Eternal Life; " The Man that doeth thefe Things fhall live in them," *Gal.* iii. 12. If, therefore, we fhould feem at any Time to fpeak flightingly or difparagingly of the Divine Law, we would not be underftood as fpeaking of the Law fimply and abfolutely, but only relatively, i. e. with Regard to our Weaknefs and Inability to fulfill it, and the Impoffibility of our obtaining Heaven by it. " The Law is Weak thro' the Flefh," *Rom.* viii. 3. We are " Carnal, fold under Sin," vii. 14. The Law is Holy, but we are Unholy; the Law is Perfect, but we are full of Sin and Imperfection. The Fault is not in the Law, but in Perfons who are under the Law. The Law is a Good Schoolmafter; but the Children who are his Scholars are very Dull, Stupid and Difobedient. All the Blame therefore lies not upon the Scoolmafter, but upon the Scholars.

Secondly, A Schoolmafter is one that hath Care of Children, and of fuch as are in their Minority. Accordingly the Word the Apoftle here ufes, fignifies a Guide, or Teacher of Children. We do not fend Perfons of Three or Four-fcore Years of Age to School; but Boys and Girls who are under Age are fent thither for Education and Inftruction. So all who are under the Law are in their Minority; they are Weak in Faith, they are Carnal, even as Babes in Chrift; they are not come to Years of Maturity; nor are they Perfect Men of Full Age, 1 *Cor.* iii. 1. *Heb.* v. 13, 14. But if awakened Souls are in great Diftrefs, and we

fce

fee plainly they are yet under the Law, fhall we fay they are not Children of God? Far be it. For how frequently do People who have known God, or rather are known of God, yet like the " *Galatians* turn again to the Weak and Beggarly Elements, whereunto they defire again to be in Bondage?" But then, obferve, fuch Perfons are Minors in Chriftianity; they are " fallen from Grace, and are again entangled in the Yoke of Bondage." They are the Children under the Pedagogy and Difcipline of the Law. And " the Heir as long as he is a Child, differeth nothing from a Servant, tho' he be Lord of all, but is under Tutors and Governors, until. the Time appointed of the Father. Even fo we, when we were Children, were in Bondage under the Elements of the World: But when the Fulnefs of Time was come, God fent forth his Son to redem them that were under the Law, *Gal.* iv. 1, 2, 3, 4, 5, 9.——v. 1, 4.

Thirdly, the Law is compared to a Schoolmafter for its ftrictnefs and feverity. Schoolmafters fet Boys their Leffons, and ftrictly charge and command them to get their whole Tafk; and do not allow them to mifs any part of it. So the Law fets before us Two Tables of Commandments, and obliges us to keep them every one perfectly. The Law requires Perfect Obedience: It makes no Grains of Allowance for our Weaknefs or Infirmity, but requires us to keep every Jot and Tittle of its Precepts without Exception and without Referve. And as fevere Schoolmafters, if their

Boys

Boys do but mifs one Word in their Leffon, take them up and whip them immediately ; fo the Law, if Perfons offend tho' but in one Point, pronounces them " guilty of all," *Jam.* iii. 2. and threatens them with Vengeance, Death and Condemnation. If we think School-mafters very Rigid and Severe for laying a Few Stripes upon the Bodies of their Dull Scholars, how Severe muft the Law be, who, for any the leaft violation of its Commands, fends both Body and Soul to Hell? For fo faith the Law, " Curfed is every one which con-tinueth not in all Things which are written in the Book of the Law to do them," *Gal.* iii. 10. What a fharp Schoolmafter then is the Law? Who would come under his Lafh? Or who that is under his Difcipline, but would be glad to be deliver'd from it ? And who that is once fet free from the Law would ever defire to go to School to fuch a fevere Mafter again ? I only appeal to you who are fet at Liberty from this Pedagogue, would you come under his Do-minion again for a Thoufand Worlds? Are you not heartily glad you are out of the Reach of his Whip ? Therefore keep clear of the Curfe and Condemnation of the Law. Ye are Chrift's Freemen. Affert your Chriftian Free-dom with Faith, and a Zeal according to your Knowledge. Be of Good Courage. Do not return to the Burden and Slavery of the Law again. Think that you are under the Law, and you will be in Bondage in a Moment. But think of Chrift, and you are fet at Liberty, and walk in much fweetnefs of Soul. As for you
who

who are under the Law, I pity you in this
Senfe, viz. with Refpect to the Toil and Vexation you undergo; for you are faft bound in
Mifery and Irons: but then I rejoice in Hope
of the End hereof; for I wifh that Terrible
Schoolmafter the Law may take his Rod in his
Hand and whip and fcourge you, till he drives
you out of his School to Chrift, that you may
take Chrift for your Mafter and Saviour, and
return to *Mofes* no more.

Fourthly, the Law refembles a Schoolmafter
in this Refpect. Schoolmafters teach Boys the
Elements or Firft Principles of Grammar, Rhe-
toric, Poetry, Oratory and Philology. Juft
fo the Law taken at large, and confider'd as
including all the Writings of the Old Teftament, plainly taught and made known to the
Jews the Firft Principles of Chriftianity. In
this fenfe the Word Law is primarily underftood in this Text; and this makes the Apoftle
fay in the foregoing Verfe, " before Faith came
we were kept under the Law, fhut up unto the
Faith, which fhould afterwards be revealed,
Gal. iii. 23. That the Gofpel was preached
to the *Jews*, the Apoftle plainly fhews in *Heb.*
iv. 2. " Unto us was the Gofpel preached, as
well as unto them"——which without doubt
implies that the Gofpel was preached unto
them. This the Apoftle exprefsly afferts again,
Gal. iii. 8. " And the Scripture forefeeing that
God would juftify the Heathen thro' Faith,
preached before the Gofpel unto *Abraham*, faying, in Thee fhall all Nations be blefled."
We find the Doctrine of Juftification by Faith,

which

which is the Main Fundamental Article of Chriſtianity, deliver'd in *Gen.* xv. 6. " He *(Abraham)* believed in the Lord; and he count- ed it to him for Righteouſneſs." *Iſa.* liii. 11. " By his Knowledge ſhall my Righteous Ser- vant juſtify many: for he ſhall bear their Ini- quities." And *Ch.* xlv. *Ver.* 25. " In the Lord ſhall all the Seed of Iſrael be juſtified, and ſhall glory." The " Prophets teſtified beforehand the Sufferings of Chriſt and the Glory that ſhould follow," 1 *Pet.* i. 11, 12. Hence our Saviour, " beginning at Moſes and all the Pro- phets, expounded to them in all the Scriptures the Things concerning himſelf—All Things muſt be fulfilled which were written in the Law of *Moſes*, and in the Prophets, and in the the Pſalms, concerning me," *Luke* xxiv. 27,— 44. *Moſes*, the Prophets, and the Pſalms, all ſpeak of Chriſt. As Schoolmaſters teach their Scholars the Rudiments of Grammar or Science, ſo the Law, i. e. the Scriptures of the Old Teſ- tament, inſtructed the *Jews* in the Firſt Prin- ciples of the Doctrine of Chriſt, as the Apoſtle ſpeaks, *Heb.* vi. 1: Which naturally leads me to ſhew

II. For what End the Law was our School- maſter, viz. " to bring us unto Chriſt that we might be juſtified by Faith. As the Twilight is an Introduction to the Meridian Light, ſo the Law was an Introduction to the Goſpel; " for the Law was the Introduction or bringing in* of a better Hope. The Jewiſh Diſpenſa-

---

* *Heb.* vii. 19.

tion

tion introduced Chriftianity, and then ceafed. *John* the Baptift was the Fore-runner of our Saviour; but when Chrift came, he muft increafe, (faith *John*) but I muft decreafe; intimating thereby, the Declenfion and Abolition of the Jewifh Religion and Hierarchy. "*John* truly baptized with Water, but ye fhall be baptized with the Holy Ghoft," *Acts* i. 5. xix. 4. *John* directed all his Difciples to Chrift, *Matt.* iii. 11. And fo Souls are commonly led from the Baptifm of *John* to the Baptifm of JESUS. The Law is a Schoolmafter to bring us to Chrift. This may be applied either to the Ceremonial or to the Moral Law.

Firft, The Ceremonial Law centred in Chrift. It was fulfilled in him and abolifh'd by him. This the Apoftle *Paul* fhews at large in his Epiftle to the *Hebrews*. " The Law was a Shadow of Good Things to come, but the Body is of Chrift, *Col.* ii. 17. All the Rites and Ceremonies of the Mofaic Law pointed to Chrift. The True Believers under the Old Teftament plainly faw this, fuch as *Simeon* and *Anna*, together with all who "looked for Redemption in *Jerufalem*, waiting for the Confolation of *Ifrael*," *Luke* ii. 25—38. 'Tis true the Carnal *Jews*, like Formal Profeffors of Religion in our Day, refted in the Ceremony, and took up with the Shadow inftead of the Subftance. For this the Lord juftly rebukes them, *Ifa.* lxvi. 3. " He that killeth an Ox, is as if he flew a Man: he that facrificeth a Lamb, as if he cut off a Dog's Neck: he that offereth an Oblation, as if he offereth Swines Blood: he

that

that burneth Incenſe, as if he bleſſed an Idol"—
All the Jewiſh Sacrifices were but Types or
Figures of Jeſus Chriſt, who appeared to put
away Sin by the Sacrifice of himſelf, *Heb.* ix.
26. And *Eph.* v. 2. " Chriſt hath given him-
ſelf for us, an Offering and a Sacrifice to God
—The Paſchal Lamb was a Type of Chriſt,
who therefore is called " the Lamb of God that
taketh away the Sin of the World," *John* i. 29.
And 1 *Cor.* v. 7, " Chriſt our Paſſover is ſlain
for us. Almoſt all Things are by the Law
purged with Blood"——All Believers under the
Goſpel are purged by the Blood of Chriſt.
" Without ſhedding of Blood is no Remiſſion,"
Heb. ix. 22. And yet " 'tis Impoſſible for the
Blood of Bulls and of Goats to take away Sins,"
x. 4. But " the Blood of Jeſus Chriſt his Son
cleanſeth us from all Sin," 1 *John* i. 7. Accordingly it is ſaid, " Not by the Blood of
Goats and Calves, but by his own Blood he
entered once into the Holy Place," *Heb.* ix. 12.
What a high Value is to be put upon the Blood
of Chriſt! It is called the Blood of God, " his
own Blood," *Acts* xx. 28. Is the Blood of
Chriſt the Blood of God? How then can we
make too much of it? Is there any Danger of
idolizing the Blood of Chriſt? Indeed you
may as ſoon make an Idol of Chriſt as of his
Blood. Do you allow the Divinity of Chriſt?
Do you allow the Unity of his Perſon? Is
Chriſt both God and Man in one Perſon? How
then can you ever enough extol the Blood of
Chriſt, which in Reſpect of his Perſonality may
be look'd upon (yea, and is look'd upon in
the

the Text before cited) to be Divine? All who know the Influence of Chrift's Blood upon their Hearts, own the Divinity of it, acknowledge the Myftery, and bow and worſhip the Perſon who ſhed it.

Further, what a ſtreſs do the Scriptures lay upon the Blood of Chriſt! How much do they aſcribe to it! All our Redemption from firſt to laſt is reſolv'd into it. We are ſaid to *have Redemption thro' his Blood*, Eph. i. 7. to be *waſhed in his Blood*, Rev. i. 5. to be *purchaſed by his Blood*, Acts xx. 28. to be *purged by his Blood*, Heb. ix. 14. We are *juſtified by his Blood*, Rom. v. 9. and *ſanctified by his Blood*, Heb. xiii. 12. Chriſt hath made *Peace through the Blood of his Croſs*, Col. i. 20. *We are made nigh by his Blood*, Eph. ii. 13. We were *redeemed by his Precious Blood*, 1 Pet. i. 18, 19. *For unto you which believe he is Precious*, ii. 7. Therefore do not loath the Blood of Chriſt; do not look upon it as Light Bread, as the *Iſraelites* did their Manna, *Num.* xxi. 5. Do not count the Blood of the Covenant an unholy or common* Thing. Look to the Blood of the Lamb, love his Blood. Worſhip " him whom God hath ſet forth to be a Propitiation thro' Faith in his Blood," *Rom.* iii. 25. Never be wearied of hearing of the Blood of Chriſt; never think you can hear too much of it; never think you can hear enough of it. O! 'tis Precious Blood, 1 *Pet.* i.

---

* *Heb.* x. 29.

19. If

19. If any are otherwife minded, it is becaufe they err, not knowing the Scriptures, nor experiencing the Power of Chrift's Blood upon their own Hearts.

Secondly, The Moral Law is a Schoolmafter to bring us unto Chrift. All our Morality will never merit Heaven. " Tho' thou wafh thee with Nitre, and take thee much Sope, yet thine Iniquity is marked before me, faith the Lord God." The Law convinces us of Sin, and worketh Wrath, *Rom.* iv. 15. vii. 7. When Sinners are firft awakened, they frequently fly to the Law for Relief; but all in vain: for by the " Deeds of the Law fhall no Flefh be juftified in his Sight," *Rom.* iii. 20. " If I wafh myfelf with Snow Water, and make my Hands never fo clean; yet fhalt thou plunge me in the Ditch, and mine own Cloaths fhall abhor me." *Job* ix. 30, 31. The Law is a Means of fhewing us the Difeafe, and forces us to look out for a Remedy; the Law fhews us our Danger, and makes us look out for Deliverance. The Law itfelf indeed affords no Relief. The Sinner who fees himfelf loft and condemned by the Law, is obliged to fly unto Chrift for a Reprieve. Therefore is the Law faid to be our Scoolmafter to bring us unto Chrift. To bring is not in the Original, but is fupplied by the Tranflators: and befides, 'tis too Soft an Expreffion; for the Law does not barely bring or lead Sinners to Chrift, but it compels and conftrains, and obliges them to fly unto the Saviour; it drives them to him; and they fly for their Lives, juft as Murderers fly to a City of

Refuge

Refuge, while the Avenger of Blood is pur-
fuing clofe behind them. Chriftians, have you
not found it fo? Have you not been terrified
with the Thunderings and Lightenings of Divine Vengeance? Have you not made more
hafte from *Sinai* than *Lot* did from *Sodom?*
Have you not " efcaped with the fkin of your
Teeth?" *Job* xix. 20. And as for you who ftill
feek Salvation by the Law, **O that you faw your**
Danger! Flee from the Wrath to come. Lay
hold on the Hope fet before you in Chrift Jefus. You may hold the Law as faft as you
pleafe, and continue under it, and contend for
it as long as you will, yet you muft come off
from it at laft, or elfe you will never be faved.
There is no getting to Heaven by your ftricteft
Adherence to, and exacteft Obfervance of the
Precepts of the Law. The " Law came by
Mofes, but Grace and Truth came by Jefus
Chrift. But if Righteoufnefs come by the
Law, then is Chrift Dead in vain," *John* i. 17.
Gal. ii. 21. But methinks, my dear Friends,
you who are under the Servitude and Hard Labour of the Law, fhould rejoice to hear of Deliverance from it. How is it with your Souls?
Do you not find the Law fuch a Yoke of Bondage as neither we nor our Fathers were able to
bear? I am fure I found it fo. I had been feeking Eternal Life by the Law for fome Years;
but I was always Miferable, and fometimes at
the Point of Defpair. And when I firft heard
of Juftification by Faith, I could fcarce venture
to believe the Report, left I fhould be deceived;
but I faid, " 'tis a comfortable Doctrine, if it

A a

" be

" be True."   Indeed the Law was a fevere Schoolmafter to me; he treated me with nothing but Terrors, Curfes and Condemnation. This made me willing to leave his School, his Lafh, his Yoke, his hard Tafks. And when you, my Brethren, have fuffer'd more from this infinitely Juft and Vindictive Pedagogue, you will be more glad to leave him. The fooner you are free from the Curfe of the Law, the better. Therefore throw off the Yoke and Burden of the Law at once; and take Chrift's Yoke upon you: for his " Yoke is Eafy and his Burden Light," *Matt.* xi. 30.

But for what Intent doth the Law bring us to Chrift? That we might be juftified by Faith. To talk of Juftification by Works, is Death to a Soul that is convinced of Sin, and fees the Purity of the Divine Law; but the Doctrine of Juftification by Faith, is fweet and comfortable to a Soul in this Condition. But fome are offended: they think we make the Way to Heaven too Eafy. Indeed the Grace of Chrift makes Hard Things Eafy. The " Highway of Holinefs is fo Plain, that way-faring Men, tho' Fools, fhall not err therein," *Ifa.* xxxv. 8. Moft Men are like the Young Man, *Matt.* xix. they are for doing fome good or great Thing to inherit Eternal Life; and when we tell them to believe in Chrift and be faved, they know not what to make of it; they begin to reafon about it, and fo are apt to conclude Salvation cannot be fo Free for Sinners as we reprefent it. We may obferve, the feeming Eafinefs of a Thing is fometimes an Objection againft it, and makes
People

People backward to comply.   Thus when *Eli-sha* the Prophet bid *Naaman* " wafh feven Times in *Jordan, Naaman* was wroth," he expected fome great Ceremony to be performed; " I thought, he will furely come out to me, and ftand and call on the Name of the Lord his God, and ftrike his Hand over the Place, and recover the Leper.   Are not *Abanah* and *Phar-pah* Rivers of *Damafcus*, better than all the Waters of *Ifrael?* So he turned and went away in a Rage," 2 *Kings* v. 11, 12, 13. He flighted the Prophet's Prefcription, as too Frivolous and Trifling : and 'twas with great Difficulty his Servants prevailed with him to comply with the Prophet's Direction.   Juft fo it is ; when we fay, believe, wafh in the Blood of Chrift, and be Clean, People think it fo Eafy a Way of being faved, that they will not comply with it.   Indeed the Way to Heaven is Difficult only to Unbelievers and Self-righteous Perfons. 'Tis the Eafieft Thing to believe, when Chrift gives us Power.   As for thofe who object againft this Way of Salvation, becaufe it is fo Eafy; we may often obferve how Hard it is to perfuade fuch to believe in Chrift. Ufe what Arguments we will, we can fcarcely convince fuch Souls that Chrift loves them.   Thofe who believe are juftified.   The Doctrine of Juftification by Faith I have enlarged upon in another Place,* and fo I need not infift upon it here.   I only

---

* Marrow of the Church, Part I. Ch. II.

                    obferve,

obferve, that thofe who believe in Chrift are Happy; they are juftified; they are deliver'd from the Law, which was the Third Thing I propos'd to fhew.

III. We are " no longer under the Law." And if there was no other Text in the Bible to prove this, yet one would think the Apoftle's Words in this Place might be fufficient to convince us of it. " After that Faith is come, we are no longer under a Schoolmafter." What Words can be Plainer? Yet this is not the only Place wherein the Apoftle delivers this Doctrine: He makes mention of it in feveral other of his Epiftles, that he may more effectually remove all Queftions and Scruples upon this Head, and fettle Believers in the Full Perfuafion and Affurance of the Truth and Certainty of it.

Thus 1 *Tim.* i. 8, 9, 10. " We know that the Law is Good, if a Man ufe it lawfully"—And that we may not be at a Lofs to know what it is to " ufe the Law lawfully," he adds, " Knowing this, that the Law is not made for a Righteous Man." Whom doth the Apoftle here mean by a Righteous Man? Certainly by Nature " none are Righteous, no, not one," *Rom.* iii. 10. And as for thofe who truft in their own Righteoufnefs, they are certainly under the Law, and under the Curfe. The Righteous Man, therefore, is he who renounces his own Righteoufnefs and trufts in Chrift's, who believes in Chrift, who hath Forgivenefs of Sins in the Blood of Chrift, and is juftified by Faith
in

in the Active Obedience of Chrift. This is the Righteous Man for whom the Law is not made. Wherefore then ferveth the Law? For whom was it made? "It was added becaufe of Tranfgreffions, till the Seed fhould come," *Gal.* iii. 19. And it was made, as the Apoftle tells us, " for the Lawlefs and Difobedient, for the Ungodly and for Sinners, for Unholy and Pro-phane, for Murderers of Fathers and Murderers of Mothers, for Manflayers, for Whoremon-gers, for them that defile themfelves with Man-kind, for Men-ftealers, for Liars, for perjured Perfons, and if there be any other Thing that is contrary to Sound Doctrine." What clearer Proof can you defire that the Law is not for Believers, but for Unbelievers, and for the long Catalogue of Sinners which the Apoftle here reckons up?

And we may obferve, that the Apoftle keeps clofe to his Text; for he maintains the fame 'Truth in his Epiftle to'the *Romans, Cb.* vii. *Ver.* 4. " Wherefore, my Brethren, ye are alfo be-come Dead to the Law by the Body of Chrift; that ye fhould be married to another, even to him that is raifed from the Dead, i. e. Chrift. ——A Man that is Dead is void of Life, Senfe and Motion; a Chriftian who is Dead to the Law hath no Legal Life, no Legal Senfe, no Legal Motion in his Heart. A Man that is Dead hath loft all Communication with this World; a Soul that is Dead to the Law hath loft all Communication with the Law: He hath no more to do with it than a Dead Man hath with the Things of this Life. This the Apoftle

afferts

aſſerts, and this he illuſtrates by a very beautiful Similitude, Ver. 1, 2, 3. Suppoſe a Woman marries a Huſband, and he dies, and ſhe
then is married to a ſecond Huſband; what a
Piece of Folly and Inconſiſtency would it be
for ſuch a Woman to talk of being married to
her firſt, i. e. her Dead Huſband again? Now
the Application of this is Eaſy; for who do
you think this firſt Huſband is? It is the Law;
this is our firſt Huſband, and to him we are
all married by Nature; but when by Grace we
believe in Chriſt, our firſt Huſband dies; we
become Dead to the Law, and the Law is Dead
to us; then we are married to another, i. e. to
Chriſt; and to talk then of being married to
the Law again would be juſt the ſame Contradiction, yea (I had almoſt ſaid) Impoſſibility,
as it would be for a Woman whoſe firſt Huſband was Dead, and ſhe married to a ſecond,
to talk of being married to her firſt, i. e. her
Dead Huſband again.

And obſerve, what is the Conſequence of
Souls being Dead to the Law and married to
Chriſt, they "bring forth Fruit unto God."
And none "bring forth Fruit unto God," till
they are married to Chriſt; all the Fruit they
bring forth before this Marriage is ſpurious and
odious in the Sight of God. People commonly
think, if they would live to God, they muſt be
alive to the Law; but the Apoſtle's Experience
was quite the contrary; for he ſaith, "I thro'
the Law am Dead to the Law, that I might
live unto God," *Gal.* ii. 19. Do you then de-
ſire to know how to live unto God? Then become

come Dead to the Law.— Indeed this is the only Way. When you are Dead to the Law and Married to Chrift, then you live unto God, your Fruits and Good Works will be acceptable to him. Do what you will or can, you will never live unto God, till you become Dead to the Law. There is no fuch Thing. It is abfolutely Impoffible.

In *Heb.* vii. 19. the Apoftle tells us, "the Law made nothing perfect," and fo *Ch.* x. *Ver.* 1. By Law here the Apoftle means the Law of *Mofes*, as he calls it, *Acts* xiii. 39. This made nothing perfect——The Apoftle doth not fay, it made no Perfon perfect, but it made no Thing perfect. For the Law does not perfect us in any one Thing; in any one Virtue, Grace or Fruit of the Spirit; the Law does not perfect us in Faith, in Hope, Love, &c. What Efforts or Attempts foever Perfons under the Law may make, how far foever they may go in Outward Chriftianity, yet they " perfect nothing, they bring forth no Fruit to Perfection." All our Perfection is in Chrift, and we know of no other; and the Law is a bringing or Introduction to Chrift, in whom we have a better Hope than ever the Law could give us, by which Hope we draw nigh unto God.

There are two Covenants; the Covenant of Works and the Covenant of Grace: all Unbelievers are under the former, and all Believers are under the latter. Now 'tis Impoffible for a Perfon to be under both thefe at the fame Time. Do you then believe in Chrift? If you do, you are no longer under the Covenant of Works,

but

but under the Covenant of Grace. " For there is verily a Difanulling of the Commandment going before, for the Weaknefs and Unprofitablenefs thereof——For if the Firft Covenant had been Faultlefs, then fhould no Place have been fought for the Second. For finding Fault with them (not with the Covenant itfelf, but with the Perfons who were under it) he faith, behold, the Days come (faith the Lord) when I will make a New Covenant with the Houfe of Ifrael, and with the Houfe of Judah—In that he faith, a New Covenant, he hath made the Firft old. Now that which decayeth and waxeth old, is ready to vanifh away." Therefore thofe who are in Chrift are in the New Covenant; and to fuch the Old Covenant is decayed and vanifhed away. The Lord taketh away the Firft Covenant, that he may eftablifh the Second; which indeed is eftablifhed in every Believer's Heart, *Heb.* vii. 18.——viii. 7, 8, 13. ——x. 9.

Gal. v. 3. " I teftify again to every Man that is circumcifed, that he is a Debtor to do the whole Law——if ye be circumcifed, Chrift fhall profit you nothing. *Ver.* 2. Chrift is become of no Effect to you——ye are fallen from Grace," *Ver.* 4. You fee here the Danger of turning back to the Law again. Such Perfons are fallen from Grace; they make the Crofs of Chrift of no Effect, and lay themfelves under an Abfolute Obligation of keeping the whole Law. So then can you bear thus to fruftrate the Grace of God? Are you willing to take fuch a Burden upon you? Yet if you feek to be

juftified

juftified by the Law, or if after juftification you revolt to the Law again, and feek Salvation by it, you renounce Chrift, and lay yourfelf under a Neceffity of fulfilling the whole Law.

Further, the Martyr *Stephen* charges the *Jews* with not keeping the Law, *Acts* vii. 53. " Who have received the Law by the Difpofition of Angels, and have not kept it." And our Saviour brings the fame charge againft them, *John* vii. 19. And indeed who is there that doth keep the Law? Therefore all Mankind are accurs'd and condemn'd by the Law. What fhall we fay then? If Perfons are under the Law, and yet do not keep the Law, what is the Confequence? The Apoftle anfwers the Queftion by letting us know, that " as many as are of the Works of the Law are under the Curfe: for it is written, Curfed is every one, &c." *Gal.* iii. 10. A broken Law and a Curfe are Infeperable. How then fhall we efcape? " Chrift hath redeem'd us from the Curfe of the Law, being made a Curfe for us: for it is written, Curfed is every one that hangeth on a Tree," *Ver.* 13. But altho' the Children of God are redeemed from the Curfe of the Law, are they delivered from the Law? The Apoftle refolves this Queftion plainly and fimply, *Rom.* vii. 6. · " Now we are deliver'd from the Law" —He does not fay, we are delivered from the Curfe of the Law; for that he afferts in the Text before mentioned: but he faith we are delivered from the Law, to acquaint us that we are delivered from the Law itfelf; for if the Children were free from the Curfe, yet if they

B b

were

were not delivered from the Law itſelf, they would always be in Bondage. Beſides, does not Perſons eſcaping the Curſe plainly ſhew that they are no longer under the Law? To talk of being under the Law and breaking it, and yet eſcaping the Curſe of it, is the greateſt Inconſiſtency that can be. Therefore let us ſtick cloſe to the Apoſtle's Words, " But now we are delivered from the Dead or Dying Law* in which we were entangled, that we ſhould ſerve in Newneſs of Spirit, and not in the Oldneſs of the Letter."

It is evident, therefore, that Believers are delivered from the Law; they are no longer under it; they are redeemed from the Curſe of it; they eſcape the Penalty of it. They have no more to do with the Covenant of Works than if no ſuch Covenant ſubſiſted. Happy are your Souls, my dear Brethren, who taſte of this Sweet Liberty. Rejoice in it; ſtand faſt in it. " If ye be dead with Chriſt from the Rudiments of the World; why, as tho' living in the World, are ye ſubjeƈt to Ordinances?" *Col.* ii. 20.

But will not this Doƈtrine lead People into Sin and Licentiouſneſs? " Shall we continue in Sin that Grace may abound? God forbid. How ſhall we that are Dead to Sin live any longer therein?—For he that is Dead, is freed

---

* So the Tranſlation from the Greek plainly ſignifies, and is agreeable tc Ver. 4, For whether we are ſaid to be *Dead to the Law,* or *the Law Dead to us,* the Meaning is ſtill the ſame.

from

from Sin—Likewife reckon ye alfo yourfelves to
be Dead indeed unto Sin, but alive unto God
thro' Jefus Chrift our Lord—Let not fin therefore reign in your Mortal Body that you fhould
obey it in the Lufts thereof—For Sin fhall not
have Dominion over you: for ye are not under the Law, but under Grace. What then?
Shall we fin becaufe we are not under the Law,
but under Grace? God forbid, *Rom.* vi. 1, 2,
7, 12, 14, 15. Every Evangelical Doctrine is
liable to Abufe. Thus what Doctrine was
ever more abufed than that of Free Juftification? For which Reafon the Apoftle *James*
writes againft the Abufers of it with great Juftice and Severity. So if Carnal People abufe
the Doctrine of Chriftian Liberty and Freedom from the Law, and 'turn the Free Grace
of Chrift into Lafcivioufnefs, their Blood is
upon their own Heads. The Doctrine is not
to be condemned upon this Account. You fee
plainly from the Teftimony of an Apoftle that
the Doctrine confider'd in itfelf hath no Tendency to lead Men into Corruption of Life or
Manners. What do you defire more

Some indeed think that St. *Paul* was under
the Law, becaufe he faith, " being not without
Law to God, but under the Law to Chrift—
1 *Cor.* ix. 21. But I have fhew'd in another
Place* that the Greek Wo d which the Apoftle
here ufes properly fignifies in a Law. And ob-

---

* Marrow of the Church, Part II. Chap. I. p. 48.

ferve,

ferve, he does not fay in a Law to *Mofes*, but in a Law to Chrift; which plainly fhews that he here means the fame Law that he calls " the Law of Faith," *Rom.* iii. 27. " the Law of the Spirit of Life in Chrift Jefus," *Ch.* viii. *Ver.* 2. and " the Law of Love," *Ch.* xiii. *Ver.* 10. This St. *James* calls " the Perfect Law of Liberty," *James* i. 25. This Law I wifh from the bottom of my Heart all who call themfelves Chriftians were well eftablifhed in. As for you, my very Dear Friends and beloved in the Lord, who are in this Perfect Law of Liberty, remember, " ye have been called unto Liberty; only ufe not Liberty for an Occafion tó the Flefh, but by Love ferve one another—For fo is the Will of God, that with well-doing ye may put to Silence the Ignorance of Foolifh Men: As Free, and not ufing your Liberty for a Cloak of Malicioufnefs, but as the Servants of God," *Gal.* v. 13. 1 *Pet.* ii. 15, 16.

But if Believers are delivered from the Law, what Rule have they to walk by? " Chrift hath once fuffered, leaving us an Example, that ye fhould follow his Steps: Who did no Sin, neither was Guile found in his Mouth: Who when he was reviled, reviled not again; when he fuffered, he threatned not; but committed himfelf unto him that judgeth righteoufly— Confider him that endured fuch Contradiction of Sinners againft himfelf, left ye be wearied and faint in your Minds—He went about doing Good. Our Saviour does not fend us unto *Mofes* to be taught; but (fays he) " Learn of ME, for I am Meek and Lowly in Heart"—

Never

Never therefore think of learning any thing of
Mofes; but think of Chrift, learn of him, follow his Example; and you will never do amifs.
Chrift is our Rule, and where can you find a
better? " As many as walk according to this
Rule, Peace be on them, and Mercy, and upon
the Ifrael of God——He that faith he abideth
in him, ought himfelf alfo to walk as he walk-
ed." 1 *Pet.* ii. 21, 22, 23. *Heb.* xii. 3. *Acts*
x. 38. *Matth.* xi. 29. *Gal.* vi. 16. 1 *John*
ii. 6.

Thus, my beloved Brethren, I have endeavour'd to fet this Truth before you in the
Plaineft Manner. I have laboured to remove
thofe Prejudices and Hindrances that lay in the
Way. And what Objections yet remain upon
your Minds, I pray the Lord Jefus to take
away; and I doubt not but he will. I only
fpeak for the Good of your Precious and Immortal Souls. " We then as Workers together
with him, befeech you alfo, that ye receive not
the Grace of God in vain." My Heart's Defire
and Prayer to God for all of you is, that ye
may be " delivered from the Bondage of Corruption, into the Glorious Liberty of the Children of God." Then the Service of our Saviour will be Perfect Freedom to your Souls.
" *Jerufalem* which is above, is Free, which is
the Mother of us all——We, Brethren, as *Ifaac*
was, are the Children of Promife. But as then
he that was born after the Flefh perfecuted him
that was born after the Spirit, even fo it is now
---So then, Brethren, we are not Children of the
Bond Woman, but of the Free," *Gal.* iv. 26.

B b 3   NOTES

N O T E S

ON THE

SERMON,

ON THE LAW.

Page 292. *Thofe who have once tafted the Grace of Chrift do again gende to Bondage*.---If this was not the cafe, what need would there be of thofe cautions and exhortations which are given, particularly by St. Paul, to ftand faft in the liberty wherewith Chrift has made us free ? St. Paul found a law in his members bringing him into captivity, i. e. into bondage; in this lies the myftery of iniquity, which yet works, more or lefs, in the hearts of God's children, and will work ; for as long as we are in this world, we fhall find a pronenefs to go back to the Law, and we fhall find what the Scriptures call the luft, or wifdom of the flefh, by which we defire to be fomething, to have fomething, and to do fomething ; inftead of being nothing in ourfelves, and having nothing but what we receive out of Chrift's fullnefs. There is nothing fo much to be guarded againft as a legal fpirit. Depend upon it, legal principles will ever produce licentious prac-tice. How earneft is St. Paul on this one point ? Ye fuffer, fays he, if a Man bring you into bondage ; and again, he fays, do any fuffer and I burn not ? How zealoufly affected was this Apoftle for the glory of God, and the comfort and happinefs of the Church and Children of God !

Page 374.

Page 308. *After that Faith is come we are no longer under a Schoolmaster.*---What words can be plainer! Strange infatuation! That Men fhould be fo enflaved by the traditions of Men, and the cunning craftinefs of thofe who lie in wait to deceive, as to fubmit to the authority of Men rather than to the authority of God; and pay more refpect to the words which Man's wifdom teacheth, than to the words of an infpired Apoftle! What clearer proof can be given that the Law is not for Believers, than may be found in St. Paul's Epiftles? You are certainly fighting againft your mercies, when you caft the word of God behind your backs, looking for doctrines to the commandments of Men.

Page 310. *We become dead to the Law, and the Law is dead to us.*---If it be fo, (and the Apoftle Paul pofitively declares that we---meaning himfelf and all Believers---are dead to the Law, and the Law is dead to us) then what communion, connection, or communication can there be between a Believer and the Law? That being dead by which he was once held.

Page 314. *To talk of being under the Law and breaking it, and yet efcaping the curfe of it, is the greateft inconfiftency that can be.*---It is commonly faid that the Law has power to command the Believer, but no power to condemn him. What is this, but a Law without a fanction? The fanction of the moral Law of Ten Commandments is the curfe: but, the fanction of the Law which proceeds from Zion, is the bleffing; for there the Lord promifed his bleffing and life for evermore.

Page 314. *But will not this Doctrine lead People into Sin and licentioufnefs?*---No; but the reverfe: It is impoffible to live to God till we are dead to the Law. Many are delivered from the Law in their experience, who are neverthelefs entangled with it, in their judgments. I would afk fuch, how do you find your corruptions fubdued, is it by looking to the Law, or by looking to Jefus who hath fulfilled it? When do you find your hearts warmed with the love of God? When do you find fin moft exceedingly finful? When do you feel the deepeft refignation to your heavenly Father's will? When are you delivered from the fear of death? When do you feel a longing defire to depart and be with Chrift? Is it when you are looking to Law? Or, is it

·B b 4

when

when you are loooking to that friend for eternity who died.
to redcem you from the Law ?

Page 316. *If Believers are delivered from the Law what rule
have they to walk by ?---*I will anfwer, " *The* WILL *of God as
revealed in the* GOSPEL." I mean that good will by which
he commended his love to us when Sinners. The Law faith,
the Soul that finneth it fhall die; to tell a Sinner to walk by
this rule, is the fame as to knock a Man down and tell him
to ftand. If we cannot ftand upon this ground how can we
walk upon it ? There is text upon text to prove that the example of Chrift is the Believer's rule, but not one fingle text,
from Genefis to Revelations, to prove that the Moral Law is
the Believer's only rule of conduct.

The following Hymns are Mr. *Hammond*'s own Com-
pofing, and are extremely fuitable to the Subjects
treated of in the preceding part of the Book.

Jer. xvii. 9.

*The Heart is deceitful above all things, and defperately wicked,
who can know it?*

I.

HOW full is my Heart of Sin!
  Oh! where fhall my Tongue begin!
How fhall I relate my Cafe,
All my Sin and Wretchednefs?
What Contraries in me rife!
If I fpeak I tell all Lies:
Nothing do I fee or feel
But a Heart as hard as Steel.

II.

I next Moment freely own
I am fenfelefs as a Stone;
I do neither fee nor feel
Love of Heav'n or fear of Hell.
Oh my curfed Unbelief!
Yet how little is my Grief!
Why fhould I of Sin complain,
When I feel no inward Pain?

III. Oh

III.

Oh this wretched Heart of mine !
How perverfely does it twine !
How I wander in a Maze !
When I ftrive to trace its Ways !
) Into me new Light inftill,
Unto me myfelf reveal,
Shew me, LORD, this Myftery,
Give me Grace myfelf to fee.

IV.

Surely none but GOD alone
Can difcover and make known
All the windings of my Heart,
Wherewith I from GOD depart.
What innumerable Hofts
Of repugnant Evil Lufts
In my Heart at once arife,
Juft like Hell before my Eyes !

V.

How the Brute and Devils ftrive
Which fhall moft profufely live !
Sin pollutes my Heart all o'er,
Pride increafes more and more.
I deferve the hotteft Hell ;
This I fay, but do I feel ?
Jesu, touch me to the Quick,
Let me feel as well as fpeak.

VI.

How I dread myfelf to fee !
Oh ! the Weight's too great for me :
Yet I dare not reft within,
While Corruption is unfeen.
Inconfiftencies agree,
Contradictions meet in me ;
Something, Nothing, Darknefs, Light,
Faith and Fear in me unite.

VII. LORD

VII.

LORD, I cannot come to Thee;
Oh! do Thou ſtoop down to me:
Filthy Creature as I am,
Love me freely, ſlaughter'd Lamb.
LORD, convert this Heart of mine,
Make me Holy and Divine:
All anew in me create,
Fix me in a Perfect State.

Juſtification by Faith.

From JOHN iii. 16.　v. 24.　vi. 29.　ROM. iii.
20, 28.　v. 1.　ix. 33.

I.

BEHOLD the Love of GOD
　To *Adam*'s fallen Race!
His Son he gracioufly beſtow'd,
　To fuffer in our Place:
　His only Son he gave,
　That Sinners who believe
Might Pardon and Redemption have,
　Aud in his Kingdom live.

II.

　Enlarge your Hearts, and praiſe
　Your Saviour and your LORD;
Admire the Riches of his Grace,
　And lean upon his Word:
　The Soul that comes to me,
　By True and Living Faith,
Is from all Condemnation free,
　And Life Eternal hath.

III. This

III.

This is the Work of GOD,
His SPIRIT's Work alone,
To give us Faith in JESU's Blood,
And draw us to the Son.
The Soul on God relies,
Thro' JESUS reconcil'd,
And GOD, the Father, juftifies
His Poor Rebellious Child.

IV.

Not one of *Adam*'s Race,
However juft and good,
Shall by his Works of Righteoufnefs
Be juftified with GOD;
The Works which we have done
Are all, alas! Unclean;
But we are fav'd by Faith alone;
And freely cleans'd from Sin.

V.

The further Men go on
In Legal Righteoufnefs;
The more they fee themfelves Undone
Unlefs redeem'd by Grace.
The Law denounces wrath;
Its Terrors never ceafe
'Till we are juftified by Faith,
And have Eternal Peace.

VI.

The LORD fent down his Son,
To call and fave his Flock;
The *Jews* fell on this ftumpling Stone,
And fplit upon this Rock.
The *Pharifees* of old,
And Moral Sinners now
Are too Self-righteous and too Bold
To JESU's Grace to bow.

VII. But

VII.

But Sinners full of Grief,
  Deferving to be damn'd,
Look up to JESUS for Relief,
  And fhall not be afham'd :
  Their inmoft Souls rely,
  They with the Heart believe
Their Spirits, Souls and Bodies fly
  To him who bids them LIVE.

VIII.

'To Life and Peace reftor'd,
  'Their Tongues o'erflow with Praife ;
Great is the Glory of the LORD—
  They fing in all his Ways :
  'Then all their Powers awake ;
  Their warm Affections rife,
Like Eagles they mount up, and take
  Poffeffion of the Skies.

CHRIST's Rightcoufnefs Imputed.

om Isa. xlvi. 12, 13.   xlv. 24.   Psal. xxiv. 5.
xxi. 16.   xl. 9, 10.   Rom. iii. 21.   iv. 3, 23, 24.
v. 19.   x. 3, 4.   1 Cor. i. 30.   Phil. iii. 8, 9.
2 Cor. v. 21.   Heb. vii. 22.

I.

Isa. xlvi. 12, 13.
SINNERS, hearken unto me,
  And let my Words take Place.
What tho' you ftout-hearted be,
  And far from Righteoufnefs ?
  I my Righteoufnefs bring near,
And my Salvation fhall not ftay ;
  I in *Zion* will appear,
    And fave without Delay.

II. I am

II.

Isa. xlv. 24.

I am GOD of all below,
  And all above poffefs;
Ev'ry Knee to ME fhall bow,
  And ev'ry Tongue confefs.
Surely, fhall the Sinner fay,
CHRIST is my Strength and Righteoufnefs;
  Gladly I his Voice obey,
  And glory in his Grace.

III.

Psal. xxiv. 5.

Happy he whoe'er believes
  The Embaffy of Peace,
Who at Jesu's Hand receives
  The Gift of Righteoufnefs;
GOD is his Salvation's GOD,
The LORD is his Almighty Shield;
  He with Grace fhall be endow'd,
  And then with Glory fill'd.

IV.

Psal. lxxi. 16.

Jesu, I defire to go,
  Depending on thy Grace;
Nothing I defire to know
  Befide thy Righteoufnefs:
Let me mention it alone,
And in my Heart feel what I fpeak;
  All Self-Righteoufnefs tread down,
  And ev'ry Idol break.

V.

Psal. xl. 9, 10.

I with boldnefs will reveal
  Thy Miracles of Grace,
In the Congregation tell
  Of thy Pure Righteoufnefs:

How

How can I my Lips refrain?
Thy Righteoufnefs I muft impart;
LORD, fhall I for fear of Man
Conceal it in my Heart?

VI.

Rom. iii 21.

Mofes at a Diftance faw
The Righteoufnefs Divine;
In the Volume of the Law,
How clearly doth it fhine!
Holy Men and Prophets Old
Beheld from far the Bleeding Lamb,
Of his Righteoufnefs foretold,
And trufted in the fame.

VII.

Rom. iv. 23, 24.

Abraham the LORD obey'd,
Believing in his Grace,
And was eminently made
An Heir of Righteoufnefs.
Was it written for his Sake?
Or doth it not belong to us,
Who of Righteoufnefs partake,
By Faith in JESU's Crofs?

VIII.

Rom. v. 19.

Did the Sin of *Adam* flay,
And Ruin all his Race?
JESUS takes our Sins away,
By fuff'ring in our Place;
He perform'd what GOD requir'd,
And anfwer'd all the Law's demands:
In his Righteoufnefs attir'd,
The True Believer ftands.

IX.

ROM. x. 3, 4.

How perverfely did the *Jews*
    His Righteoufnefs difcard !
Shall we then his Love abufe,
    And flight his great Reward ?
Of the Law he is the End,
And after we have done our beft,
    On his Grace we muft depend,
    And in his Merits reft.

X.

1 COR. i. 30.

What a Fulnefs in him dwells,
    Of Mercy, Truth and Grace !
In the LORD, the Sinner feels
    Eternal Righteoufnefs.
He enlightens Blinded Eyes,
With Heav'nly Wifdom from above
Filthy Souls he Sanctifies,
    And perfects them in Love.

XI.

PHIL. iii. 8, 9.

What Self-righteous Moralift
    Can glory like St. *Paul ?*
Yet lo ! he to fhare in CHRIST
    Freely renounces all :
In himfelf he no more trufts,
His Soul in JESUS CHRIST is found
In whofe Righteoufnefs he boafts,
    And is with Honour crown'd.

XII.

2 Cor. v. 21.

What a Myftery of Love
    In GOD's Defigns appears !
JESUS coming from Above
    Our Sin and Torment bears :

GOD

GOD imputes our Sins to him ;
Imputes to us his Righteoufnefs;
Guilty he doth him efteem,
And Guiltlefs us confefs.

XII.

HEB. vii. 22.

JESUS is our Surety too,
   And thus his Love reveals;
What we were oblig'd to do,
   He in our ftead fulfils :
He for Sinners liv'd and died;
His Life, his Death is all our own :
   We fhall foon be glorified,
   And with our LORD fit down.

Settled in CHRIST,

From 1 Pet. v. 10.

I.

THRICE happy they whofe Souls are built
   On that Foundation which is fure ;
They are difcharg'd from all their Guilt,
   And ftand eternally fecure.

II.

Their Doubts and Fears are fled away,
   They live in conftant Joy and Light,
They walk with GOD throughout the Day,
   And fleep at Peace with him by Night.

III.

Corruption reigns in them no more ;
   They have no Place, nor Love for Sin,
Abfolv'd its Guilt, fubdu'd its Pow'r,
   And Jesu's Kingdom is within.

C c

IV. How

IV.

How do they feel Seraphic Love
   Exciting in them Heav'nly Fires !
To GOD their flaming Spirits move
   In never-ceasing strong Desires.

V.

The World in vain displays its Charms,
   And spreads its Glories all abroad ;
Their Souls are safe in JESU's Arms,
   They live, they move, they breathe in GOD.

VI.

Philosophy and vain Deceit
   Cannot their stable Souls beguile ;
In CHRIST their Head they stand complete,
   And perfect in their Father's Will.

VII.

Satan may all his Hosts unite,
   And strive to vex their Peaceful State :
Not Men, nor Fiends, nor Depth, nor Height
   Shall them from Jesus separate.

VIII.

Death may put on his Terrors now,
   And come with all his Ghastly Train ;
They scorn to dread so mean a Foe,
   To live is CHRIST, to die is Gain,

IX.

The Rocks and Mountains may decay,
   The Everlasting Hills remove ;
Yea, Heav'n and Earth may pass away,
   Yet GOD can never change his Love.

GAL.

GAL. ii. 19. iii. 24, 25.

I through the Law am dead to the Law——The Law was our Schoolmaster to bring us unto CHRIST, that we might be justified by Faith. But after that Faith is come, we are no longer under a Schoolmaster.

I.

THE Law is Holy, Just and Good;
  A Transcript of the Will of GOD:
But I am Carnal, sold to Sin,*
Yet still the Law can't make me Clean.

II.

As Masters whip their Boys at School,
So the Law whips the Legal Soul;
This Pedagogue † implacable,
Commands, " Do this, or go to Hell."

III.

But what the Law cold not attain,
GOD sent his Son like *Sinful* Man ;
And he for Sin condemn'd all Sin,
And Perfect Righteousness brought in.

IV.

The Law, the Devil, Sin and Death
Give way unto *the Law of Faith.*§
No other Law do I now see
Besides *the Law of Liberty.*‖

----

* Rom. vii. 12, 14.
† That is, Schoolmaster; for so the Law is called, Gal. iii. 24. And this exactly answers to the Greek Word which the Apostle there uses.
‡ Rom. viii. 3.   § Rom. iii. 7.   ‖ James i. 5.

                    V. The

V.

The Law of Works no more takes Place,
For I am in the Law of Grace :
I joy in CHRIST, I ſtand by Faith ;
And I will be thy Death, O Death.

VI.

With Jesus I am crucified,
And in his Death the Law hath died:
From Condemnation I am Free ;
The Law, the Law is Dead to me.

VII.

Since I am waſh'd in JESU's Blood,
I am *not without Law to GOD :*
I'm *in a Law* * to GOD's dear SON,
CHRIST is my Law, and CHRIST alone.

VIII.

And Peace ſhall be on ev'ry Soul
That walks *according to this Rule* ;†
Peace on the *Iſrael* of GOD,
Who live by Faith in JESU's Blood.

Eph. v. 15.

*See then that ye walk circumſpectly, not as Fools, but as
Wiſe.*

I.

JESUS is a Holy Child ;
 Keep your Garments Undefil'd,
Otherwiſe in vain you claim
A Relation to the Lamb.

---

* So the Greek Word properly ſignifies, 1 Cor. ix. 21.
† Gal. vi. 16.

II. How

II.

How do Minifters delight
To behold their Flock in White,
Following the Will of GOD,
In the Way which JESUS trod?

III.

Would you credit JESU's Caufe?
Walk uprightly in his Laws:
Would you Souls to JESUS win,
Let your Lives be Free from Sin.

IV.

When Profeffors Chrift forfake,
What Advantage Sinners take!
Satan's Troops more daring grow,
" There, there, we would have it fo."

V,

Did the *Jews* our LORD deride?
Did the *Romans* pierce his Side?
Do not Wolves adorn'd like Sheep
Give his Soul a Wound more deep.

VI.

When the Saints their Saviour leave,
How do they his Spirit grieve!
He withdraws his Vital Pow'r
Warning them to fin no more.

VII.

When a Soul from JESUS flies,
Oh! what Doubts and Fears arife!
" All my Cries and Tears are vain,
" Chrift will not return again."

VIII.

Do not ye Backfliders know
What it is from Chrift to go?
Can Ten Thoufand Worlds repair
All the Horrors of Defpair?

IX. Let

IX.

Let your Walk be Honeſt then,
Blameleſs in the Eyes of Men;
Have you here more brightly ſhone?
You ſhall wear the brighter Crown.

---

2 TIM. iii. 5.

*Having a Form of Godlineſs, but denying the Power thereof:
from ſuch turn away.*

GAL. vi. 15.

*For in Jeſus Chriſt neither Circumciſion availeth any Thing,
nor Uncircumciſion, but a new Creature.*

I.

THE Moral Duties we have done,
　　Our Acts of Faith and Works of Love,
Will never draw one Bleſſing down,
　　Nor lift our Souls to Joys above.

II.

Can Notions ſwimming in the Brain,
　　And never ſinking to the Heart
A Pardon for one Sin obtain,
　　Or Life Divine to us impart?

III.

Can Ceremonial Rites or Forms,
　　Or Prayers, or Faſts, or Alms, or Tears
Atone for us Rebellious Worms,
　　Or plead our Cauſe when Chriſt appears?

IV.

Can Rules and Orders form'd by Man
　　Quiet our Souls, or make our Peace?
All theſe are Carnal, dead and vain,
　　To give a wounded Conſcience Eaſe.

V. And

V.

And tho' with Chriſtians we diſcourſe,
    And often in their Tents are ſeen,
This makes our Caſe ſo much the worſe,
    Becauſe we feel no Chriſt within.

VI.

LORD, work an Inward Change in me,
    Elſe Outward Worſhip all is vain :
Convert my Nature unto Thee,
    And let my Soul be born again.

VII.

Create my Heart ſo Pure and Clean,
    That I like Thee in Love may ſhine,
Fill'd with a Senſe of GOD within,
    Poſſeſs'd of Holineſs divine.

VIII.

Be Thou a Sea of Bliſs to me,
    Withdraw my Heart from Things below,
My Springs of Life are all in Thee,
    The Source from whom all Comforts flow.

GAL. iii. 10, 11.

*For as many as are of the Works of the Law, are under the
Curſe : for it is written. Curſed is every one that continueth
not in all Things which are written in the Book of the Law
to do them. But that no Man is juſtified by the Law in the
Sight of GOD, it is evident : for, the Juſt ſhall live by
Faith.*

I.

THUS ſaith our Good and Gracious GOD,
    The Juſt by Faith ſhall live ,
They feel the Pow'r of JESU's Blood,
    And Life and Peace receive.

II.

Believe that JESUS for you died;
   Your Sins are all forgiv'n :
Believe, and you are juftified,
   And foon will be in Heav'n.

III.

How dreadful is the Cafe of thofe
   Who on the Law depend ?
They to themfelves and CHRIST are Foes,
   And Hell will be their End.

IV.

In vain we hope for Righteoufnefs,
   From Works or Pow'rs within ;
For all we are is Filthinefs, ·
   And all we do is Sin.

V.

JESU, we lean upon thy Grace,
   To bring us near to GOD ;
Oh ! cloath us with thy Righteoufnefs,
   And cleanfe us by thy Blood.

VI.

While we continue here below,
   Thy Praife fhall fill our Tongue ;
And when to upper Worlds we go,
   Thy Love fhall tune our Song.